Contemporary Christian Communications

A Chriscom Book

CONTEMPORARY CHRISTIAN COMMUNICATIONS

Its Theory and Practice

JAMES F. ENGEL, Ph.D.

Chairman
Communications Department
Wheaton Graduate School

THOMAS NELSON PUBLISHERS
Nashville New York

Second printing

Excerpts from *Let the Earth Hear His Voice,* © 1975 by World Wide Publications, are used by permission.

Scripture quotations marked NASB are from the New American Standard Bible, © The Lockman Foundation 1960, 1962, 1963, 1968, 1971, 1972, 1973, 1975 and are used by permission.

Scripture quotations marked TLB are from *The Living Bible* (Wheaton, Ill.: Tyndale House Publishers, 1971) and are used by permission.

Scripture quotations marked NIV are from the New International Version of the Bible, © 1978 by The New York Bible Society International. Used by permission.

Scripture quotations marked TEV are from the *Good News Bible,* Old Testament © 1976, New Testament © 1966, 1971, 1976, by the American Bible Society.

The Scripture quotation marked "Phillips" is from J. B. Phillips: *The New Testament in Modern English.* ©J. B. Phillips 1958, 1960, 1972. Used by permission of Macmillan Publishing Co., Inc.

Published in Nashville, Tennessee, by Thomas Nelson, Inc., Publishers and distributed in Canada by Lawson Falle, Ltd., Cambridge, Ontario.

Printed in the United States of America.

Library of Congress Cataloging in Publication Data

Engel, James F
Contemporary Christian communications, its theory and practice.

"A Chriscom book."
Includes bibliographical references and index.
1. Communication (Theology) I. Title.
BV4319.E52 253.7 79-432
ISBN 0-8407-5152-4

Dedicated to the author's colleague and abiding friend—Dean H. Wilbert Norton—a man whose life always epitomizes the lordship of Christ.

Contents

Contents

Preface

It is interesting to look back and ask who had the greatest culture shock in 1972, the author or the Wheaton Graduate School? That was the year God prompted the author and his family to leave the safe haven of Ohio State University, at least temporarily. Through a combination of events, He led them to Wheaton, where the author and his wife intended primarily to study Bible and theology. But there was this small new department of Christian communications, and the author found himself more and more caught up in what it was trying to do. One thing led to another, and a new career began.

The author had served with a leading evangelistic organization as director of its ministry to college and university faculty. While this was just a part-time thing, it did enable him to visit 160 different institutions and learn the meaning of evangelism and discipleship in the "trenches," so to speak. Those were invaluable years, and the lessons learned are reflected in this book.

Interestingly enough, however, the author was teaching business students how to analyze their audience and be effective in advertising strategy, on the one hand, while ignoring that same teaching in his evangelism on the other. It was at Wheaton, under the stimulation of an exciting group of students and colleagues, that the two areas began to merge. Soon Christian organizations and churches began to recognize that the cutting edge of evangelism and discipleship ministries had grown exceedingly dull. They were all asking the same types of questions. Thus began a research-oriented approach to finding solutions. These experimental efforts tested new evangelistic concepts, ideas, and methods; the knowledge gained is absolutely priceless.

In just a few short years, an analytical approach to problem solving has evolved from being a curiosity to a widely recognized necessity. We still are in the "testing stage," and probably always will be. But some definite principles are now emerging, thus making this book possible.

The purpose of this book is twofold. First, and probably most important, it is written to provide help for the practitioner in Christian communications who is genuinely seeking to be a better steward of his or her efforts. The local church is a particular focus all the way through. Secondly, there is a need for books that can be used as texts in courses on Christian communications. Such courses are emerging with surprising rapidity in Christian colleges and universities, graduate schools, and seminaries. Other than the writings of Eugene Nida, Marvin Mayers, Em Griffin, and a few others, there is not much material to draw upon.

This is not an easy subject, because it has roots both in theology and in the behavioral sciences. The author has not hesitated to draw upon the latest thinking in both where necessary. Nevertheless, the focus is always on the practical. If it does not make a difference in what we do in the real world, why write about it? As a result, the writing style, it is hoped, is relatively light, readable, and interesting and will not fall under the charge leveled by D. Elton Trueblood toward some of his colleagues: "Part of the shame of the theology of the recent past is that sometimes it has been made deliberately foggy, under the fatuous assumption that what cannot be understood is somehow more profound."[1]

Most of the content of this book has been taught in the classrooms at the Wheaton Graduate School and in seminars held literally around the world. The feedback given has been quite helpful, and those who offered it deserve a sincere "thank you." Others have willingly waded through the typed manuscript and have given freely of their insights. Special acknowledgment must be given, first of all, to the author's longtime friend, Pete Gillquist, of Thomas Nelson Inc., who has made this text and the series in which it appears possible. Others who have been of considerable help are Howard A.

[1]D. Elton Trueblood, *A Place to Stand* (New York: Harper & Row, 1968), p. 8.

Snyder of Light and Life Men in Winona, Indiana; Stan Gundry, Department of Theology, Moody Bible Institute; and these friends and colleagues from the Wheaton Graduate School: Dean Wil Norton, John Gration, Fran White, Chuck Horne, and Jim Johnson. Their suggestions have been taken seriously.

This is the author's sixteenth book, and it is becoming more and more evident that the closest thing to writing a book is giving birth. Both are accompanied by some readily verbalized labor pains, as this author's wife and three daughters will attest. Those who are closest to an author always bear the brunt of his frustrations, and my family's patience has been encouraging and deeply appreciated. In particular, the author is grateful for their willingness to permit him to escape to Lost Grove, a family retreat in southwest Wisconsin, for periods of undisturbed writing amidst the beauty of nature.

JAMES F. ENGEL
Wheaton, Illinois
September, 1978

Contemporary Christian Communications

CHAPTER 1

We've Only Just Begun!

Those were the days, my friend. So go the words of a song made popular a few years ago. How well they express the sentiments of many Christians who look back perhaps too longingly to the life of the church in the first century. There is no question that the Christians of that day possessed a spiritual virility and a sense of joyous spontaneity that makes much of contemporary Christianity pale by comparison.[1] Everyone was a witness. Evangelism was a natural part of daily life (Acts 2:4–47). The transforming love of Jesus Christ was evidenced by a quality of life that could not be ignored by their contemporaries, and as a result, Christianity made an impact on society that seldom has been equaled in history. (However, the early church was not without its flaws.)

Nearly two thousand years have passed, and the message of Christianity and its moral and ethical mandates have not changed. With some notable exceptions, however, the cutting edge of the church has become exceedingly dull. The delegates at the International Congress on World Evangelization held at Lausanne in 1974 were shocked to hear that somewhere between 2.5 and 3.0 billion people

---

[1]Michael Green, "Methods and Strategy in the Evangelism of the Early Church," in J.D. Douglas, ed., *Let the Earth Hear His Voice,* (Minneapolis: World Wide Publications, 1975), pp. 159–180.

are presently beyond the direct witness of the church and yet to be reached effectively with the gospel![2]

Some look to the United States as a kind of evangelical mecca, but this can be misleading. George Gallup, Jr., has estimated that somewhere between forty and fifty million Americans claim to have had a "born again" experience. The most recent evidence, however, reveals that the typical U. S. evangelical is a white female Southerner over the age of fifty, with a high school education or less and below average income. Only one in eleven lives in a large city, and sixty percent reside in rural areas or small towns.[3] The facts are clear: Evangelical Christians are a minority, even though they became more visible during the 1970s because of media exposure. More than two thirds of Americans do not claim to have a personal relationship with Jesus Christ, even though most claim nominal church membership.

The middle 1970s were labeled the "era of the evangelicals" by secular media such as *Time* and *Newsweek.* These articles report an increase of eleven percent between 1963 and 1976 in the number of those who claim to have had a "born again" experience.[4] Furthermore, fifty-six percent of all adults say that religious beliefs are important to them, compared with only twenty-seven percent in Europe. In fact, India is the only nation in the world in which interest in religion exceeds that of the United States, with eighty percent claiming that their faith (non-Christian) is an important part of their life.[5] A careful analysis, however, shows a remarkable stability in religious interest and expression throughout the history of the United States and the more recent decades in particular.[6] The supposed fact of a "third great awakening" quickly dissolves when this longer time perspective is taken, and Wills has come to the conclusion that the current evangelical "boomlet" represents little

---

[2]Ralph D. Winter estimated that the figure was 2.8 billion in 1975. See "The Highest Priority: Cross-Cultural Evangelism" in Douglas, *Let the Earth Hear His Voice,* p. 225. In fact, the *MARC Newsletter* of September, 1974, estimates that 2 billion people live in countries where little or no Christian activity is allowed. The *MARC Newsletter,* January, 1978, gives the estimate of 2.4 billion unreached people.

[3]"Who Are the Evangelicals?" *Christianity Today* (January 27, 1978), p. 42.

[4]George Gallup, Jr., "Religion in Moderation?" (Address given to the 65th General Convention of the Episcopal Church, September 21, 1976).

[5]*Ibid.*

[6]Garry Wills, "What Religious Revival?" *Psychology Today,* vol. 11 (April, 1978), pp. 74–81.

more than greater availability of survey data and secular media exposure.[7]

We also must face the sobering reality that true religious awakening is given validity by profound moral and social change. The fact is that moral and ethical standards are deteriorating in North American society at large, crime rates are skyrocketing, corruption is rampant in politics and business, and restraints on previously taboo behaviors are disappearing. This has led church historian David Wells to conclude that, "Evangelicals have never been so numerous; the impact of Christian values on society has seldom been less."[8] It seems apparent that orthodox Christianity has not turned the world upside down as it did in the first century according to the Book of Acts (17:6).

Once again the words of a popular song state the truth quite aptly—"We've only just begun!" The historic mandate of the church to proclaim and exemplify the kingdom of God still remains, but we must recognize, of course, that ultimate fulfillment awaits Christ's return. The outcome is "... *God's redeeming Lordship successively winning such liberating power over the hearts of men, that their lives and thereby finally the whole creation ... become transformed into childlike harmony with His divine will.*"[9] This, in a nutshell, is what this book is all about. It represents an attempt to wrestle in the context of the twentieth century with the meaning and practical significance of Christ's command to "...go and make disciples of all nations" (Matt. 28:18–20, NIV). While the primary emphasis is placed on communication, the moral and ethical dimensions of Christian life-style cannot be ignored. Indeed, the very actions of the church, both individually and corporately, lie at the heart of the Christian message.

THE GREAT COMMISSION OR THE GREAT COMMOTION?

While we've only just begun, the church has evidenced during the 1960s and 1970s quite a resurgence of interest in Christian orthodoxy and the premium it places on evangelism. Christ's commands to make disciples in all nations is referred to by some as the Great Commission, and this term has become a central rallying

[7] *Ibid.*

[8] David Wells, "The Gospel of Razzmatazz," *Christianity Today* (April 7, 1978), p. 32.

[9] Peter Beyerhaus, "World Evangelization and the Kingdom of God," in Douglas, *Let the Earth Hear His Voice,* p. 286.

theme of evangelical outreach. Slogans and Bible verses appear everywhere, even on bumper stickers. While there is no doubt that a vital church will be an evangelistic church, it is unwise to accept all of this current activity uncritically. Indeed it is possible that the execution of the Great Commission at times is little more than a great commotion!

The effectiveness of Christian communication *can* be measured. Some immediately object that the results are in God's hands and are not for us to question. Isaiah 55:11 is cited as a proof text. God said, ". . . My word . . . shall not return to Me empty, Without accomplishing what I desire . . ." (NASB). Whatever this verse means, it is clear from its context and from the rest of God's Word that it cannot be cited to justify poor stewardship. It is our obligation to attract the attention of the hearer and to convey the intended message in such a way as to communicate the relevance of the Word of God. When this does not take place, one cannot shift the responsibility to God. Failure to establish relevance is nothing more than faulty stewardship.

An analytical evaluation of the contemporary scene is justified because of the growing evidence that some Christian communication is misfiring. It is instructive to analyze a number of examples in detail to see what common denominators emerge.

A Postmortem Analysis

The term "postmortem" often creates images of digging something up to see why it died. That is not the point at all. Any effective communicator will critically analyze results after the fact for the simple reason that "Anyone willing to be corrected is on the pathway to life . . ." (Prov. 10:17, TLB). We learn from experience.

The examples cited here all represent worthwhile outreaches by men and women who take their Christian responsibility seriously. All have both strengths and weaknesses, and we can profit from their experiences. The whole intent is to be analytical without being critical.

The Church in Japan. The country of Japan has presented a dilemma for evangelism and missions. The majority of the populace is religious, but this takes the form of worship of multiple gods. Christianity has been embraced by less than one percent, even though the country has more than 2,000 missionaries, over fifty Christian publishers, and several major Christian broadcasting centers. There certainly has been no dearth of evangelistic activity. In fact one

Japanese leader told the author that the total of reported decisions for Christ since World War II probably would exceed the number of people who live in the country! Obviously the effects of all this activity have not penetrated below the surface, and this is all the more discouraging in view of the fact that Japan has one of the largest missionary forces in the entire world.

The dilemma, in a nutshell, is that Christianity has not been viewed by the great majority as being a valid option for their lifestyle. A good deal of "North American cultural baggage" still accompanies the gospel message, and that has not helped. The need now is to rethink all that has been done with a view toward establishing the relevance of Christianity in a strictly Japanese context without the overhang from alien cultures.

Here's Life America. A twentieth century phenomenon has been the high visibility of parachurch organizations working alongside of the church without being an official part of its local structure. One of the most active, Campus Crusade for Christ, International, probably has done more than any other to encourage the church to take its evangelistic responsibility seriously. During 1976 and 1977 this organization undertook an ambitious effort to mobilize churches and utilize all forms of media to "saturate" some 250 metropolitan areas in the United States with the claims of Christ.[10] The result was the "Here's Life America" campaign with the widely displayed slogan, "I found it."

Campus Crusade took seriously its expressed purpose of uniting local churches in evangelism. Many reports have indicated that the internal life of churches was changed and that many Christians for the first time are now sharing their faith on a regular basis.[11]

The results beyond church walls were less positive, however. More than one half million indicated they had received Christ, but fewer than three percent became church members as a result.[12] While church growth is just one of several measures of evangelistic success, the fact that ninety-seven percent of alleged converts did not unite with the church either indicates that they never made a valid decision in the first place or that church follow-up effort was woefully weak.

Furthermore, it was contended that 175 million people were ex-

---

[10]Bill Bright, "It Can Happen All Over the World. By the Grace of God It Will," *Worldwide Challenge* (December, 1976), pp. 29–33.

[11]C. Peter Wagner, "Who Found It?" *Eternity* (September, 1977), pp. 13–19.

[12]*Ibid.*

posed to the claims of the gospel.[13] Because of media saturation, this figure could be accurate, but exposure and comprehension are very different matters. In a survey undertaken at the Wheaton Graduate School it was discovered that about eighty percent of those living in Upper Arlington, Ohio (a wealthy suburb of Columbus), indeed were aware of the "I found it" theme, but only forty percent understood the message. And at least half of this forty percent were already Christian or Christian-oriented. The majority never comprehended what it was trying to say.

While the final evidence is not yet available, it is apparent that Here's Life fell far short of its goals. One of the main reasons apparently is that the outreach was varied little from one city to the next, even though the climate for Christianity was better in some places than in others. There is no strategy that works everywhere.

Sermon Comprehension. The author's students have conducted over 1,000 interviews in churches in the greater Chicago area asking basically one question: "What was the main point of the sermon this morning?" A minimum of five people from each church are interviewed immediately after termination of the service. Over half of those interviewed cannot accurately state the main point of what they have heard, and two key factors always are evident. First, there may have been no main point because of a barrage of material presented; hence, the ability to recall is substantially hindered. Second, the essential content is missed because it does not touch practical, everyday living. Thus a lecture is heard, comprehended only in part, and lives remain untouched.

Those sermons that do get high recall are usually characterized by simplicity and clarity; the exposition is not covered with fine points from the original languages and philosophical speculation. Furthermore, the topic discussed is relevant for the needs of the hearer and gives that person some points of application. The pastors who give such sermons, in turn, seem to be well acquainted with the needs of their flock.

Listenership to Christian Radio Programs. A mission in Alaska operates a radio station as part of a multifaceted program of outreach. It offers both secular and Christian content. In fact, at the time of a listenership study conducted by the author, it was virtually a lifeline

---

[13]"A Letter From Bill Bright," *The President's Report* (San Bernadino, Ca.: Campus Crusade for Christ, Winter, 1978), p. 5.

for listeners. Few had telephones; there was no other available radio signal, and televison had not yet been beamed into this remote area.

Listenership to secular programming was high, and the station received excellent marks for its music, news, and local programs. The Christian programs, on the other hand, were responded to quite differently. Most were ignored by all but those who were already Christians, even though some programs were aired with a goal toward evangelism. Over sixty percent listened to the 6:00 P.M. news, for example, but only sixteen percent remained tuned to a well-known Bible preaching program aired at 7:30. The sound of the radios being turned off is almost audible on a clear Alaskan night.

A Magazine Written for Non-Believers. On college campuses an evangelistic organization distributes a magazine intended for non-Christians. The head of this organization always includes an article containing nothing other than a simple presentation of the plan of salvation. A survey of readers' response disclosed that this regular article was ignored by the vast majority, whereas a series of articles and editorials presenting a Christian perspective on a variety of pertinent issues was widely read. These articles apparently had relevance for the reader, whereas the former did not.

Bible Distribution. Through the generosity of a major publisher, a popular paraphrase of the New Testament was made available for free distribution to all inmates in prisons in the United States. One could, on the face of it, claim that all prisoners were being "reached with the Word." It came as quite a shock when it was discovered after a survey that ninety percent of the Testaments found their way into the trash can, thus leading to waste of over $250,000. The strategy was revamped so that the Testaments were given by chaplains only to those who indicated they wanted a Bible, and many were helped through this selective distribution of Scripture.

A Local Church With a Starving Membership. A church of 650 members seems to be successful from all external indications. Its pastor takes the Bible seriously and is attempting to build a genuine spiritual maturity in the members and to stimulate outreach. Yet a survey of the congregation showed that only twenty percent attempted to share their faith in the past few weeks; just thirty percent opened their Bible as often as three times a week; twenty-one percent had some form of devotions at home; seventy percent confined their church involvement to one hour on Sunday; ten percent could identify their spiritual gift; and fifty percent claimed that they were not being fed spiritually in the church.[14] It is not surprising that this church has had only minimal impact on its community, for its members are starving in the pews.

So What Does It All Mean?

This postmortem could be extended at length, but one point certainly is clear: Ministry effectiveness must be evaluated and not simply assumed. There are some churches and parachurch organizations today that have reached the point of an effectiveness crisis in their ministry. Many are little more than empty shells carrying on "business as usual." Unfortunately, this is all too often tolerated on the fatuous assumption that there is no need to evaluate effectiveness as long as contributions or offerings do not slump too seriously. Such a disregard of stewardship would never be allowed in a business that must face the discipline of the profit motive.

Fortunately, it has been the experience of the author and his colleagues that Christian leaders around the world are recovering a keen sense of stewardship. It is most encouraging to see the strongly expressed need in so many quarters to communicate effectively.

A major purpose of this book is to develop an attitude of inquiry and procedures in strategy development and execution that avoid effectiveness crises. Before proceeding further, however, it is necessary to isolate some of the major factors that can lead to a dulled cutting edge in ministry.

A Contaminated Message. Too often the message itself is blurred and uncertain. It can become contaminated in three important ways: (1) a severing of biblical roots; (2) cultural syncretism; and (3) ignoring the cost of discipleship.

(1) A Severing of Biblical Roots. This point will be developed more fully later, but it should be noted at the outset that a segment of the church has become quite equivocal regarding the Bible. A debate rages on about which sections, if any, can be taken as authoritative and which parts should be discarded. Historically, the Bible has been viewed as the final and complete authority for all that it affirms. If this is no longer held with conviction, then the "trumpet give[s] an uncertain sound," and "who shall prepare himself to the battle?" (1 Cor. 14:8, KJV). As Schaeffer notes, ". . . there is a line being drawn

[14]This church, typical of so many others, serves as the example in the book coauthored by the author and H. Wilbert Norton entitled, *What's Gone Wrong With the Harvest?* (Grand Rapids, Mich.: Zondervan, 1975).

between those who take a full view of Scripture and those who do not."[15] If the Bible is no longer fully authoritative, then the church does not have a certain and firm foundation for its message and there is no reason for modern man to take it more seriously than other philosophies.

(2) Cultural Syncretism. One of the easiest traps is to integrate the biblical message and cultural norms in such a way that the two become almost indistinguishable. The message then becomes so contaminated that its truth is obscured, and critical prophetic issues go untouched. Some issues become off limits, and the prophetic voice of the church is silenced. It is worth reflecting on John Perkins' warning: "It's okay to criticize the political system, the welfare system, or even the church. But as soon as we question the economic order we're in real trouble and are labeled as communists or anything else."[16] As Padilla has said,

> When the church lets itself be squeezed into the mold of the world, it loses the capacity to see and, even more, to denounce the social evils in its own situation. Like the color-blind person who is able to distinguish certain colors, but not others, the worldly church recognizes the personal vices traditionally condemned within its ranks, but is unable to see the evil features of its surrounding culture.[17]

(3) A Cheap Grace. A common error is to stress the promise Jesus gave of an abundant life and to under-emphasize a life of obedience to Him. The Lausanne Covenant affirmed that, "In issuing the Gospel invitation we have no liberty to conceal the cost of discipleship."[18] Discipleship includes a rigorous set of moral and social demands adhered to by the new community of believers in Jesus Christ. This imperative is often recognized more sharply by Christian leaders from the third world. Listen to the words of Orlando Costas:

> . . . we are sent to proclaim, in word and deed, the good news of this new order of life *in* the multitudinous structures of society—family and government, business and neighborhood, religion and education, etc. In doing so, we must stand as Christ did, in solidarity with the poor and the

[15]Francis A. Schaeffer, "Form and Freedom in the Church," in Douglas, *Let the Earth Hear His Voice,* p. 365.

[16]John Perkins, "Stoning the Prophets," *Sojourners,* vol. 7 (February, 1978), p. 8.

[17]René Padilla, "Evangelism and the World," in Douglas, *Let the Earth Hear His Voice,* p. 137.

[18]This clause of the Covenant appears in Douglas, *Let the Earth Hear His Voice,* p. 4.

oppressed. Further, we must engage actively in their struggle for life and fulfillment.[19]

One Way Communication. Chapter 2 will focus on audience response to communication, and one point is perfectly clear: *People are not robots.* They see and hear what they want to see and hear through a complex procedure of information processing. Because they have this God-given ability to ignore us if they choose, it places a demand on the communicator to be audience-oriented. As Jess Moody has observed, "The church needs to be informed that the world isn't obligated to pay any attention to us."[20] The apostle Paul was a master communicator who put forth this highly relevant principle: ". . . Yes, whatever a person is like, I try to find common ground with him so that he will let me tell him about Christ and let Christ save him." (1 Cor. 9:23, TLB).

A Disregard of Spiritual Decision Processes. Much of this book centers around the various ways in which people make spiritual decisions and grow in the faith. Common sense would argue that this occurs as a process, which usually takes place over time with a variety of influences. Some people are quite open and ready to give their life to Christ, whereas others are far from the point of decision. Yet, evangelism, as taught throughout the church, centers on the decision itself and utilizes a variety of methods designed to persuade someone to "give his life to Christ." If a person is not ready for such an act, our communication falls on deaf ears. When we face someone who has real doubts about the Bible, the sinfulness of mankind, or other cardinal Christian doctrines, we tend to become tongue-tied.

Unfortunately, community surveys undertaken in a variety of settings at the Wheaton Graduate School are demonstrating that most people in North America are content with life and, at the very most, are at the earliest stages of the process that might, someday, result in a personal relationship with Jesus Christ. Yet, we go on assuming, often without merit, that most people feel a great void in their life and are open and ready to receive Jesus Christ. This is increasingly becoming an invalid premise, and we must take the consequences seriously if our witness is ever going to have much impact.

An Institutionalized Church. Howard Snyder shocked many of the

[19]Orlando E. Costas, *The Church and Its Mission: A Shattering Critique From the Third World* (Wheaton, Ill.: Tyndale, 1974), p. 309.

[20]Jess Moody, "A Drink at Joel's Place," *Today* (August 24, 1969), p. 3.

delegates at the Lausanne Congress by his claim that about eighty percent of church structures are tradition and culture bound.[21] He later elaborated this statement in two significant books in which various models for the church are contrasted.[22]

The first is the institutional model based on hierarchy, formality, and delegation of authority. An inevitable distinction develops between pastor and laity. The latter tend to take their place as mere cogs in a program determined by others, executed, and maintained even in the face of radical change. The outcome is a church destined for effectiveness crisis, because it has embraced some nonbiblical patterns.

Snyder much prefers the model of the church as a charismatic organism. It is charismatic in the sense that it is empowered by the grace of God. It is an organism composed of redeemed people, endowed with gifts, functioning under the leadership of Christ as Head. While it also may have some institutionalized elements, it will not fall prey as readily to a program orientation and resistance to change.

As the church becomes institutionalized, outward forms of Christianity become embodied as a life-style, often in disregard to pertinent biblical teaching. One of the more serious forms is what the author would designate as "Great Commissionitis." This is when evangelism is defined as the sum and substance of both individual and corporate Christian life. Evangelism, of course, is central, but it does not lie at the core of spirituality. The unfortunate outcome is that other phases of church life centering on the maturity and vitality of the believer become downgraded and secondary to outreach. The inevitable result is a starved laity who, in the final analysis, are unable to witness to a good news that they are not experiencing.

A principle stressed below is that the church is both message and medium. It is the channel for the Good News, but it also is an end in itself. If it is not alive and vital, all the exhortation in the world will not generate effective outreach. A central theme of this book is that *the health of the church must be taken seriously or the cause of world evangelization is futile.*

---

[21]Howard A. Snyder, "The Church as God's Agent in Evangelism," in Douglas, *Let the Earth Hear His Voice,* p. 354.

[22]*The Problem of Wineskins* and *The Community of the King* (Downers Grove, Ill.: InterVarsity Press, 1975 and 1977, respectively).

Unscriptural Autonomy of Parachurch Organizations. It was Snyder who popularized the distinction between the church and the parachurch organization, the essential difference being that the latter is called to work along side the local church without being a direct part of it.[23] As such, it is a service agency and can include denominational structures, mission boards, broadcasters, publishers, and so on. Furthermore, its existence is warranted only insofar as it is still needed. There is no divine mandate for perpetuation whatsoever.

So long as the service function is kept primary, fine. But there has been a tendency for the parachurch organization to dominate the local church and thereby overstep its bounds. It is no exaggeration to say that the supposed "arm of the body" can control the body, and that makes for a strange-looking organism. Many examples could be given, but one will suffice. One evangelistic agency conceived a city-wide evangelistic program that it now has taken to all parts of the world. A delegation of church leaders from one Asian city approached the author with this plea: "How do we keep organization X from pressuring us to do something we feel is totally wrong for our country? They have said our failure to cooperate will set back the whole cause of Christ."

Here is a case in which the arm of the church used utterly unwarranted pressure tactics to execute its will. It no longer was a servant because the initiative and power came from itself and not from the local churches. In fact, the churches wanted nothing to do with it, because they had their own plans. Unfortunately, the parachurch group went right ahead, bypassed the leadership, and held their evangelistic "blitz" anyway. One cannot help wondering in such instances whether or not man's methods are getting in the way of God's agenda for His church.

SOME PRINCIPLES OF CHRISTIAN COMMUNICATION

It is not the purpose of the author to be negative and to center unduly on postmortem analysis; yet it must be stressed once again that we learn from experience. These examples and numerous others from the history of the church can prove helpful in isolating key principles that should motivate and guide Christian work. There

[23]Snyder, "The Church as God's Agent in Evangelism."

is a keen difference between communication in general and Christian communication, and there are seven distinct principles, which if heeded will help avoid effectiveness crisis.

Goal-Oriented Communication Is Imperative

Some will argue that evangelism is uncalled for in a pluralistic world in which many religions compete for man's loyalty. Live and let live is the guiding philosophy. While this does sound quite tolerant, it completely violates the mandate of Scripture to *go and make disciples in all nations* (Matt. 28:18–20). This command is as contemporary today as it was in the first century.[24] The church is to be salt and light in the world (Matt. 5:11–13) and always ". . . prepared to give an answer to everyone who asks you to give the reason for the hope that you have" (1 Pet. 3:15, NIV). So the issue is not debatable at all if one takes Scripture seriously.

The Bible Is the Only Infallible Rule of Faith and Practice

The words of the Lausanne Covenant affirm the historic Christian position with respect to the Word of God: "We affirm the divine inspiration, truthfulness and authority of both Old and New Testament Scriptures in their entirety as the only written Word of God, without error in all that it affirms, and the only infallible rule of faith and practice."[25] The Christian message finds its source in the Scriptures, and it is the only message of any type communicated to modern man based in absolute, unchanging truth. Anything that deviates from this standard cannot truly be called Christian.[26]

Many have referred to the late 1970s as the "battle for the Bible" era. Unfortunately, there has been a tendency to utilize theologically technical criteria and to spread doubt on the biblical fidelity of many who could fully accept the terms of the Lausanne Covenant cited above. The author agrees with Clark Pinnock who has stated unequivocally that there is ". . . little solid evidence that a determination to follow Jesus behaviorally has any part in the motivation behind this furious battle."[27]

The apologetic task of the church is best carried out through

---

[24]David M. Howard, *The Great Commission for Today* (Downers Grove, Ill.: InterVarsity Press, 1976).

[25]Douglas, *Let the Earth Hear His Voice,* p. 3.

[26]Harold J. Ockenga, "The Basic Theology of Evangelism," *Christianity Today* (October 28, 1966), pp. 9–14.

[27]*Ibid.*

proclamation, in word and action, to the world. Saying this, however, is far different from doing it, because we must face the rigorous demands of scholarship required for biblical interpretation (hermeneutics). The battle for the Bible, in actuality, is secondary to the problem of hermeneutics put so clearly by Julius Scott:

> Many evangelicals feel trapped. On the one hand, they are determined to remain faithful to the principles for the literal, grammatical, historical interpretation of the scriptures as the objective, authoritative, unchanging Word of God. On the other hand, they wrestle with the seldom-voiced conviction that the rules for interpretation, especially the traditional ones, have proven ineffective in meaningfully applying Biblical revelation to the complex needs of modern man and societies.[28]

So, in the final analysis, the demand is for biblical scholarship that can help in communicating the relevance of the Word of God for modern man.

The Church Is Both Message and Medium

One frequently hears the one-sided view that the church is on earth for one solitary reason—evangelism of the lost. If that were true, then the church is nothing more than a communication medium. But there also is a very real sense in which the church is the message as well. Consider these words:

> Unless the fellowship in the Christian assembly is far superior to that which can be found anywhere else in society, then the Christians can talk about the transforming love and power of Jesus till they are hoarse, but people are not going to listen very hard.[29]

In the final analysis, *the church is both message and medium, exemplifying and proclaiming the kingdom of God.*

The kingdom of God was announced by Jesus as embodying His reign over all of life. It is a way of life for the church based on the lordship of Jesus in every sphere in which the Christian exists, recognizing, of course, that the full expression of the kingdom awaits Jesus' return to earth. As a life-style, however, the kingdom is the message for the church in which there can be no distinction between evangelism and social action. The church, in turn, provides

---

[28]J. Julius Scott, Jr., "Some Problems in Hermeneutics for Contemporary Evangelicals" (unpublished paper, Wheaton Graduate School, 1978), p. 5.

[29]Green, "Methods and Strategy in the Evangelism of the Early Church," p. 169.

the medium as it shares the offer of *"God's redeeming lordship successively winning . . . liberating power over the hearts of men."*[30]

Viewing the church as both medium and message has powerful implications. At the very least, it is obvious that a church not exemplifying the kingdom is moribund and ineffective in the whole cause of world evangelization. Indeed, it is the author's conviction that insurance of the health and biblical fidelity of the church must precede evangelistic strategies. Our tendency usually is to place the cart before the horse, and it is little wonder that evangelism so often has proved futile. We have reversed God's priorities.

The Message Must Be Adapted to a Sovereign Audience

The next principle is that the audience is sovereign; the message must be adapted to audience members without sacrifice of biblical fidelity if it is to have relevance. As was stated earlier, Chapter 2 will verify that audience members are sovereign *at any given point in time* in that they will see and hear what they want to see and hear. Their attention is captured and held only when the message is seen to be relevant for their life at that point. It is in this sense that Green affirms the need to let the world set the agenda in a sense and to answer it imaginatively in the light of the New Testament witness to Christ.[31]

Adapting the message does not mean *changing* the message as it is affirmed in the Scriptures. It requires, instead, that ability to focus historic truth on contemporary issues, and this requires the most demanding of biblical scholarship. As Stott has said with his usual clarity,

> Now it is comparatively easy to be faithful if we do not care about being contemporary, and easy also to be contemporary if we do not bother to be faithful. It is the search for a combination of truth and relevance which is exacting.[32]

Becoming a Disciple Is an Unending Process

Contrary to what some writers say on this subject,[33] the author is convinced that the weight of biblical scholarship argues for the fact

[30]Beyerhaus, "World Evangelization and the Kingdom of God," p. 286.

[31]Green, "Methods and Strategy in the Evangelism of the Early Church," p. 164.

[32]John R.W. Stott, *Christian Mission in the Modern World* (Downers Grove, Ill.: InterVarsity Press, 1975), p. 43.

[33]C. Peter Wagner argues, for example, that a person becomes a disciple upon receiving Christ as Savior. See his *Frontiers in Missionary Strategy* (Chicago: Moody Press, 1971).

that becoming a disciple is an unending process with many influences. The word "disciple" is translated as ". . . one who follows the precepts and instructions of another."[34] Christ's mandate to make disciples is not fulfilled merely by exposing another to the gospel message and giving opportunity for response. A convert is to be baptized and taught to observe all that Christ has commanded. Therefore, discipleship continues as a process over a lifespan as believers are conformed to the image of Christ (Phil. 1:6).

Perhaps this may seem to be a hair-splitting argument, but it is much more than that in view of the rallying cry to "fulfill the Great Commission in this generation." If one can maintain that a person fully becomes a disciple upon receiving Christ, then there is a sense in which it can be said that the Great Commission can be fulfilled. The danger, however, is to place primary emphasis upon the act of soul-winning and neglect the cultivation of the new believer. The result is a spiritual impotence that renders the church only a very shallow reflection of the true meaning of the kingdom of God. The Great Commission will never be fulfilled in any final sense, prior to Christ's return because there are two distinct aspects of discipleship: (1) the sense in which a person becomes a disciple upon receiving Christ; and (2) the other sense in which one grows in discipleship throughout a lifetime.

Christian Communication Is a Cooperative Effort

If man alone could be instrumental in stimulating spiritual decisions, there would be no need for this book. Indeed, it would be possible to consult any secular book on communications and follow the principles of promotional strategy. On the other hand, if God is totally responsible for the whole process, then the Christian need have no concern about a ministry of communication. Obviously both of these positions are in error as J. I. Packer succinctly states: "While we must always remember that it is our responsibility to proclaim salvation, we must never forget that it is God who saves."[35] Thus, both God and man cooperate in the process.

Disciplined Planning Is the Obligation of the Church

In more complete terms the principle here is that disciplined planning under the leadership of the Holy Spirit is the key to

---

[34]Kenneth S. Wuest, *Studies in the Vocabulary* (Grand Rapids, Mich.: Wm. B. Eerdmans, 1945), p. 25.

[35]J.I. Packer, *Evangelism and the Sovereignty of God* (Downers Grove, Ill.: Inter-Varsity Press, 1961), p. 27.

effective strategy. The temptation, of course, is to delve deeply into secular management theory, make our plans, and then ask God to bless. In so doing, "a man may ruin his chances by his own foolishness and then blame it on the Lord!" (Prov. 19:3, TLB). Proverbs 16:9, on the other hand, states clearly that it is necessary and appropriate to make plans, but the key is "counting on God to direct us" (TLB).

The frequent objection to this principle is that it is distinctly North American. Even worse, it is often said to reflect the excesses of Madison Avenue. A leading third-world leader has laid that objection completely to rest, however. Gottfried Osei-Mensah, now coordinator of the Lausanne Continuation Committee, clearly has stated that the Holy Spirit helps us by keeping spiritual vision in focus and using our resources wisely. As he put it:

> Nothing is more calculated to check our tendency to sloth than a clear spiritual vision articulated in concrete objectives and well-defined principles for action. Spiritual goals give meaning to commitment, inspire perseverence in prayer, and promote self-discipline for their realization.[36]

So, Where to From Here?

Properly viewed and utilized, these principles can do much to remedy the effectiveness crisis so much in evidence in some quarters of the church today. Hopefully they will provide a sharp telescope through which to view contemporary realities. Each will be elaborated at length throughout the book, and the last chapter will address an agenda for the church if world evangelization is to become a reality.

[36]Gottfried Osei-Mensah, "The Holy Spirit and World Evangelization," in Douglas, *Let the Earth Hear His Voice,* p. 265.

PART I
THE FOUNDATIONS OF CHRISTIAN COMMUNICATION

The basic principles discussed in Chapter 1 focus on three foundational issues: (1) the nature of communication itself, especially within a Christian context, (2) the decision process followed as people come to Christ initially and grow in the faith, and (3) the nature of the church as both medium and message. The chapters that follow probe deeply into these issues and hence provide essential background for later chapters. Chapter 3 is of particular importance because of its focus on biblical mandates for communication, the spiritual decision process, and the implications for the communicator.

CHAPTER 2

What Is Communication All About?

Sally Anderson faced a dilemma. For two years she had served as one of six script writers for "Morning Sounds," a program aired via shortwave radio to Russia, Eastern Europe, the Far East, India, and Australia.[1] Each of the script writers was responsible for one program per week. These writers never met as a group, however, and Sally's frustration grew.

As she reflected on her ministry, Sally soon came to some conclusions that led her to feel that she, in effect, was doing nothing more than one-way communication:

1. No one at this large Christian shortwave broadcasting station ever determined with clarity what this program was designed to do.
2. No specific listening audience was designated, particularly since it was beamed to such a wide segment of the world.
3. It was assumed that those who listened were ready to make a decision for Christ and merely needed to be stimulated to "pray the sinner's prayer."
4. Cultural, religious, and life-style differences in the potential audience were completely overlooked.
5. Each of the writers had an entirely different concept of program sound, style, and format. Thus a listener tuning in from one day to the next would be baffled.

[1]While the name and geographic locations are changed, this example is based on a true situation.

Unfortunately, this example is all too common in Christian communication, although there are *many* positive exceptions. No clear target audience is specified, the potential listeners are just unidentified objects "out there" presumably waiting for the gospel to be dished out in haphazard fashion, and there are no measurements of effects. The tragedy is that this type of effort is nothing more than poor communication by any standard, and it becomes a travesty when assessed against the example of Jesus. Jesus lived, walked, and talked among people. He built a unique bond of trust by using the vernacular and speaking to people in terms they could understand. Never for a moment would He have tolerated the sloppy stewardship we sometimes cover with such a spiritual facade. In the final analysis, irresponsible stewardship does not show love and respect for the other person.

Is faulty communication stewardship simply a result of hardened spiritual arteries? This can happen, of course, but more often than not we have a shaky grasp of what communication is all about. Therefore, it is necessary to start at square one, so to speak, and wade through some basic material from communication theory. The first issue to be considered is the nature of communication itself, with special emphasis on the difference between interpersonal and mass communication. Next, we will examine the subject of audience sovereignty, which, as the reader will recall, forms the basis of one of the communication principles discussed in Chapter 1. Finally, we will come full circle to the example of Jesus to demonstrate how remarkably He exemplified the communication principles that many think have been pioneered only on Madison Avenue. In reality, Madison Avenue has much to learn from the Master.

THE NATURE OF COMMUNICATION

Most authorities agree that communication takes place when a message has been transmitted and the intended point is grasped by another.[2] In this sense, interpersonal and mass communication do not differ, but there are a number of other considerations that differentiate the two.

[2]For a review of the many definitions that have appeared in the literature, see *Interpersonal Communication: Survey and Studies,* ed. D.C. Barnlund, (Boston: Houghton Mifflin, 1968), pp. 4-5.

Interpersonal Communication

Mr. X and Ms. Y are engaged in conversation. Figure 2.1 represents the nature of the communication between them. This model is a composite of the many theories and models that have appeared in the vast literature on this subject. There are differences in details, but most agree on the fundamental elements of the process.[3]

FIGURE 2.1.

Interpersonal Communication

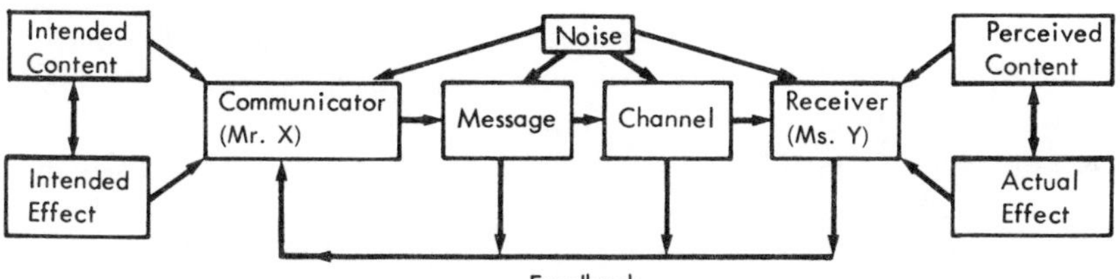

Mr. X has something he wants to say to Ms. Y. Certain words are selected that then are arranged in a pattern or sequence to be communicated. The technical word for this is "encoding." This encoded message has both an intended content and an intended effect. It is next transmitted through a channel of some type, probably the spoken word. Now, the hope is that Ms. Y will attend to the message and attempt to decode it. The actual effect of the whole process, however, is determined by her *perception* of what is said, not by its intended content.

---

[3]Among the standard sources are C. David Mortensen, *Communication: The Study of Human Interaction* (New York: McGraw-Hill, 1972); Wilbur Schramm and Donald F. Roberts, eds., *The Process and Effects of Mass Communication,* rev. ed. (Urbana, Ill.: University of Illinois Press, 1971); David K. Berlo, *The Process of Communication* (New York: Holt, Rinehart and Winston, 1960); Joseph A. DeVito, ed., *Communication: Concept and Processes* (Engelwood Cliffs, N.J.: Prentice-Hall, 1971); George A. Borden and John D. Stone, *Human Communication: The Process of Relating* (Menlow Park, Ca.: Cummings, 1976); Eugene A. Nida, *Message in Mission* (New York: Harper & Brothers, 1960); C. Shannon and W. Weaver, *The Mathematical Theory of Communication* (Urbana; Ill.: University of Illinois Press, 1949); D.C. Barnlund, "A Transactional Model of Communication," in K.K. Sereno and C.D. Mortensen, eds., *Foundations of Communication Theory* (New York: Harper & Row, 1970), pp. 83–102; B. Westley and M. MacLean, "A Conceptual Model for Communications Research" *Journalism Quarterly,* vol. 34 (1957), pp. 31–38; George Gerbner, "Toward a General Model of Communication," *Audio-Visual Communication Review,* vol. 4 (1956), pp. 171–199; and P. Watzlawick, J. Beavin, and D. Jackson, *Pragmatics of Human Communication* (New York: Norton, 1967).

Ms. Y's perception is dependent on things other than the message sent by Mr. X. For example, Mr. X can communicate a great deal by his nonverbal behavior. The environment in which the interaction takes place and Ms. Y's mental and physical states also make a difference. In addition, "noise" can enter. This is anything introduced into the communications channel that the sender did not intend.[4] It might be actual audible noise or other distracting elements that compete for attention.

The responses given by Ms. Y are termed feedback. Mr. X also can misperceive that feedback, however, because of noise and all of the other factors mentioned above.

The Communicator. Mr. X begins with both the intended content and the intended effect. For him to encode this message, he must be able to place himself in Ms. Y's shoes, so to speak, if he is to have any chance at success. This process, which is called empathy, is basic in communication.

Empathy begins early in life as we learn to take the role of another person. The child imitates his father or mother in play, for example. In the process of maturation, the child then becomes acquainted with the expectations of other people. Sooner or later it is possible to acquire a pretty good understanding of the meanings and definitions by which others regulate their lives. Taking the role of another thus becomes possible, and effective communication is facilitated.

The Message. Mr. X now encodes the message so that it can be sent to Ms. Y in either verbal or nonverbal form. The most common form, of course, involves use of spoken or written language.

Languages are composed of *signs* and *symbols.* A sign is something that indicates the existence of something within a context and hence can be readily grasped. A symbol, on the other hand, can be used quite apart from the context at hand and is just a label used to identify something.[5] Ideally, symbols acquire a more or less common meaning through social consensus, but this often does not take place as Nida points out:

> If only the right words could equal the right beliefs, and if right formulations would guarantee right relations with God, then the words would no longer be the words of life, but words substituted for life. In fact, the most grievous errors and pathetic failures in Christianity have resulted from a wrong understanding of its verbal symbols.[6]

---

[4]See Wilbur Schramm, "The Nature of Communication Between Humans," in Schramm and Roberts, *The Process and Effects of Mass Communication,* pp. 3–54.

[5]Nida, *Message in Mission,* p. 65.

[6]*Ibid.,* p. 69.

Communication certainly is helped when the two people are as much alike as possible. In other words, there should be substantial overlap in the sum total of influences on their behavior. Imagine what would happen if this were not the case. Anyone who has visited a foreign country is quite aware of the confusion resulting when two people attempt to communicate in entirely different languages, or even in the same language.

On the face of it, it is surprising that people ever can achieve a match between intended content and effect and perceived content and actual effect. Several additional factors come to our rescue. First, as Nida points out, human reasoning processes do not differ radically from one culture to the next. All people have at least some experience in common, and everyone possesses some capability to adjust to the expectations of others.[7] Also social norms provide approximate uniformities in behavior and ways of thinking. Probably both Mr. X and Ms. Y are subject to common influences of this type. Perhaps they both are members of the same church, residents of the same suburban community, and employed within the same company. Similarities in thinking and behavior are expected, and they should be able to anticipate one anothers' reactions.

The Channel. The channel usually will be the spoken word, but the importance of nonverbal modes should not be overlooked. Much is communicated by body movement (kinesic behavior), paralanguage (voice qualities and nonlanguage sounds such as laughing or yawning), skin sensitivity to touch and temperature, and use of cosmetics or dress.[8]

The Receiver. As has been stressed earlier, Ms. Y possesses full ability to miss the point of what Mr. X is trying to say. This perceptual selectivity is the greatest obstacle the communicator faces, and it will be discussed at length in the next section of the chapter.

Feedback. A smile from Ms. Y, a reply of some type, a frown, or some other response (or no response at all) allows Mr. X to determine whether or not the other person has "gotten the message." If it seems to be off target, he can try again and modify the message so as to achieve a more successful result.

The instantaneous feedback makes interpersonal communication highly efficient in the sense that both sender and receiver can keep trying until effective contact is made. Quite the opposite is true in mass communication as later discussion will demonstrate.

---

[7]*Ibid.,* p. 90.

[8]See S. Duncan, "Nonverbal Communication," *Psychological Bulletin,* vol. 72 (1969), pp. 118–137.

Mass Communication

In mass communication the message is sent to a large group at roughly the same point in time. The model of this process appears in Figure 2.2. Notice that the sender is now represented as an organization, because more likely than not many people interact in the message's design. Also, the audience is an interconnected group of receivers, each of whom interacts with others who may, in the process, affect the content. In fact, the content that emerges after social interaction may bear little resemblance to that which was sent, much to the communicator's dismay.

FIGURE 2.2

Mass Communication

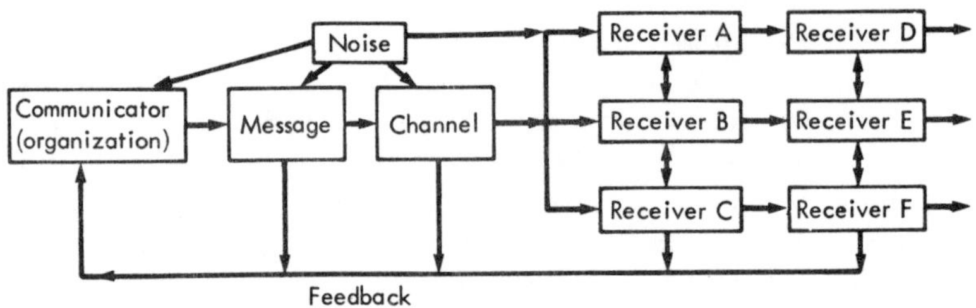

Source: James F. Engel, Hugh G. Wales, and Martin R. Warshaw, *Promotional Strategy,* 3rd ed. (Homewood, Ill.: Richard D. Irwin, Inc., 1975) p. 27. Used by special permission.

Mass communication also is profoundly affected by the social structure in which it takes place. The mass media as a complex social system is depicted in Figure 2.3. Of major concern in the contemporary world is the extent to which the various agencies can censor the free flow of information and deprive substantial segments of the population of the very information they need for survival.[9]

Arrows connect the various subsystems in Figure 2.3 to show how the flow of influence is expressed. Unfortunately, this complex of influences has only recently become the subject of concentrated inquiry, because most mass communication research to date focuses on persuasive effects of messages on individuals.

[9]Luis R. Beltran, "Research Ideologies in Conflict," *Journal of Communication,* vol. 23 (Spring, 1975), pp. 35–41.

FIGURE 2.3.

The Mass Media as a Social System

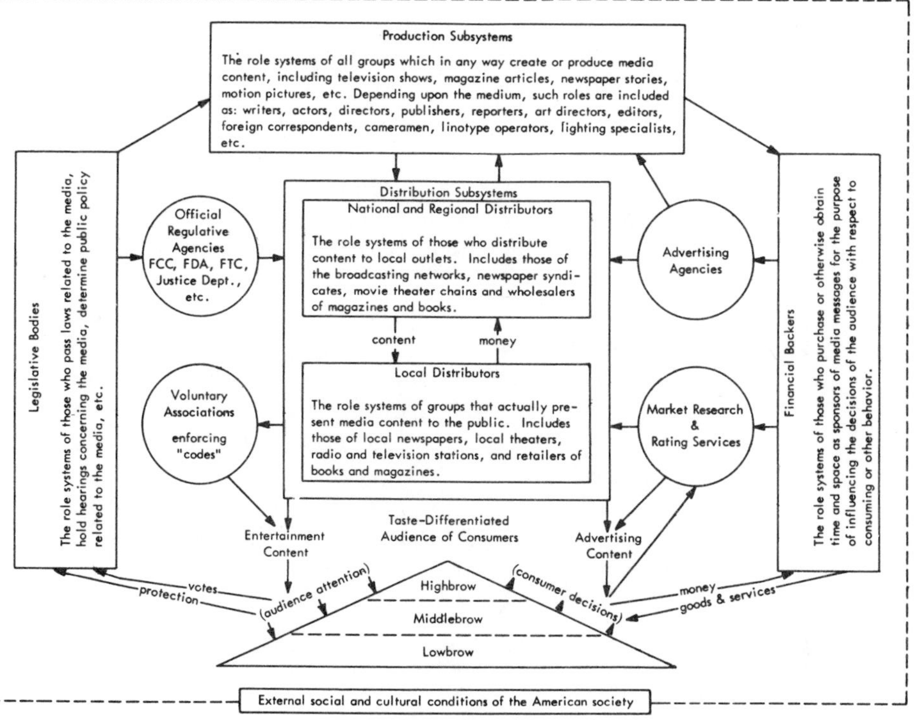

Source: Melvin L. DeFleur and Sandra Ball-Rokeach, *Theories of Mass Communication,* 3rd ed. (New York: David McKay Co. 1975), p. 166. Used by special permission.

The Communicator. The sender of the message through mass media most often is a governmental, educational, or commercial agency. The goal generally is to persuade people to accept some point of view or to inform and educate with respect to a particular topic. Many individuals interact in the process of message design. As a result, the need for collective decision can reduce both the speed and effectiveness of communication.

The Message. Message format does not necessarily differ from that of its interpersonal counterpart, because it also uses both verbal and nonverbal symbols. The primary difference is that it usually must be more impersonal due to the fact that it is directed toward a group rather than to an individual person. The result is that it is difficult to design it to achieve maximum impact on any one person in the audience. This message inflexibility is a primary disadvantage.

The Channel. Channels used include newspapers, radio, television, films, books, and so on. Usually these media are published, aired, or viewed at regular, spaced intervals with the result that both speed and flexibility in communication are further reduced. Also, communication tends to be indirect because of the obvious fact that both parties are not simultaneously present in space or time. The counteracting advantage, however, is that many people can be reached quickly at a lower cost than would be possible if face-to-face interaction was used.

The Receivers. The audience is a group of individuals, no one of which is directly known to the communicator. Selective perception is particularly likely because the message is designed for many people. As a result, it frequently will be off target for an individual and hence will be ignored, distorted, or forgotten. This is yet another disadvantage of the mass media.

Feedback. Finally, the physical separation of communicator and recipient means that effective feedback is nearly impossible. At the very least, feedback will be delayed because it must take the form of some type of audience survey. Examples would be readership surveys or questionnaires asking what television programs are viewed.

Audience surveys of these types are time-consuming and expensive. The greatest problem is that the feedback comes too late to permit altering the message during the communication process itself. Feedback is useful only for future efforts.

A Comparison of Mass and Interpersonal Communication

Obviously, the two modes of communication differ. There is an important generalization that must be grasped at this point because of its significance for Christian communication: *The basic role of the mass media is to change existing beliefs and attitudes, thus moving a person closer to decision.*[10] *The actual decision, however, usually is stimulated through face-to-face conversation.* To evaluate mass media efforts solely in terms of so-called "decisions" is to force a role on this form of

[10]This principle has emerged from decades of communications research. For an especially helpful discussion see Wilbur Schramm, *Mass Media and National Development* (Stanford, Ca.: Stanford University Press, 1964), p. 132ff.

communication for which it is not suited. However, the powerful impact of the media on *attitude changes* has been evidenced for decades. The problem lies in the inflexibility required to speak to groups rather than identified individuals and the profound delay of feedback.

The pros and cons of the two types of media are summarized in Figure 2.4.

FIGURE 2.4.

Comparative Advantages and Limitations of Interpersonal and Mass Media

	Interpersonal	**Mass**
Ability to stimulate a final act of conversion	High	Relatively Low
Reaching a large audience:		
Speed	Slow	Fast
Cost per individual contacted	Very high	Low
Feedback:		
Direction of message flow	Two way	One way
Speed of feedback	Instantaneous	Delayed
Accuracy of feedback	High	Low

Adapted from James F. Engel, Hugh G. Wales, and Martin R. Warshaw, *Promotional Strategy,* 3rd ed. (Homewood, Ill.: Richard D. Irwin, 1975), p. 30.

Using the Mass Media

Although this subject will be addressed again later, there are some initial generalizations about the use of mass media that should be grasped at this point.

Isolation of Audience Segments. Because the mass message must be directed to many recipients, it is necessary to isolate relatively homogenous *segments* of a total audience so that communication can take place. The target audience, for example, might be young, midwestern mothers in the middle social classes married to junior executives with college degrees. Each of these factors (young, midwestern, mother, middle class, college educated, junior executive) implies certain common ways of thinking and behaving. Thus messages directed to them probably can succeed in their intended effect if these common factors are kept in focus.

It is absolutely imperative to define the target audience and to study the background and motivation of its members *before* mass communication is undertaken. The same also is true in face-to-face interaction, but it is easy to correct a misfire in that situation. All is lost in mass communication if the message isn't perceived as intended.

How should audience segmentation be undertaken? This will be a topic discussed at greater length in Part II, but the major premise is to *seek out those who have factors in common who are likely to be receptive to the message at this point in time.* Sometimes this is referred to as the *fertile field principle*—sow your seed where it is likely to grow. It does not exhaust all options for strategy, but it will be an important building block.

Design of the Message. Communication through mass media requires that the story be told so that it can speak effectively to a group—an inflexibility that will cause the message to miss the mark with some. If the audience has been properly segmented, the probability of success is increased. The goal of segmentation is to achieve homogeneity so that one message will be suitable for many individuals. The odds of success are further increased by pretesting the message so that the probability of effectiveness can be gauged before funds are invested. This also will allow necessary modifications to be made.

Response Feedback. The mass communicator must use measures to analyze readership, message comprehension, attitude change, and so on. These will require some research expertise and expenditures as well. This is not an option, however, but an imperative if the mass media are ever to be used with any degree of precision.

AUDIENCE SOVEREIGNTY

In the early 1970s CBS introduced a program that was destined to become one of the most popular in its history—*All in the Family,* featuring Archie Bunker. Archie is an intriguing character, but he is known for two distinguishing characteristics—his prejudice and bigotry. One might logically assume that most viewers would perceive Archie for what he is, but an audience survey disclosed some surprising results.[11] Many saw Archie as a hero, and it turned out

[11]Neil Bidmar and Milton Rokeach, "Archie Bunker's Bigotry: A Study in Selective Perception and Exposure," *Journal of Communication,* vol. 24 (Winter, 1974), pp. 36–47.

that they embraced the very same patterns of prejudice. The non-bigoted, on the other hand, had the opposite reaction.

What has happened here? Both groups saw the same programs, but their responses were diametrically opposed. The first thing is the obvious fact that an audience is not just a group of passive recipients. The fact that they tend to see and hear what they want to see and hear is demonstrated by the fact that, on the average, only forty-four percent of those exposed to print advertisements notice a particular ad and, thirty-five percent read enough to identify the brand mentioned, and only nine percent say that they read most of the copy.[12] Thus human information processing is *highly selective.*

In order to appreciate the significance of audience sovereignty, it will be necessary to dig into the subject of *cognitive processes,* which is the study of the manner in which information is "transformed, reduced, elaborated, stored, recovered, and used."[13] It will be demonstrated as we look into the organization and functioning of memory that people are fully capable of resisting attempts to influence them, and there is no magic power available to the communicator. It is this all-important point that underlies the principle mentioned in Chapter 1: Success comes only as we *adapt communication content to the audience* without sacrifice, of course, of biblical fidelity.

Information Processing

The study of memory has emerged as one of the great concerns of contemporary psychology, because an understanding of its functions directly affects all attempts at communication.[14] Obviously memory, as with all psychological processes, can never be studied directly. The analyst must rely largely on verbal responses and make inferences as to what is taking place "upstairs." As a result, myriads of theories have surfaced, and who is to say which is closest to representing the actual processes themselves?[15] All that can be done

---

[12]Herbert Krugman, "What Makes Advertising Effective?" *Harvard Business Review,* vol. 53 (March/April, 1975), pp. 96–102.

[13]Ulrich Neisser, *Cognitive Psychology* (New York: Appleton, 1966), p. 4.

[14]McGuire has designated analysis of memory as one of the highest priorities of communications research. See William J. McGuire, "Some Internal Psychological Factors Influencing Consumer Choice," *Journal of Consumer Research,* vol. 2 (March, 1976), pp. 302–319.

[15]There are two excellent summaries for the interested reader. See Leo Postman, "Verbal Learning and Memory," in *Annual Review of Psychology,* ed. Mark R. Rosenzweig and Lyman W. Porter, vol. 26 (Palo Alto, Ca.: Annual Reviews, Inc., 1975), pp. 291–335 and Robert W. Chestnut and Jacob Jacoby, "Consumer Information Processing: Emerging Theory and Findings," in Arch G. Woodside, Jagdish N. Sheth, and Peter Bennett, eds., *Consumer and Industrial Buying Behavior* (New York: Elsevier North-Holland, 1977), pp. 219–234.

here is to give the best of contemporary thinking on this subject and recognize that much is as yet unknown.

Until recently most theorists distinguished between *short-term memory* (sometimes referred to as primary memory) and *long-term memory* (or secondary memory). Short-term memory was felt to be distinctly limited in capacity, and the goal was to understand how information moves from there into permanent storage.[16] About the only thing that could be said for certain was that a good bit of the information we take in never moves into long-term memory and hence is lost.

The two-stage memory theory has begun to give way to an emphasis on *active memory.*[17] Active memory is essentially similar to a desk top on which many things are assembled when one is working on a problem, and then later these things are put away. In effect, active memory is thought to function so that the individual can make sense out of in-coming information. New information and that already stored in long-term memory are brought together, and, in this way, the new input is categorized and interpreted.

Obviously not everything within long-term memory will be available for active memory. Probably the most important consideration is the extent to which memory contents are recirculated and used in problem solving.[18] If this recirculation does not take place, content more or less becomes buried in memory and increasingly inaccessible.

Memory, on the other hand, is always changing as new information enters. Figure 2.4 shows how this is thought to take place.

The first step is actual *exposure* and activation of the senses. The new information input moves into active memory, and it can be said that *attention* has been attracted. But this by no means guarantees that the message will be *received* (comprehended and retained) as the sender intends, because the stimulus may become changed as analysis takes place within memory. The last stage is some type of response, depicted here only as new *information and experience.* This could lead to change in beliefs, attitudes, and behavior. Each of the

---

[16]A good source is Robert G. Crowsers, *Principles of Learning in Memory* (Hillsdale, N. J.: Lawrence Erlbaum Assoc., 1976).

[17]For some of the evidence leading to this revised perspective, see Michael I. Posner, *Cognition: An Introduction* (Glenview, Ill.: Scott Foresman, 1973) and F.I.M. Craik and R.S. Lockhart, "Levels of Processing: A Framework for Memory Research," *Journal of Verbal Learning and Verbal Behavior,* vol. 11 (December, 1973) pp. 425–438.

[18]Donald A. Norman, *Memory and Attention* (New York: Wiley, 1969), p. 86.

FIGURE 2.4

The Stages in Information Processing

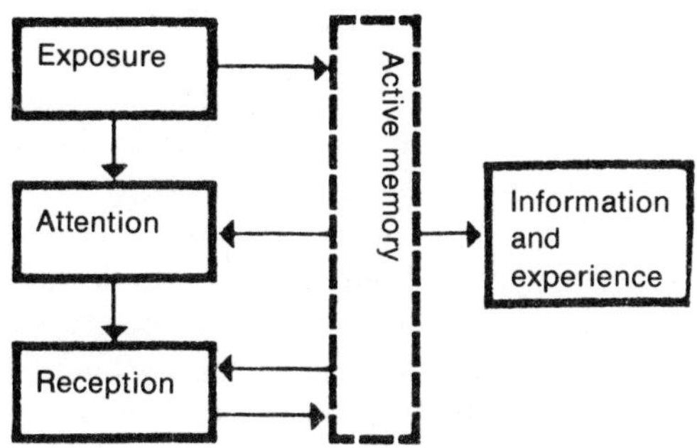

four stages in information processing (exposure, attention, reception, and response) is discussed in greater depth in the following pages.[19]

Exposure. Information processing commences when energy patterns, in the form of stimulus inputs, activate one or more of the five senses. For this to happen, of course, the communicator must select media, either interpersonal or mass, that reach the individual at the time and place where he or she happens to be. This principle of media selection is little more than common sense, but it is more difficult to implement than it might seem. For example, one Christian author wrote a book for "all who are seeking to know more about God." Now, what in the world does that mean? There will be wide differences in interest in this subject, and his goal is so vague as to be meaningless. Furthermore, he assumes that everyone will be a reader who will go to a Christian bookstore in a mass rush for his words of wisdom. What about those who never go near such outlets? Enough said?

Attention. Nearly a century ago, the famous psychologist William James offered this definition of attention:

> . . . the taking possession by the mind, in clear and vivid form, of one out of what seems several simultaneously possible objects or trains of thought. Focalization, concentration, of consciousness are of its essence. It implies withdrawal from some things in order to deal effectively with others.[20]

---

[19]The discussion here, of necessity, will be brief. Those interested in more detail should refer to James F. Engel, Roger D. Blackwell, and David T. Kollat, *Consumer Behavior,* 3rd ed. (Hinsdale, Ill.: Dryden Press, 1978), ch. 13.

[20]William James, *The Principles of Psychology,* vol. 1 (New York: Henry Holt and Co., 1890), pp. 403–404.

This definition is still used today with only one essential difference:[21] Attention is now viewed as the conscious end product of the process in which incoming information is categorized and given initial meaning. There are two distinct stages here: (1) preliminary classification and (2) analysis for pertinence.

In preliminary classification the stimulus is analyzed on an initial basis largely in terms of such physical properties as loudness, pitch, and so on.[22] Categories of meaning[23] that help in this process are stored within memory. For example, a thin object consisting of many pages between two covers is usually seen as a book. This conclusion is based on years of past experience with such objects. Such processing takes place virtually instantaneously without conscious awareness.

Analysis for pertinence refers to the way in which active memory functions to admit some information while excluding other information. Selection is made on the basis of information that is pertinent or relevant for the individual at a given point in time. Obviously, this is a selective process and it is profoundly affected by both needs and attitudes functioning as a part of active memory.

Active memory, in effect, functions as a kind of filter that opens and shuts in response to needs, values, and attitudes. The key for the communicator is to pinpoint these felt needs and use them as an entry point to attract attention. Otherwise the filter is likely to close. The psychological literature is full of pertinent illustrations. For example, hungry people are more likely to give a food-related response when exposed to a purposefully ambiguous stimulus. Psychological need can have the same effect as was demonstrated by the fact that those with a strong need for love and affiliation are much more likely to attend to and identify pictures of people from a larger grouping of pictures than will those who do not have a similar felt need.[24]

In an interesting series of studies it has been found that important values influence the speed of recognition for value-related words.

---

[21]See especially Neisser, *Cognitive Psychology*, and Norman, *Memory and Attention*, for elaboration.

[22]Neisser has popularized the distinction between preliminary classification and analysis for pertinence.

[23]The basic source on the nature of categories of meaning is J.S. Bruner, "On Perceptual Readiness," *Psychological Review*, vol. 64 (1957), pp. 123–152.

[24]J.W. Atkinson and E.L. Walker, "The Affiliation Motive and Perceptual Sensitivity to Faces," *Journal of Abnormal and Social Psychology*, vol. 53 (1956), pp. 38–44.

This type of selective attention is referred to as *perceptual vigilance.*[25] The reverse also happens through *perceptual defense* whereby recognition of threatening or low-valued stimuli is delayed or even totally avoided.[26] The underlying dynamic seems to be the perceived pertinence of the stimulus for the individual, and information processing is either augmented or inhibited.[27]

Finally, human beings have a persistent tendency to resist changes in strongly held attitudes and beliefs.[28] Because this is such an important phenomenon, it is discussed in a later section of the chapter.

Reception. The fact that attention has been attracted does not imply that intended message content and effect will equal actual content and effect. Whether or not information processing will proceed as intended depends upon *reception* (accurate comprehension of meaning and acceptance of that input into permanent memory).

(1) Comprehension. The filtering effect of active memory begun earlier also affects comprehension, and the outcome can be a surprising degree of distortion. In one landmark study, for instance, it was found that children from lower economic classes overestimate the size and value of coins when feeling them without seeing them.[29] In this case economic deprivation and the derived needs affect the whole process of perception. The literature now is full of such studies.

Miscomprehension also can enter due to the fact that a person's reaction to something often reflects his or her expectations about that stimulus and not the actual stimulus itself.[30] A soft-drink company introduced a new product that proved to be unsuccessful.[31] A taste test was undertaken in which this brand was compared with

---

[25]L. Postman and B. Schneider, "Personal Values, Visual Recognition, and Recall," *Psychological Review,* vol. 58 (1951), pp. 271–284.

[26]D.P. Spence, "Subliminal Perception and Perceptual Defense: Two Sides of a Single Problem," *Behavioral Science,* vol. 12 (1967), pp. 183–193.

[27]*Ibid.*

[28]For a thorough review, see E.E. Jones and H.D. Gerard, *Foundations of Social Psychology* (New York: Wiley, 1967), ch. 7.

[29]J.S. Bruner and Cecile C. Goodman, "Value and Need as Organizing Factors in Perception," *Journal of Abnormal and Social Psychology,* vol. 42 (1947), pp. 33–44.

[30]For a classic study, see A.L. Edwards, "Political Frames of Reference as a Factor Influencing Recognition," *Journal of Abnormal and Social Psychology,* vol. 38 (1941), pp. 34–50. See also Norman, *Memory and Attention.*

[31]"Twink: Perception of Taste," in Roger D. Blackwell, James F. Engel, and David T. Kollat, *Cases in Consumer Behavior* (New York: Holt, Rinehart and Winston, 1969), pp. 38–43.

others both with and without labels. When it was unlabeled, this unsuccessful brand was preferred by consumers over others, but exactly the opposite occurred when the label appeared. Apparently the brand name or company image strongly affected taste ratings. As a result, the whole promotional program was revamped, whereas the formulation of the product was left unchanged.

(2) Acceptance. Correct comprehension also does not guarantee that a message will be accepted into long-term memory where it will have a chance to modify beliefs, attitudes, or behavior. For instance, supporters of former President Nixon tended to remain unchanged in their convictions regarding his presidency for a long period after Watergate, in spite of all the contradictory evidence.[32] Once again this is an example of strongly held beliefs and the tendency to resist change.

This blocking effect works in interesting ways. In the first place, the person can miss the point completely, as was demonstrated by the Archie Bunker study cited earlier. A second response is to dismiss the source of the message as being biased and not worthy of consideration. Further, the message itself can be distorted in two ways.[33] The first is to sharpen or change it to make it consistent with present beliefs. The second, referred to as leveling, consists of blurring some details to bring about consistency with established predispositions.

Response. The final stage in the whole process is the entry into long-term memory in the form of new information and experience. The result then will be the response anticipated by the sender.

Resistance to Communication

The filtering effect of active memory is now quite apparent, and the upshot is that the individual has a God-given defense against unwanted persuasion. Some of the ways this affects use of the media have yet to be discussed, however, and that is the purpose of this section. The key point to be elaborated is this: *People resist change in strongly held beliefs and attitudes* and do so through selective information processing.

---

[32]Garrett J. O'Keefe, Jr. and Harold Mendelsohn, "Voter Selectivity, Partisanship and the Challenge of Watergate," *Communications Research,* vol. 1 (October, 1974), pp. 345–367.

[33]Thomas R. Donohue, "Impact of Viewer Predispositions on Political TV Commercials," *Journal of Broadcasting,* vol. 18 (Winter, 1973–74), pp. 3–16.

Selective Exposure. It came as a surprise to political observers in the 1940 presidential campaign that "exposure to political communications . . . is concentrated in the same group of people not spread among the people at large."[34] It has been found repeatedly that political rallies and campaigns sponsored by a given party attract mostly those from that party and vice versa. It seems commonplace for people to avoid unwanted persuasion simply by not being in the audience when they are forewarned.[35] Katz argues that we maintain beliefs in this way:

> . . . (a) . . . an individual self-censors his intake of communications so as to shield his beliefs and practices from attack; (b) . . . an individual seeks out communications which support his beliefs and practices; and (c) . . . the latter is particularly true when the beliefs or practices in question have undergone attack or the individual has otherwise been made less confident of them.[36]

Not all authorities agree with Katz on this assessment,[37] but the balance of evidence points this way.

Selective Attention. Earlier it was pointed out that the typical advertisement (or any mass media message, for that matter) is attended to by only a subset of all who are exposed. Assume, for instance, that a *Playboy* reader is exposed to the advertisement appearing in Figure 2.5. Furthermore, assume, as is likely, that he is quite happy with his life as it is and is not, as yet, really considering any change in the so-called "good life." Quite likely he will not pay any attention to this ad at all, even if he is exposed to it, and it is doubtful that any substantial changes will occur in beliefs or attitudes. Those seeking a change in life might react quite differently.

The logical strategy for the mass communicator in particular is to direct efforts to those who already are neutral or even sympathetic

---

[34]P.F. Lazarsfeld, B.B. Berelson, and H. Gaudet, "Radio and the Printed Page as Factors in Political Opinion and Voting," in W. Schramm, ed., *Mass Communications*, (Urbana, Ill.: University of Illinois Press, 1949), p. 484.

[35]See, for example, M.T. O'Keefe, "The Anti-Smoking Commercials: A Study of Television's Impact on Behavior," *Public Opinion Quarterly*, vol. 35 (1971), pp. 242–248.

[36]E. Katz, "On Reopening the Question of Selectivity in Exposure to Mass Communications," in *Theories of Cognitive Consistency: A Sourcebook*, ed. R.P. Abelson et. al. (Chicago: Rand McNally, 1968), p. 789.

[37]See D.O. Sears, "The Paradox of De Facto Selective Exposure Without Preferences for Supportive Information," in *Theories of Cognitive Consistency*, ed. Abelson et. al., pp. 777–787.

FIGURE 2.5.

An Appeal to the Playboy Reader

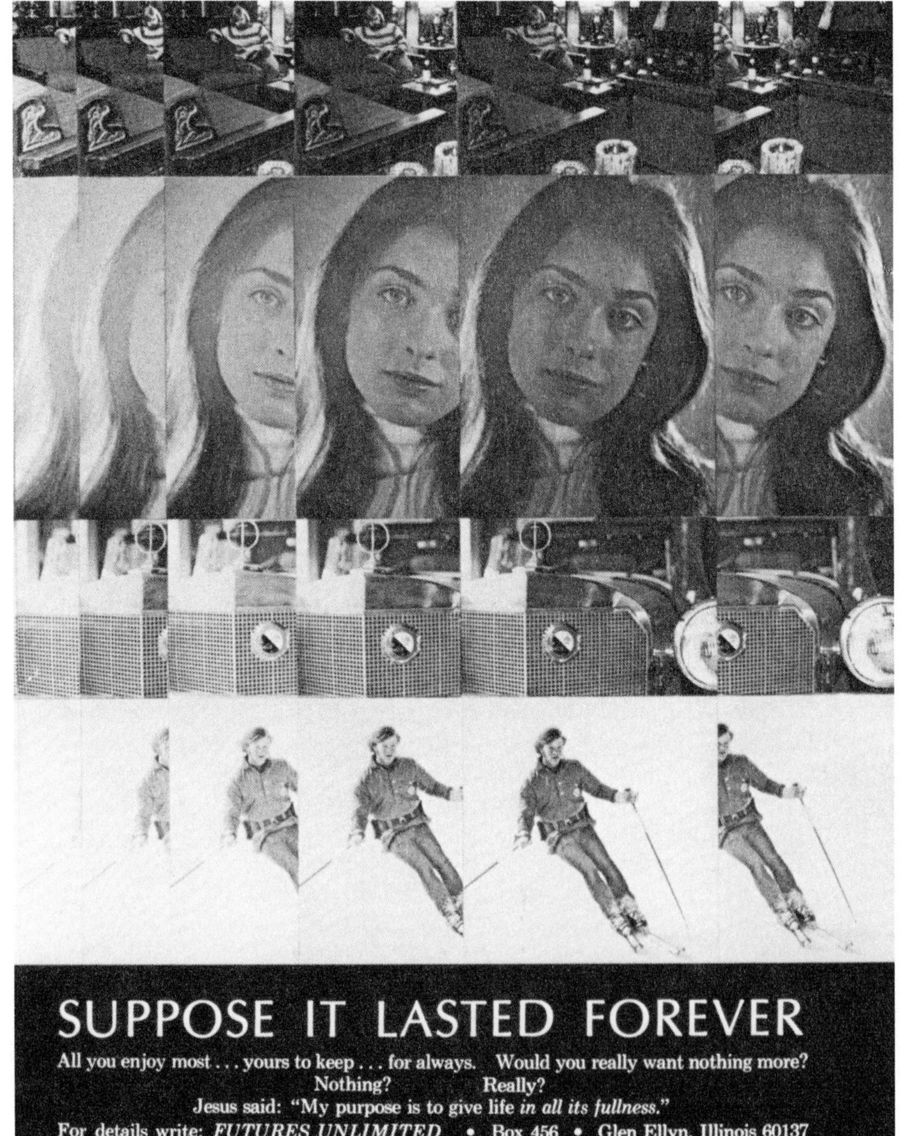

Courtesy of *Playboy* Magazine.

toward the point of view being advocated and to avoid those who are not. The probability of substantial inroads into the latter group is not high. This principle was referred to earlier as *audience segmentation,* and the concept is to focus, where possible, on fertile fields. Another possibility is to search for those whose beliefs are wavering for one reason or another. It is quite possible that some readers of *Playboy* are asking the question implied in the headline in Figure 2.5 and will be open to the advertisement's message. The hope is that there will be enough reponse from the audience to make the expenditure worthwhile.

Selective Reception. It is a surprising fact that the possibility of miscomprehension and lack of acceptance of a persuasive message was overlooked until about the time of World War II. Propagandists assumed (along with many Christian communicators yet today) that simply exposing people to the message would bring about the desired response. It came as a surprise that propaganda films did not succeed in making members of the Allied forces more eager to fight.[38] Other studies began to document selective reception, especially in the political arena:

> In the course of the campaign . . . strength of party support influences the perception of political issues. The more intensely one holds a vote position, the more likely he is to see the political environment as favorable to himself, as confirming his own beliefs. He is less likely to perceive uncongenial and contradictory events or points of view and hence presumably less likely to revise his own original position.[39]

It was found that strong party members saw the stand of preferred candidates as being in harmony with their own beliefs, regardless of reality.

As was mentioned earlier, a common means of miscomprehension is to reject the source, the content, or both as being biased. In one famous study, favorable reactions were expected to increase as the distance decreased between the recipient's viewpoint and that advocated in the persuasive message.[40] Opinions were measured toward the issue of repeal of prohibition, a hot topic in Oklahoma at that

[38]C.I. Hovland, A.A. Lumsdaine, and F.D. Sheffield, *Experiments in Mass Communication,* vol. 3 (Princeton, N. J.: Princeton University Press, 1949).

[39]B.R. Berelson, P.F. Lazarsfeld, and W.N. McPhee, *Voting* (Chicago: University of Chicago Press, 1954), p. 223.

[40]C.I. Hovland, O.J. Harvey, and M. Sherif, "Assimilation and Contrast Effects in Reactions to Communication and Attitude Change," *Journal of Abnormal and Social Psychology,* vol. 55 (1957), pp. 244–252.

time. Subsequent communications were administered differing in varying degrees from the categories of public opinion on this topic. When the recipient viewed the discrepancy as large, the message was perceived as less fair, less informed, less logical, and so on.

Now let's return to our *Playboy* reader and the advertisement in Figure 2.5. It is entirely possible that he will read it but distort the message. He might not even see that the intent is to present Jesus Christ as an alternative to his life-style. Acceptance could be prevented by concluding that "there go those Christian brainwashers again." Therefore, exposure and attraction of attention by no means insure that the message will be perceived as intended.

Fortunately, the conveying of facts may be unaffected even though the persuasive intent of a message is short-circuited. For example, one orientation film for soldiers in World War II did not change their attitudes toward the British Army as allies, but there was recall about how the British were able to withstand Nazi bombings.[41] This type of effect is not uncommon.[42]

The Question of Persuasive Influence Without Awareness. Years ago an adman, James Vicary, gave rise to fears of "Big Brother" influence by supposedly inducing people to act against their desires. His method allegedly was to flash the words "Eat Popcorn" and "Drink Coke" on a movie screen at such high speeds that people were unaware of what he was doing.[43] He then reported that sales of both items jumped during intermission.

Technically it would be said that Vicary's presentation was *subliminal* or below the level (threshold) at which conscious discrimination is possible—hence the term "subliminal perception." In reality, this whole thing was a hoax, and all attempts at replication of that experiment have failed.

More recently Dixon has re-examined the whole subject of subliminal perception.[44] While subliminal influence is possible, there is no evidence whatsoever that the ability to filter out unwanted persuasion is in any way circumvented. Furthermore, the stimulus presented is so fractional in nature that the odds of ever capturing

---

[41]Hovland, Lumsdaine, and Sheffield, *Experiments in Mass Communication.*

[42]E.J. Baur, "Opinion Change in a Public Controversy," *Public Opinion Quarterly*, vol. 24 (1962), pp. 212–226.

[43]J.J. Bachrach, "The Ethics of Tachistoscopy," *Bulletin of Atomic Scientists,* vol. 15 (1959), pp. 212–215.

[44]Norman F. Dixon, *Subliminal Perception—The Nature of the Controversy* (Maidenhead-Berkshire, England: McGraw-Hill Publishing Co., Ltd., 1971).

attention are weakened.[45] Given the present state of the art there is nothing to be gained through use of subliminal influence as a strategy.

A Final Word on Sovereignty

The individual *is* sovereign, with full abilities to screen out messages contradicting strongly held predispositions. The only way to overcome this filtering ability is to gain full control of another's life, as would be possible in a prison camp setting.[46] Then one could implement hypnosis, sensory deprivation (perhaps through solitary confinement), stimulation with drugs, inducing of stress, or brain implantation with electrodes.[47] Obviously these are beyond the means of communicators in normal situations, and, as one authority has said so clearly, understanding the audience is the only clue to success:

> . . . to the social scientist, A's influence of B is not a matter of art, but of the witting or unwitting application of known or unknown scientific principles and must be looked upon as such. The scientific analysis of human behavior is perhaps the single most potent weapon in A's arsenal. If he fails to make use of this powerful tool, he does so at his own risk.[48]

IN THE STEPS OF THE MASTER

It is hoped that the reader has survived this brief but intensive review of some essentials of communication theory. Catch your breath now, and let's return to the story of Sally Anderson whose dilemma triggered this whole discussion. It should be abundantly apparent that the approach to programming followed by her organization violates every tenet of communication theory. But there is even a more serious side to this situation: *It also fails to capitalize upon the very example of Jesus* who left us a clear model to follow. This example had four dimensions: (1) knowing the nature of man, (2) respecting audience sovereignty, (3) communicating the relevancy of the word of God, and (4) avoiding "canned" strategies.

---

[45]J.V. McConnell, R.L. Cutler, and E.B. McNeil, "Subliminal Stimulation: An Overview," *American Psychologist,* vol. 11 (1958), p. 230ff.

[46]J.V. McConnell, "Persuasion and Behavioral Change," mimeograph (Ann Arbor, Mich.: University of Michigan, 1959).

[47]A.D. Biderman and H. Zimmer, eds., *The Manipulation of Human Behavior* (New York: Wiley, 1961).

[48]McConnell, "Persuasion and Behavioral Change," p. 73.

Knowing the Nature of Man

The fact that Jesus completely understood the nature of man (John 2:25) was quite apparent in all He said and did. In the first place, He knew, as is made clear in the creation accounts, that man, by a willful act of disobedience, severed a personal relationship between Himself and God. This disobedience, in turn, made each person become a slave to self-seeking. There is no choice but to remain imprisoned by one's ego unless the liberating gift of salvation offered by Christ is accepted. Man without Christ, then, is incomplete, destined to live with a perceptual filter programmed around the "big I."

In spite of the fall, man is created in the image of God. This means, at the very least, he has rational capacities, problem-solving ability, and the capacity to respond to the Word of God. None of this would be possible, however, without memory. Beliefs and attitudes become formed and stored throughout life and provide a kind of "map of the world." At the heart of this is the filtering mechanism that helps us to behave in a manner consistent with basic needs and to avoid those outside influences and behavior patterns that are nonadaptive.

The ego in turn lies at the heart of the filter. Therefore, fallen man remains a self-seeker in both thoughts and deeds. When pushed to ultimate extremes, all forms of depravity result. Change comes not by self-effort but by a total rebirth and reprogramming from within (2 Cor. 5:17).

Respecting Audience Sovereignty

Jesus knew that some would accept Him and that others would not. His very words on this subject make that quite clear: "I have not come to call righteous men but sinners to repentance" (Luke 5:32, NASB). He was saying, in effect, that the "religious ones" of His day felt they had all the answers. They had scriptural proof texts for everything and did not recognize their own spiritual need. Thus filters were completely closed. Jesus' approach generally was to seek those who deeply felt a need for change in their life and to offer them the means of satisfying that need in a way they could understand.

It is interesting that Jesus never resorted to any kind of trickery or gimmickry. Joe Bayly has written incisively about a kind of "spiritual brainwashing" that stops short of nothing to stimulate a "decision."[49] Jesus exemplifed an ethical standard that many contemporary evangelists violate (we hope in innocence rather than willfully): *"Any persuasive effort which restricts another's freedom to choose for or against Jesus Christ is wrong."*[50]

One of the most frequent forms of outright biblical distortion is to present Christianity as the answer to all life's problems while ignoring its ethical demands for the new believer. Some of our rosy testimonies leave the mistaken impression that acceptance of Christ removes the problems and leads to even greater success in one's personal strivings. The words of the Lausanne Covenant again provide a good corrective:

> In issuing the Gospel invitation we have no liberty to conceal the cost of discipleship. Jesus still calls all who would follow him to deny themselves, take up their cross, and identify themselves with his new community. The results of evangelism include obedience to Christ, incorporation into his church and responsible service in the world.[51]

Communicating the Relevance of the Word of God

Missionary strategist Don Richardson has made the observation that the job of the church is *not* to make the gospel relevant but rather to *communicate the relevance of the gospel.*[52] This is a simple but profound point. Our tendency is to distort the Word of God to make it acceptable to modern man, whereas Jesus took great pains to understand His audience so that He in turn could utilize those portions of biblical truth that spoke to the needs of the moment.[53]

How did Jesus come to know so much about those whom He encountered? First, He lived among them. He met people on the streets, in the places of prayer, on the hillsides, at work in fishing boats, at weddings, at meals. This is a prime example of observational research, which then was energized by the Holy Spirit to provide remarkable insights into basic needs and motivations.

---

[49]Joe Bayly, "The Evil of Spiritual Brainwashing," in *Out of My Mind* (Wheaton, Ill.: Tyndale, 1970), pp. 86–89.

[50]Em Griffin, *The Mind Changers* (Wheaton, Ill.: Tyndale, 1976), p. 28.

[51]J.D. Douglas, ed., *Let the Earth Hear His Voice* (Minneapolis: World Wide Publications, 1975), p. 4.

[52]Distinguished Lectureship, Communications Department, Wheaton Graduate School, April 4, 1978 (tape available upon request).

[53]For an excellent analysis of the approach of Jesus, see James Bowman, "Practicing What We Preach: A Biblical View of Communicating," *Religious Broadcasting,* vol. 7 (October/November, 1975), pp. 18–19.

Next, Jesus was not a one-way communicator pontificating in "take it or leave it" style. He asked questions, listened, probed, reasoned, and dialogued. He practiced empathy and truly could put Himself in another's shoes. As John R. Stott has pointed out, dialogue is always part of true evangelism:

> Dialog is a token of genuine Christian love, because it indicates our steadfast resolve to rid our minds of the prejudices and caricatures which we may entertain about other people; the struggle to listen through their ears and look through their eyes so as to grasp what prevents them from hearing the gospel and seeing Christ; to sympathize with them in all of their doubts, fears, hangups.[54]

Through establishing empathy, Jesus was able to communicate gospel relevance in a unique fashion. In a real sense He and the first-century church "let the world set the agenda," as Michael Green reminds us.[55] Jesus began at the point of felt need and moved from there with insight to bring spiritual light on the underlying dimensions of the problems. But notice that felt needs were *not* ignored as being trivial or unimportant.

Another part of Jesus' method was to take the person from the known and familiar to the unknown through use of metaphor[56] and parables[57]—symbols with which all were familiar or illustrations from real life. Thus both the messenger and the message were received as intended because He built trust by using the vernacular and speaking to the needs of the audience.

Finally, Jesus broke all molds and stereotypes. One principle of communication theory not yet discussed is a very simple one: The greater the predictability of the message, the smaller its impact. All this means is that once the message becomes familiar, it ceases to have as much influence. God coming to Earth in the person of a man, who in turn made humanly outrageous claims about Himself, certainly shattered the predictability others had come to expect from

---

[54]John R.W. Stott, *Christian Mission in the Modern World* (Downers Grove, Ill.: InterVarsity Press, 1975), p. 81.

[55]Michael Green, "Methods and Strategy in the Evangelism of the Early Church," in Douglas, *Let the Earth Hear His Voice,* p. 164.

[56]R.T. Books, "Concerning Metaphors and Symbols—More Than English Grammar? *Christian Communications Spectrum,* vol. 3 (Winter, 1977), pp. 17–19.

[57]Brad L. Smith, "A Philosophy of Christian Communications Strategy" (unpublished paper, Wheaton Graduate School, May 28, 1975).

religious teachers of the time.[58] In the same sense, a contemporary Christian communicator breaks the predictability barrier when he or she can truly exemplify the live miracle of day-to-day living with the power of Jesus Christ.

Avoiding Canned Strategies

A careful analysis of the Gospels reveals that Jesus continuously varied His message. Obviously, truth was not distorted in the process. Rather, the message was adapted to all circumstances.

There are some today who are saying loud and clear that successful evangelism is the product of using the right methods, especially those that reduce the essence of the message to four or five basic points. Certainly there is nothing wrong with such tracts when properly used, but Stott sounds an altogether appropriate warning: ". . . we must never degrade evangelism into being merely or even mainly a technique to be learned or a formula to be recited."[59] There is no substitute for the hard work of audience analysis, the sifting out of felt needs, and the use of the gospel as a "two-edged sword" in the manner for which it is intended. Jesus proved that there is no place for simplistic, program-oriented approaches.

[58]Charles H. Kraft, "The Incarnation, Cross-Cultural Communication and Communication Theory," *Evangelical Missions Quarterly,* vol. 9 (Fall, 1973), pp. 277–284.

[59]Stott, *Christian Mission in the Modern World,* p. 125.

CHAPTER 3
The Spiritual Decision Process

"At last the Christians in Japan are emerging from the dark ages and there is hope for that great country!" This was the glowing report in a United States publication after hundreds of Japanese pastors and laymen were trained to share their faith and went door to door in one city. Thousands allegedly had accepted Christ, and the Christians presumably were emboldened to believe that they could be effective in evangelism.

Nearly two months later most of the pastors engaged in this outreach gathered at a conference attended by the author, and they were a disillusioned bunch. Follow-up efforts were showing that nearly all of those who had supposedly "accepted Christ" were largely unchanged. They were not interested in pursuing Christianity in any form—Bible study, church attendance, and so on. Accepting Christ, by the way, was defined as having prayed a prayer to invite "Christ into one's heart."

What had gone wrong? A careful analysis disclosed that the handful who showed some evidence of a truly changed life had a substantial Christian background. Those whose lives were unaffected apparently had little grasp of such terms as "God's love," "sin," "a man named Jesus who claimed to be God," and the significance of a genuine acceptance of Christ. They willingly prayed a prayer with a lay evangelist, but this could have meant many things: (1) a response of courtesy and desire not to offend; (2) "fire insurance" in which the person perceived that a prayer to Christ would be a helpful addition to prayers to Buddha, Shinto gods, and other forms of deity; (3) a way of getting rid of the evangelist; or (4) a response of genuine interest to pursue Christianity further but not a true acceptance of Christ at that point in time. The obvious conclusion is that salvation decisions had been assumed but not confirmed! This error was only compounded by the glowing report to the United States constituency.

In the final analysis the root problem illustrated here is an extraordinarily common one: *a faulty understanding of spiritual decision processes.* The method of communication used made assumptions about audience background and understanding that were unwarranted. As a result, the tenets of communication discussed in the previous chapter were violated.

This chapter elaborates two of the principles of Christian communication stated in Chapter 1: (1) goal-oriented communication is imperative and (2) becoming a disciple is an unending process with many influences. The issue of the spiritual decision process is central, because the remainder of this book rests on the premises developed here.

DECIPHERING THE TERM "DISCIPLE"

Jesus' last words to His core group of followers were, ". . .'All authority in heaven and on earth has been given to me. Therefore go and make disciples of all nations, baptizing them in the name of the Father and of the Son and of the Holy Spirit, and teaching them to obey everything I have commanded you. And surely I will be with you always, to the very end of the age' " (Matt. 28:18–20, NIV).

The first and most obvious point is that Jesus, in effect, is empowering believers with the very authority given to Him by the Father to *go* unto all the earth sharing the message that He provided by His life, death, and resurrection. This is not an option for an obedient church. This command, often referred to as the Great Commission, stands for the church until the "very end of the age."[1] From the first century until the present the church has been alive and vital only when it has taken this command seriously.[2] The best analogy is of a

[1]For a discussion in a more contemporary context, see Johannes Schneider, "The Authority of Evangelism," *Christianity Today* (October 28, 1966), pp. 4–8 and Max Warren, *I Believe in the Great Commission* (Grand Rapids, Mich.: Wm. B. Eerdmans, 1976).

[2]See Michael Green, "Methods and Strategy in the Evangelism of the Early Church," in J.D. Douglas, ed., *Let the Earth Hear His Voice* (Minneapolis; World Wide Publications, 1975), pp. 159–180.

body of water with no outlet—the water becomes dead and stagnant. When the outlet is functioning, on the other hand, there is renewal and life. So it all boils down to the issue of obedience. In the words of the Lausanne Covenant, "We need to break out of our ecclesiastical ghettos and permeate non-Christian society. . . . World evangelization requires the whole church to take the whole Gospel to the whole world."[3]

Most orthodox Christians have no difficulty with the meaning of the so-called Great Commission up to this point, but now we enter into a thorny issue. What does it mean to "make disciples"? When does a person become a disciple? One's answer to this question profoundly affects his or her whole approach to world evangelization. Thus, it is necessary to do some deciphering of the term disciple.

When Does a Person Become a Disciple?

There are many who hold the viewpoint that one becomes a disciple at the point when they accept Jesus Christ as Savior.[4] Furthermore, it is alleged that this is the meaning Jesus had in mind when He gave His challenge to the church. Therefore, the essence of the Great Commission, stated variously, is to share the gospel in such a way that people in all nations both understand it and are given opportunity to respond. This then will "fulfill the Great Commission" and essentially discharge the primary mission of the church. No one would advocate, by the way, that Christian growth is not essential, but it is not seen, according to this viewpoint, as being encompassed in the Great Commission.

Others would take quite a different point of view. Consider the words of Orlando Costas, for example:

> To separate the "make disciples" of Matthew 28:19 and the parallel expression of verse 20, "teaching them," is to force on the passage an interpretation contrary to the structure of the sentence that begins in verse 19. Further, it is to misunderstand the role of a disciple.[5]

The argument is that the true meaning of disciple transcends the act of accepting Christ. Rather, it is an unending process in which the

---

[3]Douglas, *Let the Earth Hear His Voice,* p. 5.

[4]This viewpoint is strongly advocated by two of the leading writers on church growth theory. See particularly, Donald McGavran, *Understanding Church Growth* (Grand Rapids, Mich.: Wm. B. Eerdmans, 1970) and C. Peter Wagner, *Frontiers in Missionary Strategy* (Chicago: Moody Press, 1971).

[5]Orlando E. Costas, *The Church and Its Mission: A Shattering Critique From the Third World* (Wheaton, Ill.: Tyndale, 1974), p. 142.

believer submits to the lordship of Christ and lives in such a way that Christian ethics permeate society at large.

Which viewpoint is correct? In one sense, both are, because it is an undeniable fact that one becomes a disciple once he has decided to follow Jesus (Mark 1:17).[6] Therefore, one meaning of the term "disciple" is to "follow me."[7] If this has exhausted the meaning, then the first perspective is valid and one perhaps could respond enthusiastically to the rallying cry "The Great Commission in this Generation" echoed by John R. Mott and the Christian Volunteer Movement at the turn of the century and others since that time.

There is more to the term, however, than simply being a follower. The Greek word used in the Gospels and in the Book of Acts is *Mathetes,* which denotes a pupil and continuing adherent of his master.[8] In short, discipleship requires continued obedience over time. The convert is to be *baptized* and *taught* to observe all that Christ has commanded the church. Jesus said, ". . .'If you abide in My word, then you are truly disciples of Mine" (John 8:31, NASB). Thus, becoming a disciple is a *process* beginning when one receives Christ, continuing over a lifetime as one is conformed to His image (Phil. 1:6), and culminating in glory at the end of the age. In this broader perspective, the Great Commission *never* is fulfilled but always is in the process of fulfillment. Furthermore, the obligation of the church is not released when wide-scale evangelism has taken place, because the hard work of cultivation of new believers still remains. *One cannot separate evangelism and cultivation and be true to the biblical mandate.*

What Difference Does It All Make?

Everyone agrees that we should do both evangelism and cultivation, so why split hairs? It is not as simple an issue as it might seem, however, because the separation of cultivating Christian growth from the Great Commission *can* have some unfortunate consequences if we are not careful.

Over Emphasis on Evangelism. This is what the author earlier referred to as "Great Commissionitis"—a nonbiblical tendency to de-

[6]J.B. Bauer, *Sacramentum Verbi* (New York: Herder & Herder, 1970), p. 210.

[7]Kenneth S. Wuest, *Studies in the Vocabulary* (Grand Rapids, Mich.: Wm. B. Eerdmans, 1945), p. 25.

[8]See James Hastings, ed., *A Dictionary of the Bible* (Edinburgh: T & T Clark, 1905), p. 609 and *Wycliffe Bible Encyclopedia,* vol. 1 (Chicago: Moody Press, 1975), p. 458.

fine the role of the church primarily around "saving the lost." Evangelism thus takes center stage, with the result that Christian growth is secondary. Anyone with much experience in mass evangelism can point to crusades that supposedly have reached thousands, few of whom ever show up anywhere near the church because of lack of follow-up and cultivation. Perhaps they were converted, but who knows? God certainly does not intend to have His kingdom occupied by vast numbers of spiritual babies.

All too quickly this imbalanced emphasis leads to real impotence within the church. The church becomes a center for saving the lost while the spiritual needs of believers go unmet. One Latin American church leader told the author that the church in his country has not learned the true meaning of discipleship at all. They are commanded to evangelize and they do. But, he asks, how can they give away something they possess only in the most rudimentary form? And the church lies moribund while the "Great Commission machinery" cranks on.

In a debate between good friends, Peter Wagner and the author have taken strongly opposed positions on this issue. Wagner argues, quoting Donald McGavran, that it is a grave missiological error to confuse the issues of evangelism and discipleship and treat them together in a strategy of outreach.[9] The author, on the other hand, contends that it is a grave missiological error *not* to do so for the reasons already cited. Not only does it do offense to Scripture, but it causes an imbalance in church outreach. Furthermore, recent experience with crusades of Luis Palau in South America have demonstrated that the building of the church prior to the onset of concentrated evangelism results in sharp increases both in the continued effectiveness of the church in outreach and growth of believers and in the numbers of converts who find their way into church ranks.[10] This is leading to growing recognition that a primary objective of world evangelization is to strengthen the church so it can perform its tasks with greater effectiveness.[11]

A Short-Circuiting of Ethical Mandates. A distorted priority that places evangelism over and above the spiritual maturity of the church also can have grave ethical consequences. As Costas puts it:

---

[9]See *Evangelical Missions Quarterly,* vol. 12 (July, 1976), pp. 177–180.

[10]E. Edgardo Silvoso, "In Rosario It Was Different—Crusade Converts Are in the Churches," *Evangelical Missions Quarterly,* vol. 14 (April, 1978), pp. 83–88.

[11]Edward C. Pentecost, "Time for Faith Boards to Change Goals for Strategy?" *Evangelical Missions Quarterly,* vol. 12 (October, 1976), pp. 211–217.

> The preaching of the gospel must not only be seen in its horizontal dimension. The act of discipling should also be seen in an ethical context, and not merely in terms of seeking a decision for Christ.[12]

Unfortunately, our measure of success can become the *number* of decisions for Christ, leaving the effects these decisions should have on life within society and culture largely ignored.[13] All of the pressing social issues of the day—undue materialism, racism, secularization of values, oppression of the poor, and any number of others—tend to lie dormant at least insofar as the average church member is concerned. To say that we are following Jesus and observing all that He taught is a travesty under such conditions. In the final analysis, it is outright disobedience to the gospel when viewed from a more holistic perspective.

A Broadened View of the Great Commission

This book will take a more holistic view of the Great Commission, a view which encompasses the broadened definition of discipleship stated above. In fact, the term "Great Commission" no longer will be used, because it appears nowhere in the Bible. It tends to become little more than a man-made invention used as a rallying cry for concentrated outreach, and its connotations can become unbiblical when carried to the extreme. This statement must not be misinterpreted by the reader, however. Remember our insistence that evangelism is *not* an option. The plea is for balance. Padilla summarizes the issues well in his definition of evangelism:

> To evangelize is to proclaim Christ Jesus as Lord and Savior, by whose work man is delivered from both the guilt and the power of sin and integrated into God's plans to put all things under the rule of Christ.[14]

THE PROCESS OF MAKING DISCIPLES

Our basic premise, then, is that one becomes a disciple *both initially and behaviorally* through a process that extends over a lifetime and that has many influences. Looking strictly at the act of accepting Christ initially, Scobie in his exhaustive review of research on the psychology of conversion, notes that there are three basic types of conversion: (1) sudden, (2) gradual, and (3) unconcscious.[15]

---

[12]Costas, *The Church and Its Mission,* p. 142.

[13]René Padilla, "Evangelism and the World," in Douglas, *Let the Earth Hear His Voice,* pp. 116–146.

[14]*Ibid.,* p. 122.

[15]Geoffrey E.W. Scobie, *Psychology of Religion* (New York: Wiley, 1975).

The first of these categories, sudden conversion, is most perplexing. Usually sudden converts report no prior thought, recognition of personal needs, or particular religious interest but nonetheless make a religious decision usually in a mass evangelism setting.[16] Sudden conversion was reported, for instance, by the great missionary pioneer Hudson Taylor when the gospel was presented for the first time in the interior of China. Contemporary research has shed some light on this phenomonon, however. First of all, it is relatively rare,[17] and secondly it may be more apparent than real. Colquhoun assumed that those who came forward during the 1954 and 1955 evangelistic campaigns conducted by Billy Graham in Great Britain were sudden converts.[18] A more penetrating analysis found that this was not the case at all; rather, the response of most at these crusades was one of a series of responses of various types that were made as these new converts had learned more about Christianity.[19]

Gradual conversion is by far the most common.[20] It can extend over quite a period of time, and it encompasses a progressive change from rejection of Christianity as a whole or in part to acceptance. It may climax in what appears to be sudden conversion, but the actual act of decision is secondary to the process itself.

So-called unconscious conversion takes place when an individual is brought up under the direct influence of Christian beliefs in the home and cannot document a decision point. Scobie found that thirty percent of theological students followed this pathway.[21] There is a decision process, of course, even though the culminating point cannot be recalled.

What this says is that some type of decision process is the normal route to conversion, and this has been affirmed by many writers on this subject.[22] Scripture also states that a saving faith in Christ does not require a leap into the unknown. Paul, writing to the Corinthians,

---

[16]*Ibid.*, ch. 6.

[17]*Ibid.*

[18]F. Colquhoun, *Harringay Story* (London: Hodder and Stoughton, 1955).

[19]R. Holt, *An Approach to the Psychology of Religion* (Boston: Christopher, 1956).

[20]Scobie found this to be the case in his study of the decision processes of theological students.

[21]Scobie, *Psychology of Religion.*

[22]See, for example, Viggo B. Søgaard, *Everything You Need to Know for a Cassette Ministry* (Minneapolis: Bethany Fellowship, 1975); Em Griffin, *The Mind Changers* (Wheaton, Ill.: Tyndale, 1976); Edward R. Dayton, *Planning Strategies for Evangelism: A Workbook,* 6th ed. (Monrovia, Ca.: MARC, 1978); A.R. Tippett, *Verdict Theology and Missionary Theory* (South Pasadena, Ca.: William Carey Library, 1973).

stated that a valid decision must be based on information concerning who Christ is, what He has done to make salvation possible, and what He will do in the future (1 Cor. 15:3,4). As Horne has pointed out, "Apart from such knowledge, faith would be blind conjecture at the best and foolish mockery at the worst."[23]

Finally, theologians virtually since the time of Christ have conjectured about the decision process. Technically, doctrines abound regarding the *ordo salutis,* or the order in which Christ's redeeming work is applied to man. All would agree with Berkhof when he states the essence of the issue:

> When we speak of an *ordo salutis,* we do not forget that the work of applying the grace of God to the individual sinner is a unitary process, but simply stress the fact that various movements can be distinguished in the process, that the work of application of redemption proceeds in a definite and reasonable order, and that God does not impart the fulness of His salvation to the sinner in a single act.[24]

There is substantial disagreement on the exact steps in the process, and there are at least three distinctly different viewpoints (the Lutheran, the Arminian, and the Calvinist).[25] Unfortunately, there is no definitive way to resolve differences, because Scripture does not state a fixed or complete *ordo salutis.*[26] Therefore, theological speculation of this nature can be a pretty fruitless endeavor.

This all boils down to a simple fact: People generally do not accept Christ without some understanding of the gospel and its relevance for their life. Otherwise, why would they embrace something that, from a strictly human point of view, makes little sense? The tragedy is that such an obvious point is often overlooked in evangelistic endeavors. One of the most common statements from the pulpit is that "the lost are just waiting to receive Christ if they just knew how." This presumes that all the communicator need do is to encourage unbelievers to make a decision and show them how. But, in reality, people are at all stages of the salvation process. Some have never really heard the facts of the gospel before. Others fail to see any relevance for their life. Still others may understand the whole story but feel no need for change. To call for a decision under such circumstances is to guarantee a communication misfire.

---

[23]Charles M. Horne, *Salvation* (Chicago: Moody Press, 1971), p. 55.

[24]L. Berkhof, *Systematic Theology* (Grand Rapids, Mich.: Wm. B. Eerdmans, 1941), p. 416.

[25]This is discussed in succinct fashion by Horne (see Appendix A), pp. 107–112.

[26]*Ibid.,* p. 112.

What this says, of course, is that there is no guaranteed method of evangelism because of the widespread differences between people who will be encountered. Unfortunately, there is an altogether unwarranted tendency to assume that evangelistic success depends upon knowing how to use a simple tract. Eminent pastor Richard Halverson completely devastates such assumptions:

> The one completely safe and dependable manual on personal evangelism and witness is the New Testament; yet the more one studies the New Testament, the less one can deduce from it a system of personal evangelistic methods. Jesus employed a different approach with each person.[27]

God, Man, and the Decision Process

The sixth principle of Christian communication put forth in Chapter 1 states that *Christian communication is a cooperative effort between God and man.* On the other hand, God is completely sovereign and calls those whom He chooses in the way He chooses. On the other hand, it is the responsibility of Christians to proclaim the gospel message and, when possible, to encourage a decision. As noted earlier, Packer has stated that it is necessary to accept the fact that the juxtaposition of divine sovereignty and human responsibility is an antimony (two irreconcilable propositions): "While we must always remember that it is our responsibility to proclaim salvation, we must never forget that it is God who saves."[28]

One of the worst mistakes is for humans to assume responsibility for the results of their evangelistic efforts. Evangelism *is* communication with a view toward conversion, but the results are solely God's responsibility.[29] The only role of the Christian is to be faithful, always prepared ". . . to give an answer to everyone who asks you to give the reason for the hope that you have" (1 Pet. 3:15, NIV).

Figure 3.1 depicts the manner in which God and communicator cooperate in the spiritual decision process.

Making God's Existence Known. The apostle Paul argued that no one ever could claim that God failed to reveal Himself, ". . . because that which is known about God is evident within them; for God made it evident to them" (Rom. 1:19, NASB). Through general (or natural)

[27]Richard C. Halverson, "Methods of Personal Evangelism," *Christianity Today* (October 28, 1966), p. 28.

[28]J.I. Packer, *Evangelism and the Sovereignty of God* (Downers Grove, Ill.: InterVarsity Press, 1961), p. 27.

[29]This is the whole thesis of Packer's book. Also see John R.W. Stott, *Christian Mission in the Modern World* (Downers Grove, Ill.: InterVarsity Press, 1975).

FIGURE 3.1.

God, Communicator, and the Spiritual Decision Process

Ministry	God's Role	Communicator's Role
Making God's existence known	General revelation	(no role)
Evangelism	Conviction	Proclamation of gospel
		Call for decision
Rebirth	Regeneration	(no role)
Spiritual growth	Sanctification	Follow-up of new believer
		Cultivation of new believer

revelation, God has made Himself known both through the witness of creation manifest in nature and through conscience. Obviously the communicator has no role in this form of witness.

Evangelism. As was stated earlier, the role of the communicator in evangelism is to proclaim the facts of the gospel, always showing the relevance for another's life, in the hope that a decision may be encouraged. Indeed, there is both a time and place in which a call for decision is entirely appropriate.

No one can make a spiritual decision, however, without the direct influence of the Holy Spirit through the ministry of conviction. As Jesus said regarding the Holy Spirit, " 'And He, when He comes, will convict the world concerning sin, and righteousness, and judgment' " (John 16:8, NASB). Man otherwise never would see his need of Christ. Christ also issued the great call to all mankind on the last day of the feast, "If any man is thirsty, let him come to Me and drink. He who believes in Me, as the Scripture said, 'From his innermost being shall flow rivers of living water.' " (John 7:37,38, NASB). This call is made effectual through the witness of the Holy Spirit, using the words provided by the communicator.

Rebirth. No matter how effective the evangelism has been, it can never do more than set the stage for regeneration, which is the sole responsibility of the Holy Spirit. Paul speaks of the love of God and notes that "He saved us, not on the basis of deeds which we have done in righteousness, but according to His mercy, by the washing of regeneration and renewing by the Holy Spirit" (Titus 3:5, NASB).

The act of regeneration is profound in its implications. One authority puts it like this:

> The act of regeneration made them partakers of the divine nature. This is the basis upon which the Holy Spirit works in the Christian's life. *He has in His hands now an individual who has both the desire and the power to do the will of God. He augments this by His control over the saint when that saint yields to Him and cooperates with Him.*[30]

Spiritual Growth. The decision process does not cease once the person becomes spiritually alive. Rather, the Holy Spirit now undertakes the ministry of sanctification, which provides both the motivation and the power to bring about a growing conformity to the image of Christ over a lifetime (Rom. 8:29; Phil 1:6). The communicator, on the other hand, has the responsibility of following up the new believer, thus supporting the decision that was made. Then the cultivation of growth begins as the believer is united with the church, among whom he or she is taught the fundamentals of the faith and equipped to live a life of Christian service.

Steps in the Decision Process

In reality the steps involved in spiritual activity are not greatly different from those required in any type of major problem-solving decision. There have been many models (conceptualizations) of problem solving throughout the years,[31] and the model used in this book certainly has some similarities. It is usually postulated that the process begins with need activation and is followed in varying order by search for information, formation and change in beliefs and attitudes, problem recognition, decision, and post-decision evaluation.

Need Activation. This subject is covered in detail in Chapter 5, but the basic point is simple. People will not change until they *want to change,* until that change is seen as beneficial in terms of their basic needs and desires.[32] The obvious implication is that people without felt need for change will not be receptive to spiritual things. The

---

[30]Wuest, *Studies in the Vocabulary,* pp. 94-95.

[31]See, for example, John Dewey, *How We Think* (New York: Heath, 1910); Orville Brim, David C. Glass, David E. Lavin, and Norman Goodman, *Personality and Decision Processes* (Standard, Ca.: Stanford University Press, 1962); and Robert M. Gagne, "Problem Solving and Thinking," in *Annual Review of Psychology,* ed. P.R. Farnsworth and Q. McNemar (Palo Alto, Ca.: Annual Reviews, 1959), pp. 147–172.

[32]Ward Goodenough, *Cooperation in Change* (New York: Russell Sage Foundation, 1963), ch. 3.

most basic meaning of the term "fertile field" used in preceding chapters is an uncovering of an individual or a group who are, in some way, already seeking change. The assumption is that needs have been activated, and the task now is to show the relevance of the gospel to a receptive audience. When this is not the case, evangelism may well fall on deaf ears. As the discussion in Chapter 5 will clarify, the great challenge of the church today is to discover ways of reaching those who are complacent and satisfied with life as it is. Surveys of the Western world are now disclosing that sixty percent or more of non-Christians fall into that category!

Search for Information. Once a need is activated, there is an immediate internal search of long-term memory to see if storage contains sufficient information to guide need-satisfying action. When this is not the case, there is an external search, which may take many forms. While this important issue is the subject of Chapter 6, it is worth stating once again the all-important principle of media usage developed in the preceding chapter: Mass media have their primary role in forming and changing beliefs and attitudes; conversion most often is the result of interpersonal contact.

Formation and Change in Beliefs and Attitudes. This stage in the process is an important one, and it will require greater elaboration than the first two. Let's begin with some definitions. First, beliefs are those things which an individual holds to be true. In the case of religious beliefs, their content will touch on very basic issues of life itself, and for this reason they will have two components: (1) cognitive (content) and (2) motivational (a commitment to live consistent with those beliefs). As defined here, beliefs are equivalent to Schaeffer's use of the term "presupposition." His definition is worthy of note:

> By *presuppositions* we mean the basic way an individual looks at life, his basic world view and the grid through which he sees the world. Presuppositions represent that which a person considers to be the truth of what exists. People's presuppositions lay a grid for all they bring forth into the external world.[33]

Beliefs (or presuppositions if you prefer) obviously are an important part of active memory. In turn, they provide the basis for a

---

[33]Francis A. Schaeffer, *How Should We Then Live?* (Old Tappen, N.J.: Revell, 1976), p. 19.

system of attitudes (learned predispositions to respond consistently in a favorable or unfavorable manner with respect to a given belief). Together, these variables provide a map of one's world and hence will profoundly affect behavior. Fortunately, there is an important behavioral principle that will provide real keys for evangelistic strategy: A change in beliefs leads to a change in attitudes, which, all things being equal, leads to a change in behavior.[34] Much of evangelism, then, is undertaken to bring erroneous beliefs into accord with reality as revealed by Scripture.

Modern man no longer tends to base belief systems on sacred values, and there is a real blurring between secular and sacred.[35] It is not an overstatement to say that prevailing belief systems often follow this pattern:[36]

> God, if He exists at all, is just an impersonal moral force.
>
> Man basically has the capacity within himself to improve morally and make the right choices.
>
> Happiness consists of unlimited material acquisition.
>
> There really is no objective basis for right and wrong.
>
> The supernatural is just a figment of someone's imagination.
>
> If a person lives a "good life," then eternal destiny is assured.
>
> The Bible is nothing other than a book written by man.

The message of the gospel will make little sense until such beliefs are challenged, changed, and brought into accord with reality.

We are saying, of course, that a person cannot make a valid decision for Christ until he or she is at least open to modification of belief systems in terms of these categories of biblical truth:[37]

---

[34]The research underlying this proposition will be reviewed in Chapter 7. For a summary see James F. Engel, Roger D. Blackwell, and David T. Kollat, *Consumer Behavior,* 3rd ed (Hinsdale, Ill.: Dryden Press, 1978), ch. 15.

[35]Paul W. Pruyser, *Between Belief and Unbelief* (New York: Harper & Row, 1974), p. 80.

[36]For an especially interesting discussion of modern man, see William F. Fore, "How Christ Speaks to Mass Media's Modern World," *Newsletter of the Fellowship of Christians in the Arts, Media & Entertainment* (March, 1978), p. 1ff.

[37]Robert Webber has stressed that the essence of the gospel is rooted in restoration of communication between God and man. See "Toward a Theology of Communication," *Christian Communications Spectrum,* vol. 3 (Summer, 1977), pp. 16–17.

1. There is one God, Creator, who actually existed in space and time.

2. Man, because of a willful act of disobedience, became severed from a personal relationship with the God who made him. The consequence is that man has become imprisoned and must live a self-seeking life with no possibility on his own of restoring this lost communication.

3. Jesus Christ, a human being who actually lived on earth, is God's Son who has provided, through His death and resurrection, the only way for man to be restored in fellowship with God.

4. The Bible is a valid witness to eternal spiritual truth.

5. Restoration of fellowship between God and man requires an acceptance by man of the free gift God offers, but only on the terms that God has provided.

The ultimate meaning of these truths, of course, cannot be fully grasped until one matures in the faith, but there must be at least some grasp of the content if the offer of the gospel is to make any sense and a "leap into the unknown" is to be avoided.

(1) Beliefs, Attitudes, and the Decision Process. It will be helpful to tie the discussion thus far together through use of a graphic model which appears in Figure 3.2.

Notice that we now have drawn together God's role, the communicator's role, and man's response in terms of changed beliefs and attitudes. The numbers used on these stages are arbitrary, and they progress in descending order to indicate that each change brings a person closer to the point at which they can make a valid spiritual decision. People, in turn, can fall into any one of these stages.

There will be many, especially in the non-Christian countries, who will fit into category–8. This means that their understanding of God and corresponding belief structure is based only on the witness provided through conscience and nature. Raising such issues as "sin," "the shed blood of Christ," and so on is only nonsense to them, because it is necessary to start at the very beginning with the existence of God Himself.

FIGURE 3.2.

A Model of the Spiritual Decision Process Showing Progressive Change in Beliefs and Attitude

GOD'S ROLE	COMMUNICATOR'S ROLE		MAN'S RESPONSE
General Revelation		–8	Awareness of Supreme Being
Conviction ↓	Proclamation ↓	–7	Some Knowledge of of Gospel
		–6	Knowledge of Fundamentals of Gospel
		–5	Grasp of Personal Implications of Gospel
		–4	Positive Attitude Toward Act of Becoming a Christian

Others will have at least some awareness and understanding of the basic claims of the Christian message regarding God, man, Christ, and the Bible. Depending upon their knowledge, they will fall either at –7 or –6. At these stages, however, there is no real sense of the meaning of these truths in terms of basic life-style and motivations.

Once individuals begin to grasp the implications (–5), there is growing openness and receptivity to evangelism. They now have sufficient background to understand at least something of what the Bible is saying. Moreover, they have been helped to see that it is relevant for their basic needs and strivings. Once this stage is reached it is probable that there will soon be a positive attitude toward the act of accepting Christ. (–4).

(2) The Role of the Communicator. At these stages which precede decision, especially –7 and –6, the goal of the communicator is to build awareness. Persons must come to see that there is one God, that man is an imprisoned self-seeker (sinner), that Jesus has a unique role in salvation, and that the Bible is a valid source of eternal truth. A call for decision is decidedly inappropriate, because individuals must be moved in the decision process to that point at which they clearly see Christ as a viable alternative for their lives. Witness at the

preliminary stages is designed to lay the ground for this type of problem recognition.

The real challenge is to bring about a grasp of implications. This presumes that the communicator has sufficient audience background to detect important needs and values. Furthermore, it assumes a developed sophistication in biblical knowledge so that its relevance may be communicated in a truly meaningful way. Sometimes this type of witness is referred to as "pre-evangelism," but this term is resisted by the author because of the unfortunate connotation that it is somehow not a part of the "real thing," whatever that might be. For this reason, "proclamation" is used as a substitute.

Now let's get down to some trouble spots on the subject of evangelism. First, there is only a meager list of resource materials prepared for use in witnessing to people at the outset of their decision processes. Most tracts and evangelistic approaches assume that the person is ready to receive Christ as Savior and only needs to be shown how. Therefore, *most Christians are utterly unprepared to cope with the majority of the people they will meet!*

Next, there has been an unfortunate practice of defining evangelistic success only in terms of the numbers of decisions, usually measured by a count of those who prayed the so-called "sinner's prayer." The usually unstated premise is that Christians who are not seeing many decisions of this type are a failure in their witness, and quite the opposite may be the case. It is necessary to set the facts absolutely straight on this issue: Many will never see large numbers of decisions because they deal primarily with people in stages –8 to –6. They are successful, in turn, if their witness has helped another to grasp something of the truth of the gospel in the context of his or her life-style. This will represent movement in the decision process toward that point at which they later might accept Christ. The key is to touch people where they are with biblical truth in a loving and empathetic manner. If that has been done, then there has been successful evangelism!

The author has come down hard on this point because of the tyranny under which many Christians have been forced to live. Because their witness presumably has been unfruitful in terms of decisions, the implication is that they are either unspiritual, ineffective in what they do, or both. If this has been the situation with the reader, simply realize that there is no biblical basis for this tyranny. Simply remove any unwarranted guilt and recognize that a large percentage of the evangelistic methodology in use today almost completely overlooks the realities of the spiritual decision process.

Problem Recognition. Problem recognition occurs when God, through the "quickening of the [Holy] Spirit,"[38] has brought about a perceived difference between the actual life of an individual and the ideal life as defined by scriptural truth. This is what is meant by problem recognition. Because it serves as a powerful motivating force for change, positive attitude toward the act of accepting Christ now shifts to an intention to undertake behavior to reduce the uncomfortable state of dissonance that exists. For this reason, the role of the Christian communicator is to help encourage a decision as Figure 3.3 illustrates. This, of course, is precisely what most traditional evangelistic materials are designed to stimulate.

FIGURE 3.3.
Problem Recognition and the Spiritual Decision Process

GOD'S ROLE	COMMUNICATOR'S ROLE		MAN'S RESPONSE
General Revelation		–8	Awareness of Supreme Being
Conviction ↓	Proclamation ↓	–7	Some Knowledge of Gospel
		–6	Knowledge of Fundamentals of Gospel
		–5	Grasp of Personal Implications of Gospel
		–4	Positive Attitude Toward Act of Becoming a Christian
↓	Call for Decision	–3	Problem Recognition and Intention to Act

One of the most common errors in personal evangelism is to assume without verification that the other person is in problem recognition. It is more likely that he or she is at –7 or –6, in which case a call for decision is decidedly inappropriate.

Decision and Rebirth. Figure 3.4 shows that a person who becomes a

[38]Horne, *Salvation,* p. 54.

new creature in Christ does so through repentance and faith as indicated in Romans 10:9–13. The term "believe" as used in this passage has the connotation of "betting one's life" on revealed truth. An all-out commitment must be made, and there is no normative way in which this must be done. This fact has some important implications, and these will be explored in Chapter 9. Suffice it to say at this point that the Bible does not even require a potential convert to utter a prayer. "For it is with your heart that you believe and are justified, and it is with your mouth that you confess and are saved" (Rom. 10:10, NIV). As will become apparent later, counting as converts those who pray some type of prayer is a very dangerous practice.

FIGURE 3.4.

The Spiritual Decision Process: Decision and Rebirth

GOD'S ROLE	COMMUNICATOR'S ROLE		MAN'S RESPONSE
General Revelation		–8	Awareness of Supreme Being
Conviction ↓	Proclamation ↓	–7	Some Knowledge of Gospel
		–6	Knowledge of Fundamentals of Gospel
		–5	Grasp of Personal Implications of Gospel
		–4	Positive Attitude Toward Act of Becoming a Christian
	Call for Decision ↓	–3	Problem Recognition and Intention to Act
		–2	Decision to Act
		–1	Repentance and Faith in Christ
REGENERATION			**NEW CREATURE**

Post-Decision Evaluation. It is almost inevitable that a major decision is accompanied by post-decision doubts, sometimes referred to as post-decision dissonance.[39] It is commonplace for the new convert to wonder just what has happened, and the outcome may be real doubt and confusion. This is the reason why follow-up is such an important communication task (Figure 3.5). In follow-up, teaching is given in which assurance of salvation is presented and the essentials of Christian growth are explained. If this is not done, impaired spiritual development or even retarded Christian growth may be the result.

FIGURE 3.5.

The Spiritual Decision Process: Post-Decision Evaluation

GOD'S ROLE	COMMUNICATOR'S ROLE		MAN'S RESPONSE
General Revelation		–8	Awareness of Supreme Being
Conviction ↓	Proclamation ↓	–7	Some Knowledge of Gospel
		–6	Knowledge of Fundamentals of Gospel
		–5	Grasp of Personal Implications of Gospel
		–4	Positive Attitude Toward Act of Becoming a Christian
	Call for Decision ↓	–3	Problem Recognition and Intention to Act
		–2	Decision to Act
		–1	Repentance and Faith in Christ
REGENERATION			**NEW CREATURE**
Sanctification	Follow Up	+1	Post Decision Evaluation

[39]For a review of this literature, see Engel, Blackwell, and Kollat, *Consumer Behavior,* ch. 18.

Spiritual Growth. Figure 3.6 completes the model of the spiritual decision process and depicts the stages in the cultivation of the new believer. The first requirement is to incorporate the new believer into some type of expression of the local church (stage +2). In fact, it is a basic tenet of church growth theory that uniting with a local church is the definitive measure of evangelistic success.[40] In a sense, one cannot quarrel with this, because spiritual growth will be virtually impossible unless we, ". . . consider how to stimulate one another to love and good deeds, not forsaking our own assembling together, as is the habit of some, but encouraging one another . . ." (Heb. 10:24,25, NASB). While there are doctrinal differences on this point, church membership is often accompanied by the act of baptism, signifying the forsaking of the past and a desire to serve God.

Spiritual growth now begins in earnest. The model is open-ended in this respect, because believers will be at all stages of growth when they go to be with the Lord. Thus some might be only beginning (+3), others could be at +6, +12, and so on. The important point here is that each will have unique needs that must be met through the ministry of cultivation.

For purposes of simplicity, there are three foundational areas described in which all believers must show both conceptual and behavioral growth:[41]

1. Communion with God through prayer and worship
2. Stewardship—continued commitment of all aspects of one's being to God and to His service
3. Reproduction—ministry to others, thereby reproducing the love and power of God in them (a) internally within the body of Christ through spiritual gifts and (b) externally to the world through verbal witness, social concern, etc.

This model has become known as the "Engel model," and many have found it to be helpful. But it is necessary to give credit where credit is due. It was first published in a more rudimentary form by the author's good friend and former student, Viggo Søgaard.[42]

---

[40]See McGavran, *Understanding Church Growth* and Wagner, *Frontiers in Missionary Strategy.*

[41]James F. Engel and H. Wilbert Norton, *What's Gone Wrong With the Harvest?* (Grand Rapids, Mich.: Zondervan, 1975), p. 53.

[42]Søgaard, *Everything You Need to Know for a Cassette Ministry.*

FIGURE 3.6.

The Complete Spiritual Decision Process Model Showing the Stages of Spiritual Growth

GOD'S ROLE	COMMUNICATOR'S ROLE		MAN'S RESPONSE
General Revelation		−8	Awareness of Supreme Being
Conviction ↓	Proclamation ↓	−7	Some Knowledge of Gospel
		−6	Knowledge of Fundamentals of Gospel
		−5	Grasp of Personal Implications of Gospel
		−4	Positive Attitude Toward Act of Becoming a Christian
	Call for Decision ↓	−3	Problem Recognition and Intention to Act
		−2	Decision to Act
↓	↓	−1	Repentance and Faith in Christ
REGENERATION			**NEW CREATURE**
Sanctification ↓	Follow Up ↓	+1	Post Decision Evaluation
		+2	Incorporation Into Church
	Cultivation ↓	+3	Conceptual and Behavioral Growth • Communion With God • Stewardship • Internal Reproduction • External Reproduction
		•	
		•	
		•	
↓	↓	Eternity	

Later it was revised by the author and published in various places.[43] That version, however, first of all underwent the scrutiny of students at the Wheaton Graduate School, and Richard Senzig and James Kovalik were particularly helpful in its revision. Then substantial contributions were made by Professors Charles Kraft and C. Peter Wagner at the Fuller School of World Mission. And, recently, it has been modified by others,[44] and no doubt it will be further revised in the future. So the credit really belongs to a great many friends and colleagues.

A Case Example

At one time, the Quichua Indians of Ecuador, descendents of the proud Inca tribe, were considered to be one of the most resistant fields to evangelism in the entire world. Missionary efforts begun at the turn of the century had resulted in only four baptized Christians by 1954.[45] But then something broke loose and unprecedented church growth began. Membership in the church jumped to 200 by 1964, reached 5,000 by 1973, and now has leveled off at about 10,000. The church has spread throughout Chimborazo Province and to others of the same tribe in Columbia and Peru through remarkable evangelistic zeal.

What happened to make this church growth possible?[46] For most of the years between 1900 and about 1965, the vast majority of the people were at either –8 or –7. While there was a form of Catholicism active in the province, for the most part it left pagan beliefs unchanged. Several missions, and the Gospel Mission Union in particular, began what, in retrospect, was a very well conceived strategy of proclamation:

1. There was consistent missionary presence, especially by males in a male-oriented society, which exemplified what true Christian life is.
2. The first school in the area was started by the mission, and Christian teaching was given for the first time.

[43]See, for example, James F. Engel, "The Audience for Christian Communication," in Douglas, *Let the Earth Hear His Voice,* pp. 533–539.

[44]Dayton, *Planning Strategies for Evangelism.*

[45]Ben J. Nickel, *Along the Quichua Trail* (Smithville, Mo.: Gospel Missionary Union, 1965).

[46]Jacob P. Klassen, "Fire on the Paramo" (M.A. thesis, Fuller School of World Mission, November, 1974).

3. Medical outreach was another way in which Christian love was expressed.
4. The New Testament was published in the Quichua tongue, and it began to be used as large numbers of people were taught to read.
5. Radio outreach, distinctly localized, was begun for both evangelism and teaching.
6. Numerous evangelistic meetings were held over the years with virtually no decisions but apparent change in belief structures on the part of many who were exposed.
7. Development of indigenous hymns and forms of expression.

All of these factors, in retrospect, served to move large numbers to stage −5 or even to −4. They began to see the relevance of the gospel. Still old life-styles resisted change until 1966 when land reform gave Indians title to their land for the first time in their history. Prior to that time they had lived in complete bondage to Spanish landowners and in debt to the Catholic church, which had deviated far from any legitimate spiritual roots. Once land reform occurred, in a sense old values crumbled completely, and there was an openness to new values. First one leader became a Christian, then another, and then a whole "people movement." Today the church has achieved a high degree of maturity as is exemplified by the hundreds who are engaged in theological education by extension.

None of this church growth would have happened without the decades of proclamation. In fact, one missionary worked for more than fifty years without seeing any clear-cut converts. Yet her witness is felt by many to have been one of the most influential factors in the later explosion.

WORLD EVANGELIZATION: MYTH OR REALITY?

A lot of ground has been covered in this chapter, and it is necessary now to take a breather and put the issues in a broader perspective. The example of the evangelistic campaign given at the outset is quite typical of the strategies used up until recently throughout the world. But, even today, much that we do is based on some fuzzy thinking regarding world evangelization. In fact, the theme of the Lausanne Congress, "Let the Earth Hear His Voice," may be just myth or mere sloganeering instead of reality unless we clear away some cobwebs of misunderstanding. There are three main points that emerge: (1) world evangelization requires more than evangelism, (2) an understanding of decision process is the key to strategy, and (3) strategy is a variable, not a constant.

Evangelism and World Evangelization

Evangelism is only the first step in the making of disciples, and not an end in itself. Nothing in God's mandate to the church is "fulfilled" or finished, even if everyone in a geographic area has heard and understood the basic message of the gospel. Then the hard work of cultivation begins, and that demands a life-style exemplifying the lordship of Christ over *all* phases of life. As we have stressed, the making of disciples is an unending process.

Chapter 4 will elaborate on the basic principle that the church is the primary means of world evangelization. If we are unconcerned about building spiritual maturity within the body, then all the exhortation in the world for evangelism is just so much empty talk. Evangelism simply will not become a way of life if the church is not functioning as the Scriptures instruct. Therefore, *the greatest priority in world evangelization at the moment is not evangelistic strategy but the building of the church to do the work of the kingdom.* This does not for one minute de-emphasize the importance of evangelism; rather it facilitates it as the natural outgrowth of a healthy body.

An Understanding of Decision Process

The entire communication ministry of the church is based on a proper understanding of decision processes, because only then is it possible to set realistic objectives and determine an effective combination of message and media.

First, as we have seen, a decision for Christ is just one possible evangelistic goal, and that outcome is realistic only when people are at stage +3 of their decision process. The majority of the time, the objective should be to change beliefs in such a way that they are brought into accord with revealed truth. That, in turn, will lead to movement in the process itself and predispose that person for a decision at a later point in time.

Next, the content of the message requires an unusual audience sensitivity that detects both spiritual awareness and understanding and felt needs and motivations. These determinants never can be assumed but rather must be detected through careful audience research.

Finally, the media to be used also are dependent upon decision process. A strategy often can make effective use of the mass media for leading to changes in beliefs and attitudes. A conversion, on the other hand, generally is stimulated through face-to-face conversation. This means, of course, that mass and interpersonal media should be part of a common strategy, because one without the other is likely not to be effective. If the Spirit of God has used mass media exposure to move a person to stage −3, for example, the seed which has been sown may be wasted unless church members are both motivated and trained to share their faith in an appropriate way.

Strategy Is a Variable, Not a Constant

We cannot stress too frequently that there is no such thing as a "grand evangelistic strategy" that works everywhere. By now, this should be painfully obvious, but this basic truth has yet to penetrate in many quarters. Just look at the books and tracts on personal evangelism for proof. The best thing we could do at this point is, in effect, to "begin again" and see if the strategies being used in various local situations really are succeeding in building disciples. In the final analysis, it is altogether possible that the methods used are getting in the way of the Holy Spirit.

CHAPTER 4

The Church: Medium and Message

CHURCHOTHEQUE

They're charging sixty pence
for colour posters of your
supersaints.
They're asking for 10,000
to renovate the bishop.
The public are invited
to inspect the stained glass
stripcartoons,
light a candle for the builders
and sing hosannahs
to the architect.
You can buy a booklet of its
history and an ashtray with a
picture, before guiding your
conscience past the begging
money boxes.
They have a concert there on
Tuesdays, a garden fete each
month, as well as the obligatory
service or two.
And, oh yes, I'm glad that you
asked about God.
He was made redundant in their
latest promotional campaign.
The moving finger of public
opinion wrote the obituary
on the wall.
Jesus was evicted for the
operatic society to rehearse.

Now, you'll find Him in the
houses if you care to take a
look. You'll hear Him in the
streets if you get a chance
to listen.
There's not enough room in
the churchotheque.
It's Christmas all over again.[1]

Steve Turner has a way of writing in verse what many of us feel but cannot articulate as clearly. While the church, according to Scripture, is God's only divinely appointed means for world evangelization, all too frequently local expressions of the church appear moribund. It may have all the exterior trappings of success but be inwardly devoid of the power that Christ alone can give. The fact of the matter is that Christ often is not looked to as head of the local church and is denied His rightful role by our programs and activities.

"Evangelize the World," "Solution: Spiritual Revolution," "Let the Earth Hear His Voice," "New Life for All"—so our slogans read. But what good is all this activity if the church itself lies listless and in need of a revival? There is no way to avoid the conclusion that the building of a healthy church *must* take precedence if we ever are to make disciples in all nations. The church cannot function effectively as the *medium* for world evangelization or the *message* (the lordship of Christ exemplified through His body on earth) unless this matter is given highest priority.

The purpose of this chapter, simply put, is to stimulate right thinking about the local church. Two important models of the church, the institutional and the organic, will be contrasted, and it will become apparent that too much of modern church life, especially that of North America, is built on a pragmatic foundation of success and efficiency rather than on Scriptural principles and instructions.

TWO CONTRASTING MODELS OF THE CHURCH

While there are many ways in which the church can be organized and function (this is what is meant by the word "model"),[2] two have

[1]From Steve Turner, *Tonight We Will Fake Love* (London: Charisma Books, 1974), pp. 58–59. Used by permission of the author.

[2]See Avery Dulles, *Models of the Church* (Garden City, N.Y.: Doubleday, 1974).

become especially prominent through the writings of Howard Snyder[3]—the institutional and the organic. The issues raised are absolutely basic, because one's view of the church is a direct determinant of the strategies to be followed in evangelism and cultivation.

The Institutional Model

In the institutional form, according to Dulles, primacy is placed on the formal structure of governance.[4] Hence, its activities are governed by hierarchy, delegation of authority, formality, and ministry through ever expanding programs.

The final authority rests with some type of governing board, designated by such terms as "elders," "deacons," "the official board," and so on. Usually they are elected from the membership. The board, in turn, exercises oversight with respect to the paid pastoral staff. Various committees are given responsibility for ministries of the church and are the primary source for program determination. The membership then occupies a relatively passive role except to take their part, if they so desire, in these ongoing activities.

Life in the Institutionalized Church. The discerning reader will quickly notice that this model really does not differ much from the standard organizational chart found in businesses and other formal institutions. This may seem, on the surface, to be perfectly satisfactory, but there are many outcomes that can snuff out the very life of the church.

(1) Ignoring Spiritual Gifts. "We still have three teacher openings in the Junior High Sunday school class, and the membership committee needs at least ten more callers. Any volunteers?"

Such announcements from the pulpit are not uncommon. The fact is that many churches are forced to some pretty powerful persuasion to fill the various slots in its programs. This may achieve the intended result, but it completely deviates from the means of equipping the church specified in Scripture. The church is supposed to be the body of Christ characterized by spiritual gifts present in the life of every believer. Some of the gifts mentioned in the New Testament (Romans 12, Ephesians 4, and 1 Corinthians 12–14) provide for leadership: those of prophet, apostle, teacher, and evangelist. Others are given for the work of the ministry, including

[3]See especially Howard A. Snyder, *The Community of the King* (Downers Grove, Ill.: InterVarsity Press, 1977).

[4]Dulles, *Models of the Church,* p. 32.

miracles, healing, administration, tongues, and so on. Still others are given as the need arises.

The point, of course, is that God "*. . . really cannot work through an organization chart, which is just man's invention, unless it provides for a staff equipped by God to perform the functions.*"[5] It is small wonder that the church often is characterized by impotence.

(2) A False Dichotomy Between Staff and Laity. Secular management theory often will define a good leader as one who can get things done through people. Thus, a pastor will receive high marks if the program is functioning efficiently and he (or she) is an effective organizer. In fact, leadership must have this quality if the institutional model is to work.

Once again, nonbiblical thinking rears its ugly head. The biblical job description for pastors is ". . . the equipping of the saints for the work of service, to the building up of the body of Christ" (Eph. 4:12,13, NASB). "Getting things done" is quite secondary here to the development of fellow believers into men and women of God. An emphasis on *using people* in the programs of the church is a nonbiblical dead end.

The paid staff (and perhaps a limited number of lay leaders) almost inevitably wind up in the driver's seat, and most members sit quiescently in the pews with only a minimum of involvement. Thus a dichotomy develops between staff and members. The clearest evidence that such a dichotomy is widespread is the continued use of the terms "staff" and "laity," as if there were some difference between the two, other than the source of their paychecks. This does gross disservice to the biblical meaning of *laos*—the people of God. Staff and members alike are part of the *laos,* and the New Testament does not unduly elevate the gift of pastor (or shepherd of the flock) over any other, although he or she has a unique and central role (1 Tim. 5:17,18).

(3) Program Orientation. Jacques Ellul has talked about the technological mentality that has pervaded a large segment of North American church life.[6] This outlook embraces efficiency as an absolute criterion of success and systematizes methods and resources to attain pre-established results. Activities and programs thus abound. Indeed the very life of the church depends upon the continued

---

[5]James F. Engel and H. Wilbert Norton, *What's Gone Wrong With the Harvest?* (Grand Rapids, Mich.: Zondervan, 1975), p. 141.

[6]Jacques Ellul, *The Technological Society* (New York: Alfred A. Knopf, 1964).

development and support of its programs. All too quickly program maintenance becomes a primary goal, and change that may threaten the functioning of the smoothly oiled machine is resisted.

When program orientation is carried to the extreme, the church loses its cutting edge, and effectiveness crisis enters. It can even reach the point that Christ, in effect, no longer truly functions as head of His church. Has the reader ever heard someone pray, in so many words, "Lord please bless these programs *we* have designed?"

The Organic Model

The church viewed as an organism has these essential attributes:[7] (1) one body under one head, (2) equipped by God, (3) led by God through disciplined planning, (4) ministering to one another in community, and (5) ministering to the world through proclaiming and exemplifying the kingdom of God. While there will, of necessity, be some institutionalization, it is distinctly secondary to the informal, the personal, and the communal.[8]

One Body Under One Head. The apostle Paul stated that Christians ". . . are no longer foreigners and aliens, but fellow citizens with God's people and members of God's household, built on the foundation of the apostles and prophets, with Christ Jesus himself as the chief cornerstone" (Eph. 2:19,20, NIV). Moreover, God has appointed Christ to be ". . . head over everything for the church, which is his body, the fullness of him who fills everything in every way" (Eph. 1:22,23, NIV). These verses effectively capture the biblical meaning of the term organism.

Equipped by God. We have already discussed the subject of spiritual gifts and pointed out that the institutional model can interfere with God's plan for organizing and equipping. It is not the author's purpose to develop this subject in any detail, because that has been done quite adequately by others.[9] But two factors should be mentioned. First, Wagner has stressed that evangelism is just one of the gifts of the Spirit; in fact it may be possessed by no more than ten

[7]The most extensive discussion of the church as an organism is in Dulles, *Models of the Church,* ch. 3. Also Snyder bases his entire book, *The Community of the King,* on this model as opposed to the institutional.

[8]Dulles, *Models of the Church,* p. 55.

[9] Of particular value are C. Peter Wagner, *Frontiers in Missionary Strategy* (Chicago: Moody Press, 1971); David Mains, *Full Circle* (Waco, Texas: Word Books, 1971); and Howard A. Snyder, *The Problem of Wineskins* (Downers Grove, Ill.: InterVarsity Press, 1975).

percent of all believers.[10] Some leaders place such emphasis on this gift that others are ignored and left undeveloped. This leads to the second point: Evidence is rapidly accumulating which documents that most church members either do not know what their spiritual gift is or do not know how to use it in ministry. Therefore, the church is substantially hindered in functioning as God intended.

Led by God Through Disciplined Planning. If Christ is head of the church and the body is equipped by God through spiritual gifts, how then is practical ministry carried on? How can we be sure that God is leading and that programs are initiated by Him rather than by man? The answer lies in *Spirit-led planning.* Some will immediately object that such a statement reflects North American business management principles. The truth, however, is that secular management has borrowed principles that have their roots in the Word of God,[11] a fact that is not always recognized.

The starting point is that creation did not just happen in some random fashion. God Himself is a planner. As the psalmist said, "He has decided the number of stars and calls each one by name" (Ps. 147:4, TEV). So any theology of planning and management finds its roots in the very nature of God.

The church, in turn, is a co-laborer or partner with God, created by Him to carry out His good works (1 Cor. 3:9; Eph 2:10). Therefore, if God is a planner and we are co-laborers, then there is no option but to follow His pattern, always remembering this one essential admonition: "We may make our plans, but God has the last word" (Prov. 16:1, TEV).

Spirit-led planning, then, is not an option. But, if God is to lead, there must be avenues for communication, one of which is prayer. Specific guidance and direction are received from the Holy Spirit who will ". . . guide you into all the truth . . ." (John 16:13, NASB). Christ could legitimately tell His disciples that they would be led and enabled to do ". . . greater works than these . . ." (John 14:12, NASB).

Planning requires fact finding and disciplined analysis. As the famous English rector, Dr. John R.W. Stott, once stated on the

---

[10]See C. Peter Wagner, *Your Church Can Grow* (Glendale, Ca.: Regal, 1976), p. 76. Also C. Peter Wagner and Arthur Johnston, "Intensity of Belief: A Pragmatic Concern for Church Growth," *Christianity Today* (January 7, 1977), p. 382.

[11]The author is grateful to his colleague John Gration for his insights on the theology of management spelled out in an unpublished paper at the Wheaton Graduate School, August, 1977.

Wheaton campus, "God cannot lead an empty head." There are some scriptural guidelines for this process found in the Proverbs (from the TEV):

1. *Analyze the situation to be faced and test opinions by fact.* "Enthusiasm without knowledge is not good; impatience will get you into trouble" (19:2). "Sensible people will see trouble coming and avoid it, but an unthinking person will walk right into it and regret it later" (27:12).
2. *Evaluate resources before arriving at a decision.* "Don't build your house and establish a home until your fields are ready, and you are sure that you can earn a living" (24:27).
3. *Set goals and make plans based on this information.* ". . . you must make careful plans before you fight a battle, and the more good advice you get, the more likely you are to win" (24:6). "Ask the Lord to bless your plans, and you will be successful in carrying them out" (16:3).
4. *Measure effectiveness.* "People who listen when they are corrected will live, but those who will not admit they are wrong are in danger" (10:17).
5. *Analyze results and change actions where necessary.* "It is pleasant to see plans develop. That is why fools refuse to give them up even when they are wrong" (13:19, TLB).

Ministering to One Another. How many in the church today have developed a relationship with other believers to the point that they would ". . . lay down our lives for the brethren" (1 John, 3:16, NASB)? This sense of deep love and commitment goes far beyond the usual definition of "fellowship" which tends to be quite bland and nondemanding. A healthy body will be characterized by a sense of *community,* a sense of love for each other that stands in sharp contrast to the selfish individualism and power struggles often seen in the world at large.

Henry G. Bosch relates an interesting story that has some poignant implications for contemporary church life. One morning a customer in a rural store discovered that a slow-moving clerk no longer was around:

> "Where's Eddie? Is he sick?"
> "Nope," came the reply. "He ain't workin' here no more."

"Do you have anyone in mind for the vacancy?"
"Nope! Eddie didn't leave no vacancy."[12]

There are too many Eddies in the church today who leave and no one notices because they were never taught to function as a member of the body.

The importance of community, or body life if you prefer,[13] is once again being rediscovered as the church moves from being strictly an institution toward the organic form. Indeed, the so-called *body life movement* has been a catalyst for this change. Small groups are springing up for the purpose of discovery and exercise of gifts, prayer, praise, edification, and Bible study. The Holy Spirit is being freed to teach, to heal, to work miracles. Church discipline and authority are, to a growing extent, being removed from the dusty archives of church constitutions and are being exercised to sharpen both commitment and consistency in holy living. These are all vital signs of health.

Ministering to the World. As one takes the perspective of the kingdom of God and the premium placed on Christ's lordship over all phases of life, outreach takes on a much more wholistic nature. Evangelism is the *core* of outreach when the church is attempting to exemplify the kindgom of God, but it certainly is not the *circumference.*[14] Just to make sure that priorities are in focus, consider Snyder's words:

> The individual believer's responsibility is first of all to the Christian community and to its head, Jesus Christ. The first task of every Christian is the edification of the community of believers. If we say that evangelism or soul winning is the first task of the believer, we do violence to the New Testament and place a burden on the backs of some believers that they are not able to bear. The idea that every Christian's first responsibility is to be a soul winner ignores the biblical teachings about spiritual gifts.[15]

Loving acceptance of those from all races and backgrounds, concern for fairness and justice, absence of extreme individualism, a shunning of power as a motivation for living, and other factors all are a vital part of the responsibility of the church as later discussion will elaborate.

---

[12]Henry G. Bosch, "He Left No Vacancy," *Our Daily Bread* (May, 1974), entry for May 6.

[13]Ray C. Stedman, *Body Life* (Glendale, Ca.: Regal, 1972).

[14]Snyder, *The Community of the King,* pp. 101–104.

[15]*Ibid.,* p. 75.

The Importance of Right Thinking About the Church

While no local church ever will fit either of these two models completely, a tendency toward institutionalization will almost inevitably institute a strong pull toward pragmatism. In other words, the institutional church can become preoccupied with "getting things done." This is acceptable if those "things" are in accord with biblical norms, but pragmatism can all too quickly become substituted for biblical fidelity unless some real precautions are taken. This can also happen in a church built on the organic model, but it is far less likely to occur in the first place and more amenable to correction once it does arise.

Once pragmatism replaces biblical fidelity as a guiding principle for church life, there are many pathological consequences. Two of the most serious are "bigness as a sign of greatness" and "prophetic tunnel vision."

Bigness as a Sign of Greatness. Church growth theory is one of the most significant contributions of the past two decades. Most of its principles have become an accepted part of contemporary missionary strategy, and these principles also have more recently been applied to the North American church. The author is indebted to the church growth theorists, and many of their major concepts are reflected throughout this book.

According to McGavran,[16] Wagner,[17] and other advocates,[18] a healthy church will be a growing church. Growth, in turn, should occur through conversion as opposed to expansion of numbers through transfer of members or biological growth (children of members who later join church rolls).

Most will agree that a healthy church body will be a growing body.[19] But there is not unanimity on the premise, articulated by Wagner, that a large membership is a special virtue.[20] It is his contention that larger churches have more resources for outreach

---

[16]Donald A. McGavran, *Understanding Church Growth* (Grand Rapids, Mich.: Wm. B. Eerdmans, 1970) and Donald A. McGavran and Winfield C. Arn, *How to Grow a Church* (Glendale, Ca.: Regal, 1973).

[17]Wagner, *Frontiers in Missionary Strategy* and *Your Church Can Grow.*

[18]Vergil Gerber, *God's Way to Keep a Church Going and Growing* (Glendale, Ca.: Regal, 1973); J. Robertson McQuilkin, *Measuring the Church Growth Movement* (Chicago: Moody Press, 1974); Alan R. Tippet, *Church Growth and the Word of God* (Grand Rapids, Mich.: Wm. B. Eerdmans, 1970); and Robert H. Schuller, *Your Church Has Real Possibilities* (Glendale, Ca.: Regal, 1975).

[19]See especially Snyder, *Community of the King,* ch. 7.

[20]Wagner, *Your Church Can Grow.*

and therefore are enabled to accomplish more in the way of evangelism. While this no doubt is true, the objection is twofold. First, some contend that there is no biblical teaching explicitly justifying growth as a goal for the church, let alone justifying bigness.[21] In other words, the church exists for a great deal more than evangelism, and success is to be evaluated on multiple criteria and not only on the basis of soul winning. Furthermore, bigness can aggravate the excesses of the institutionalized form, especially by increasing the distance between pastor and laity. Wagner even goes so far as to contend that a growing church must have a strong visionary pastor and cites as examples of the ideal church many churches where the pastor is the dominant figure.[22] Such a policy can accentuate the inevitable tendencies for the average member to play a passive role.

Let's face it—size can connote power, especially in the North American culture. It is not difficult to conceive that church growth principles are embraced as an attractive means of feeding pastoral egos, an outcome not envisioned by Wagner and other writers on the subject. (See Figure 4.1).

Church growth has encountered greatest criticism for its principle that a church should be made up of essentially the same type of people. This has become known as the *homogeneous unit principle.*[23] The argument goes this way: People do not like to gather with others who are different in any major way. Therefore, a church will not grow if it is heterogeneous. Dissenters point to Galatians 3:28, Ephesians 2:14–19, Colossians 3:10,11, and other passages, all of which argue that there should be no artificially imposed distinctions or barriers within the body of Christ. Sider contends, for example, that the church ought to stand as a living model to the non-Christian world of the kingdom of God in which all cultural and racial barriers are transcended in Christ;[24] other leaders agree.[25] It all comes down to this essential issue: Is the homogeneous unit principle merely an expedient means for evangelism, or does it have intrinsic biblical merit?[26]

---

[21] E. Luther Copeland, "What Do the Gospels Have to Say About Church Growth?" *Evangelical Missions Quarterly,* vol. 9 (Fall, 1973), pp. 294–300.

[22] Wagner, *Your Church Can Grow,* ch. 4.

[23] This was first put forth in the writings of McGavran.

[24] Ron Sider, "Homogeneity and Church Growth: A Search for Biblical Priorities," *The Other Side,* vol. 14 (January, 1978), pp. 62–63.

[25] See especially the comments by Ray Stedman in "Should the Church be a Melting Pot?"*Christianity Today,* vol. 22 (August 18, 1978), pp. 10–15.

[26] This issue is discussed in detail in *The Pasadena Consultation—Homogeneous Unit* (Wheaton, Ill.: Lausanne Committee for World Evangelization, 1977).

FIGURE 4.1.

Bigness Is Not Always a Sign of Greatness

Reproduced by special permission from *The Wittenburg Door* (June/July, 1975), p. 26.

The author is of the conviction that the homogeneous unit principle is an instance of making pragmatism the dominant consideration. Wagner has modified his position now to propose homogeneity only as the starting point for a new church and not as an end in itself.[27] This is a more acceptable position, but there are few instances of established churches moving from homogeneity to heterogeneity wihout serious internal disruption. It makes more sense to follow God's blueprint from the outset and not to make size and growth the determining factors.

In the final analysis, size and growth should be secondary factors, and often only reflect a North American value structure in which bigness is a sign of greatness. Scripture focuses far more directly on the total impact made by the church first of all on its members and then on society at large. Evangelism is just one aspect.

Prophetic Tunnel Vision. There is yet another unfortunate form of pragmatism that develops when there is an undue attempt made to make the gospel "palatable." Moral and ethical demands, so evident in Scripture, become muted or ignored altogether, sometimes on the assumption that people will not respond evangelistically if preaching and teaching are in any way controversial and challenge the status quo. On the other hand, Scripture demands that the church be a prophetic church, outspoken (1) in identifying satanic forces as the true enemy of the church (Eph. 6:12; 1 Pet. 5:8,9); (2) in renouncing the world's definition and practice of power (Matt. 20:20–28; Luke 9:46–48); and (3) in calling for action to bring about social justice (Luke 3:10–14; Matt. 11:4–6; Eph. 5:11).[28] When the church is silent on these issues it has fallen prey to little more than a cultural Christianity that encourages maintenance of the status quo.[29]

The Need for Renaissance.

All too often, attempts are made to recruit churches that are caught in the muck of institutionalization as participants in world evangelization. They may jump on the bandwagon for a time but show little lasting persistence. Bruce Larson has put his finger on one of the greatest needs of the worldwide church—a renaissance that restores the church to its biblical forms and practices.[30]

---

[27]See Peter Wagner's comments in "Should the Church be a Melting Pot?"

[28]Snyder, *Community of the King,* ch. 6.

[29]A number of voices have been raised on this subject, some of which may sound a bit strident and militant. Yet they need to be heard. See, for example, Clarence R. Hilliard, "The Honky Hermeneutic," *The Other Side,* vol. 5 (May/June, 1976), pp. 66–72.

[30]Bruce Larson, *The One and Only You* (Waco, Texas: Word, 1973), p. 26.

The beginning point is to move from the institutional model to the organic model. The steps required cannot be fully spelled out here,[31] but there are some important common denominators among current experiments. First, and most important, church leadership must see the need for change. In effect, some will be "dethroned" to take their rightful place as spelled out in scriptural passages on the body of Christ. Next, goal setting and planning must involve a significant portion of the total membership and not just the formal leadership structure. One useful action is to survey a congregation and then assemble a large group from the membership to wrestle with the issues that surface.[32] Finally, real change seldom occurs without development of cells or small groups in the church in which discipleship and other aspects of community are stressed.[33]

Only through such means as those mentioned above can Sunday-morning-only "churchianity" be stifled. All of this is a long, slow, and nondramatic process, but it is the author's firm conviction that this is the stuff out of which world evangelization will become a reality.

THE CHURCH AND THE WORLD

A foundational principle of Christian communication mentioned in Chapter 1 is that the church is both the medium and the message for world evangelization. It is the purpose of this section to explore these two dimensions in greater depth.

The Church as Medium

Theologian Melvin Hodges has written that, "The Church is God's agent in the earth—the medium through which he expresses himself to the world. God has no other redeeming agency in the earth."[34] The church, then has a permanent divine mandate to be the means whereby world evangelization is undertaken and the kingdom of God proclaimed and exemplified.

An obvious point? Perhaps, but the working out of this principle is anything but simple in today's world. The complicating factor is the

---

[31]See Dulles, *Models of the Church;* Snyder, *The Community of the King;* and Snyder, *The Problem of Wineskins.*

[32]This approach is discussed in Engel and Norton, *What's Gone Wrong With the Harvest?*, chs. 8 and 9.

[33] One of the organizations that has been uniquely used to help churches in this area is Churches Alive. For a description, see Kay Oliver, "One Secret of Lasting Growth," *Moody Monthly* (June, 1977), pp. 27–29.

[34]Melvin Hodges, *A Guide to Church Planting* (Chicago: Moody Press, 1973), p. 15.

rise of what has come to be known as the parachurch organization. Parachurch structures such as denominational offices, publishers, broadcasters, mission boards, and so on exist alongside of the local church but are not the church in and of themselves. Their existence is warranted only to the extent that they aid and extend the church in its mission. They are strictly man-made in this sense and are culturally determined.[35]

The problem arising between church and parachurch organization is best epitomized by a conversation held between the author and a leader of a major evangelistic organization. When queried about the fact that the efforts of this organization have not resulted in much church growth, this was his answer: "Would you want to put your converts into most of the churches in this country?" Yet, this organization is publicly positioned as an "arm of the church." Obviously something is seriously amiss. Those who are part of parachurch organizations and who hold a low view of the church apparently do not see that their actions are having the effect of letting the arm control the body. In the final analysis, the parachurch group has yanked the responsibility from the church itself and has neglected its role to build the church to carry on the work of the kingdom.

This admittedly is an extreme example, for there are many parachurch groups functioning in a remarkable way as servants. There are times, in fact, when such organizations provide services the church never could afford. Missionary Aviation Fellowship is a good example. Therefore, the parachurch organization *does* have a valid function, but only insofar as the centrality of the church is kept in focus. Executives of these parachurch organizations must keep this fact in mind, because the burden is on them to justify their continued existence by *proof* that real service is being provided and not by the all-too-frequent use of exaggerated direct mail claims, some of which make the secular advertiser appear bland by comparison.

The Church as the Message

A consistent theme in the ministry of Jesus was, "Repent, for the kingdom of heaven is near" (Matt. 4:17, NIV). And He told His

---

[35]This point was first made by Howard A. Snyder at the Lausanne Congress in his paper entitled "The Church as God's Agent in Evangelism," in Douglas, *Let the Earth Hear His Voice,* pp. 336–340. Also see Snyder, *The Problem of Wineskins,* ch. 12.

followers, "You are the salt of the earth. . . . You are the light of the world" (Matt. 5:13,14, NIV). It is clear that He was referring to something radically new, made possible through His ministry. First was an offer of a new life, of a total inner transformation. That new life was to be expressed in society as believers served as both salt and light. The outcome was to be a spiritual kingdom on earth initiated in the lives of believers once Christ was accepted as Savior and Lord. Ultimately this kingdom will be fully established when Christ comes back to reign in glory. Let's refer once again to Beyerhaus's clear and concise definition:

> *The Kingdom of God is God's redeeming Lordship successively winning such liberating power over the hearts of men, that their lives and thereby finally the whole creation . . . become transformed into childlike harmony with his divine will.*[36]

There is no denying the fact that the kingdom of God has been a controversial doctrine since New Testament times.[37] As Jonathan L. Blanchard, the first president of Wheaton College, made clear, we must object to those who ". . . locate Christ's kingdom in the future to the neglect of the present."[38] Blanchard was referring to a point of view, still popular in some quarters, that conversion is the final aim of world evangelization. If that is true, what then happens to the unambiguous New Testament doctrine that it is the work of the church (i.e., Christ in us) to reconcile all things to Jesus Christ and His lordship (2 Cor. 5:19; Col. 1:20)? Sad to say, the outcome all too often is a group of believers whose lives are scarcely different from those around them. As Escobar makes so clear, not much salt and light comes from such a church:

> The danger of evangelicalism is that it will present a saving work of Christ without the consequent ethical demand, that it will present a Savior who delivers from the bondage of spiritual slavery but not a model of the life that the Christian should live in the world. A spirituality without discipleship in the daily social, economic, and political aspects of life is religiosity and not Christianity.[39]

---

[36]Peter Beyerhaus, "World Evangelization and the Kingdom of God," in Douglas *Let the Earth Hear His Voice,* p. 286.

[37]For a thorough review of differing perspectives on this doctrine see J. Andrew Kirk, "The Kingdom of God and the Church in Contemporary Protestantism and Catholicism," in Douglas, *Let the Earth Hear His Voice,* pp. 1071–1080.

[38]Quoted by Donald Dayton, "More on Hope in Action," *The Other Side,* vol. 14 (February, 1978), p. 7.

[39]Samuel Escobar, "Evangelism and Man's Search for Freedom, Justice and Fulfillment," in Douglas, *Let the Earth Hear His Voice,* p. 310.

Blanchard also goes on to object to those who seek ". . . to construct a local heaven upon earth . . . thus shutting out the influence and motives of eternity."[40] All that can be hoped for now is a *spiritual kingdom,* authenticated through Christian lives. While society can be changed for the better, orthodox Christianity has always recognized that the world is still under the domination of satanic forces. Spiritual warfare is inevitable, and the final victory must await Christ's messianic reign on earth.

The Church as an End in Itself. When the church is viewed in terms of the doctrine of the kingdom, it is far more than a means of world evangelization. The establishment of the spiritual kingdom expressed through the body of Christ is an end in and of itself. In the final analysis, this is why Christ came. If the church is just viewed as evangelistic machinery, the result is a gross disservice to scriptural teachings.

Exemplifying the Kingdom in the World. We cannot beat around the bush on a critical issue. *A church, collectively and individually, that is not living as salt and light destroys the credibility of the gospel message.* Frankly, our verbal gospel promises and neatly packaged tracts can come across as little more than ". . . a resounding gong or a clanging cymbal" (1 Cor. 13:1, NIV). Some have written extensively on this subject.[41] The church must have a life-style that is a genuine alternative to the system of the world. Indeed, this life-style is, or should be, the result of belief in the message we offer. There are at least several critical aspects of this life-style, in turn, that tend to be neglected.

(1) A Ministry to the Oppressed. Jesus said, citing Isaiah 61:1,2: "The Spirit of the Lord is on me; therefore he has anointed me to preach good news to the poor. He has sent me to proclaim freedom for the prisoners and recovery of sight for the blind, to release the oppressed, and to proclaim the year of the Lord's favor" (Luke 4:18,19, NIV). While Jesus gave priority to the poor and the oppressed, the same certainly cannot be said of the largely white Anglo-Saxon church of North America and Europe. It is small wonder that racial tension is endemic throughout the world. Hilliard has even warned that a propensity to overlook scriptural teaching on this point may well lead the middle class church to judgment.[42] Some say such

---

[40]Quoted in Dayton, "More on Hope in Action," p. 7.

[41]See, especially, Snyder, *The Community of the King;* Escobar, "Evangelism and Man's Search for Freedom, Justice and Fulfillment"; Padilla; Beyerhaus, "World Evangelization and the Kingdom of God"; and *Partnership* (October 21, 1976), entire issue citing Enrique Guang.

[42]Hilliard, "The Honky Hermeneutic."

voices are nothing more than militant rabble-rousers, but are the words of Jesus to be taken seriously or not?

(2) Attack on Injustice. The Lausanne Covenant encompassed a clause that also must be taken seriously:

> . . . we express penitence both for our neglect and for having sometimes regarded evangelism and social concern as mutually exclusive. . . . The message of salvation implies also a message of judgment upon every form of alienation, oppression and discrimination, and we should not be afraid to denounce evil and injustice wherever they exist. When people receive Christ they are born again into his kingdom and must seek not only to exhibit but also to spread its righteousness in the midst of an unrighteous world. The salvation we claim should be transforming us in the totality of our personal and social responsibilities. Faith without works is dead.[43]

Christians have no choice but to act against all forms of injustice. The church that sits in its spiritual ghetto, comfortable in its complacency, is giving this message to the world: *We don't have any solutions either and we are not anxious to find any.*

(3) A Rejection of the World's Standards. Now we arrive at the point where we begin to sense what Christ meant when He said the way was a narrow one. The Old and New Testaments with a single voice denounce a self-centered individualism that expresses itself through striving for power and accumulation of wealth.[44] This fact simply cannot be rationalized away, and it hits most of us pretty close to home. J. D. Douglas has identified what he terms a moral sickness in the church in the developed countries:

> . . . while we rightly recoil from materialistic Communism, pervading our society is an even more insidious materialism which makes Christians short of breath through prosperity and ill-equipped to run the race that is set before them.[45]

Fallen man, by and large, has little else to live for but to achieve power and wealth. Christ is very clear that such motivations are to be forsaken by members of His body. Consider His words: "For whoever wants to save his life will lose it, but whoever loses his life for me will find it. What good will it be for a man if he gains the whole world, yet forfeits his soul?" (Matt. 16:25,26, NIV). The accumulation of wealth, according to the biblical writers, is especially sinful, because

---

[43]This appears in Douglas, *Let the Earth Hear His Voice,* pp. 4-5.

[44]For an especially good biblical perspective, see Peter Davids, "Wealth and the People of God," *Latin American Evangelist* (March/April, 1976), pp. 2–4.

[45]J.D. Douglas commenting on western civilization and the mission of the church, *World Vision,* vol. 20 (January, 1976), p. 8.

wealth is possessed by the powerful of this age who tend to gather it at the expense of others. Justice, fairness, equality, all are consistent biblical themes.

Just for a moment consider how the average nonbeliever feels who drives by our beautiful churches, notices the cars in the parking lot, and observes the premium we place on the latest fashions. What do they think when they visit our homes with the latest "all-electric kitchen" and other gadgets? Probably none of these things are wrong in and of themselves, but how is the church really an alternative to the world when it embraces the same materialistic standard?

What this boils down to is that a comfortable living standard with a measure of wealth is not necessarily a sin. But striving for such advantages has no place in the church. The clause in the Lausanne Covenant that has proved to be most troublesome to the author and many others who attended is worded as follows: "Those of us who live in affluent circumstances accept our duty to develop a simple life-style in order to contribute more generously to both relief and evangelism."[46] Accepting this and working it out in practice are two different matters, but do we have any choice?

A FINAL WORD

"And they went out and preached everywhere while the Lord worked with them, and confirmed the word by the signs that followed"(Mark 16:20, NASB). In a nutshell, this is the work of the church—a unified *body,* exemplifying the kingdom of God, with the Lord confirming His presence by signs and miracles. The church, itself, is the key to world evangelization. If it is healthy, it will, to use Tozer's words, be a ". . . formidable, moral force to be reckoned with."[47] Where that is not the case, let's shelve our grand evangelistic strategies for the time being and get about the business of restoring the missing cutting edges.

---

[46]This appears in Douglas, *Let the Earth Hear His Voice,* p. 6.

[47]A.W. Tozer, *Paths to Power* (Philadelphia: Christian Publications, n.d.), p. 5.

PART II
THE PROCESS OF MOTIVATING CONVERSION

The stages of the spiritual decision-making process were discussed briefly in Chapter 3. The stages were as follows: (1) activation of need; (2) search for information; (3) formation and change in beliefs and attitudes; (4) problem recognition and intention to act; (5) decision; and (6) post-decision evaluation.

Each of the chapters in this part focuses on one or more of these stages. Activation of need is the subject matter of Chapter 5. Chapter 6 goes on to discuss information search, whereas Chapter 7 focuses more directly on the ways in which various media may be used in evangelistic strategy. Chapter 8 explores the complex subject of formation and change of attitudes and beliefs. Because problem recognition and intention to act are the outcomes of changed beliefs and attitudes, this fourth stage of the decision-making process also is covered in that chapter. This section of the book concludes with a consideration of decision (conversion) and post-decision evaluation in Chapter 9.

This section, then, focuses specifically on evangelism in all of its phases. Evangelism is viewed as movement from one stage of the decision process to another, and the final act of conversion is merely the end point of this complex process.

CHAPTER 5
Activation of Need

A young, newly minted Ph.D. emerged from his graduate studies having garnered nearly all of the academic laurels anyone could. On his way to the faculty of one of the greatest universities of the world, he was full of visions of turning the world upside down in his field. Everything was bright and rosy.

It did not take long for this "young turk" to make quite an impact both in the classroom and in his publications. Soon he was recognized as a real "comer." Everything was going his way, or at least it seemed to be. There was little room for God at this point, even though he and his young family attended church on a fairly regular basis. Spiritual concerns were on a far back burner, except in those odd moments when there were fleeting thoughts of dissatisfaction. Attend a Billy Graham crusade? No way! "I'm doing fine, thank you, and things will just keep getting better. Sunday morning church is okay, but let's not be a fanatic about this thing!"

A few years passed, however, and the bloom began to disappear on this rosy life. "The real problem is lack of social life. Also, those old fogies on this faculty don't really appreciate what I have to offer." So, he accepted an invitation to join the faculty at another major state university, and things were fine for a couple of years. Everything was new—students, colleagues, friends, house. Yes, life was vibrant and exciting, for awhile. Then the same dissatisfactions entered, and others at the same stage of their careers felt the same thing. A discussion group formed that sought solutions to some of life's hard questions, but no one had any answers. The fairly liberal consumption of alcohol, however, stimulated some mighty lively evenings. Gradually those evenings became depressing. "There must be more to life than this!"

One evening a new friend asked an interesting question: "What would you and your wife think about getting together with a few other couples to see what the Bible has to say about life?" This couple, now in their early 30s, jumped at this invitation and were interested in doing something they never would have considered just a few years earlier. After a few months both accepted Jesus Christ as their Savior, and a new life began.

Some readers will recognize that this story is not fiction—it is a brief account of the early stages of the author's own spiritual pilgrimage. What was taking place at the various stages? First of all, the lack of interest in spiritual concerns during those earlier years is typical. All of the presumed excitement of success lay ahead, and there was no felt need for a change. One of the most basic principles that emerges from the study of human behavior is that *people will not change unless they feel a need to change.* Need activation is always the first step in any type of decision. Furthermore, there will be no interest in the gospel unless it is shown to be relevant to a person's basic life-styles and strivings. The Christian message never can be communicated effectively if it is presented as abstract principles divorced from the basic issues of life itself.

This brief story also illustrates the dramatic change in receptivity that occurred *after* life had been tasted and found to be wanting. In effect, a filter was opened to anything that promised a deeper and more fundamental answer. Human philosophies were explored for a period but fell short, and there was a growing interest in exploring the Bible. In other words, a success-oriented striver turned into a seeker, and spiritual truth was sought.

All of this suggests that human need cannot be ignored by the Christian communicator. Analysis of needs will disclose those who are receptive to the gospel at a point in time and those who are not. It also is the key to showing that the message *is* relevant to twentieth-century man.

SOME FUNDAMENTALS OF HUMAN MOTIVATION

Everyone has certain desires that he or she strives to fulfill and satisfy. When the perceived difference between the present state of affairs and this ideal state reaches a certain point, the individual is motivated to act and restore a sense of balance. Some will use the term "need" to designate these desired states.[1] Others refer to them as "wants" or "motives."[2] Call them what you will; the important issue is that we understand how they function to shape *purposeful behavior.*

Notice the use of the term "purposeful." This is quite deliberate, because the human being does not behave in capricious, random fashion. We may not agree with what someone does, but that is not the point. Pay careful attention to Snygg's and Comb's important statement:

> Laying aside, for the moment, the objective facts about behavior that some of us have learned, let each of us look at his own behavior as we actually see it while we are behaving. We find lawfulness and determinism at once. From the point of view of the behaver himself, behavior is caused. It is purposeful. It always has a reason. . . . When we look at other people from an external, objective point of view their behavior may seem irrational because we do not experience the field as they do. . . . But at the instant of behavior the actions of each person seem to him to be the best and most effective acts he can perform under the circumstances. If, at that instant, he knew how to behave more effectively, he would do so.[3]

What this says, of course, is that all of us are rational beings. We have no justification to disparage another person just because he or she is different. The only ultimate criterion is biblical truth, properly interpreted and applied.

Before proceeding further it is well to ask the important question of the relevance of *individual* needs (or motives) to the communicator who often must deal with masses. Fortunately, it usually is possible to uncover audience segments with common strivings. One authority puts it this way:

> Motives [needs] are individually acquired but certain situations will produce pleasure or pain with such regularity either through biological or cultural arrangements that the probability of certain common motives developing in all people is very high.[4]

---

[1]For one of the clearest discussions see Ward Goodenough, *Cooperation in Change* (New York: Russell Sage Foundation, 1963), ch. 3.

[2]See, for example, David C. McClelland, *Personality* (New York: William Sloane Assoc., 1951). Also the various issues are discussed thoroughly in James F. Engel, Roger D. Blackwell, and David T. Kollat, *Consumer Behavior,* 3rd ed. (Hinsdale, Ill.: Dryden Press, 1978), ch. 8.

[3]Donald Snygg and Arthur W. Combs, *Individual Behavior* (New York: Harper & Row, 1949), p. 12.

[4]McClelland, *Personality,* p. 474.

Classification of Needs

Writers in the behavioral sciences over the years have tried their hand at classifying needs and some lists attain great length. Unfortunately this often is little more than an exercise in ingenuity. Some would list one hundred or more! More recent contributors, however, have brought some needed clarity.

The Maslow Classification. Psychologist A. H. Maslow has introduced the concept of a hierarchy of needs.[5] While his writings differ somewhat on both the number of such needs and their labeling, they fall into the five categories appearing in Figure 5.1.

FIGURE 5.1.

The Maslow Hierarchy of Needs

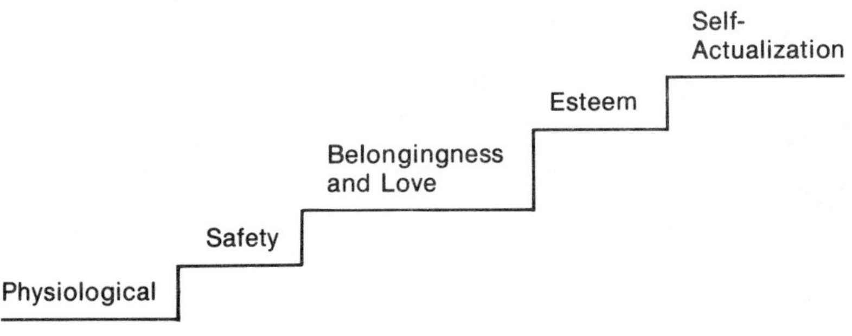

Adapted from A. H. Maslow, *Motivation and Human Behavior,* rev. ed. (New York: Harper & Row, 1970).

There are three essential dimensions in this classification: (1) survival needs, (2) needs related to acceptance by and involvement with others, and (3) needs centering around individual competency and self-expression. Each higher order of need will not function as a motivator until needs at the lower levels are largely satisfied. The hungry person, for example, cares little about geometric theorems (perhaps very few others care either). Each level contains some important insights for those attempting to understand human behavior.

[5]A.H. Maslow, *Motivation and Human Behavior,* rev. ed. (New York: Harper & Row, 1970). The implications for the Christian communicator are spelled out in Keith Miller, *The Becomers* (Waco, Texas: Word Books, 1973), chs. 12–13.

(1) Physiological. Basic bodily desires such as hunger and thirst fall into this category. If they are unsatisfied, all of the human being's resources become focused toward that end. Jesus Christ certainly was aware of this fact and cognizant that needs follow a hierarchical pattern. Consider His words in that all-important passage stating His priorities in ministry: "The Spirit of the Lord is on me; therefore he has anointed me to preach good news to the poor. He has sent me to proclaim freedom for the prisoners and recovery of sight for the blind, to release the oppressed, to proclaim the year of the Lord's favor" (Luke 4:18,19, NIV).

(2) Safety. Man also has basic needs for security and physical safety. There was a time when life was almost completely dominated by physical hardships, which shortened lifespans and rendered life a bleak and frustrating existence. This is still the situation in many parts of the world, and recent Gallup polls show that most people living under such circumstances are profoundly unhappy. Unemployment, poverty, war, and perpetual famine provide little basis for optimism and hope.

The first obligation of the church, of course, is to attempt to remedy the underlying causes of such conditions and to bring about change where possible. This is not always feasible, in which case it is proper to emphasize the rewards of the next life. The joys of heaven and life after death can become an important appeal since the present life has no lasting hope. The potency of this message diminishes, however, once safety needs are met and people are more concerned about higher-order needs. Life after death then is seen more as a "fringe benefit" of the gospel rather than a prime motivator.

Safety needs are not confined to the underdeveloped nations, however. Conditions of future shock (i.e., a sense of powerlessness in the face of unending change) give rise to a striving to maintain the known and familiar in a chaotic world.[6] Change is resisted and the familiar is embraced at all costs. The gospel message of freedom from anxiety and relief from turmoil (Phil 4:6–8) provides a powerful "safety zone" for life under such conditions.

(3) Belongingness and Love. When physiological and safety needs are largely met, most of us then focus our attention on giving and receiving love. For the first time the role of others becomes critically important, over and above their contribution to safety and survival.

[6]See Alvin Toffler, *Future Shock* (New York: Random House, 1970).

It is interesting to observe the extent to which this need has become dominant in the post-World War II generation in North America.[7] The parents of today's under-thirty-five generation were raised during the Depression of the 1930s. Hence physiological and safety needs were paramount. Only a minority had these lower-order needs satisfied to the point that they have ceased to serve as motivators. The businessman in his fifties, for example, is likely to place importance on job security, economic advancement, and ample savings. The younger generation, however, has had these needs met, for the most part. The result is a focus on love and belonging. Physical survival is assumed.

The church as the body of Christ should meet this need for belongingness through a sense of true community. Obviously this cannot come only through Sunday morning attendance, and so the widespread expression of this desire has given rise to the body life movement. Small groups and other forms of face-to-face interaction have emerged, but casual observation will disclose that those active in such groups are largely under the age of forty. Only handfuls over the age of forty seem to feel a similar need. The reason, of course, lies in the motivational differences of the two generations discussed above.

(4) Esteem. A sense of self-worth and self-respect is very much related to belongingness and love. Nothing can be more devastating than going through life with a faulty self-image. All too frequently depression and worthlessness result when performance falls short of unrealistically high standards. Among the most powerful words of Scripture is the truth that God has made us ". . . holy in his eyes, without a single fault—we who stand before him covered with his love" (Eph. 1:4, TLB). The fact of God's unconditional acceptance of the Christian is a potent healing force for a wounded self-esteem.

(5) Self-Actualization. Maslow contends that only a handful of people ever reach that point at which they can give themselves over to ultimate individual fulfillment through creative activity. Most are hung up at lower levels of need. Maslow apparently does not realize that self-actualization in its fullest sense is impossible without the indwelling power of God, without the ability simply to know and to enjoy Him.

The Need for Sensation and New Experience. There is an altogether

[7]For a more thorough discussion see Engel, Backwell, and Kollat, *Consumer Behavior,* pp. 180–189.

different category of need poignantly illustrated by Steve Turner's little poem entitled, "Tonight We Will Fake Love":

> Tonight, we will
> fake love together.
> You my love, possess
> all the essential qualities
> as listed by *Playboy*.
> You will last me for
> as long as two weeks
> or until such a time
> as your face & figure
> go out of fashion.
> I will hold you close
> to my Hollywood-standard body,
> the smell of which
> has been approved
> by my ten best friends
> and a representative
> of Lifebuoy.
> I will prop my paperback
> Kama Sutra
> on the dressing table
> & like programmed seals
> we will perform
> & like human beings
> we will grow tired
> of our artificially sweetened
> diluted & ready to drink
> love affairs.
>
> Tonight, we will fake love.
> Tonight we will be both
> quick & silent, our time limited,
> measured out in distances
> between fingers
> & pushbuttons.[8]

People tire of what they do—the familiar becomes stale and boring. Consequently, there is a need to seek new experience and high sensation.[9] Such a motivation, of course, never ceases and is ultimately futile. As Solomon said many centuries ago, ". . . Our eyes can never see enough to be satisfied; our ears can never hear

---

[8]This appears in Steve Turner's anthology entitled *Tonight We Will Fake Love* (London: Charisma Books, 1974), p. 15. Used by permission of the author.

[9]Marvin Zucherman, "The Search for High Sensation," *Psychology Today,* vol. 11 (February, 1978), p. 38ff.

enough. What has happened before will happen again. . . . There is nothing new in the whole world" (Eccles. 1:8,9, TEV). The ultimate answer, of course, lies in the gospel promise that ". . . if anyone is in Christ, he is a new creation; the old has gone, the new has come!" (2 Cor. 5:17, NIV).

The Unity and Stability of Need Patterns

Needs are not organized and expressed in haphazard fashion. Rather, one's entire psychological makeup is integrated into a meaningful whole through the functioning of the *self-concept.* The self-concept provides a means whereby basic goals and social values become internalized as behavioral standards. Rogers puts it this way:

> The self-concept, or self-structure, may be thought of as an organized configuration of perceptions of the self which are admissible to awareness. It is composed of such elements as the perceptions of one's characteristics and abilities; the precepts and concepts of the self in relation to others and to the environment; the value qualities which are perceived as associated with experiences; and the objectives, goals, and ideas which are perceived as having positive or negative valence.[10]

The self thus becomes an entity to be enhanced. The result is that certain needs become internalized as more or less permanent incentives. As Maslow indicated, self-actualization, self-esteem, and belongingness and love are all needs keyed to self-maintenance and enhancement.[11]

Uncovering Human Needs

There are a number of standardized scales used in the psychological clinic to detect both the existence and strength of needs.[12] Most of these will not find their way into the arsenal of the practical Christian communicator, however, for the reason that his purposes are different from those of clinical psychology.

Questionnaire methods are readily adaptable to group settings.[13] For example, the author and others at the Wheaton Graduate School have had success with scales listing various areas of need such

---

[10]Carl R. Rogers, *Client-Centered Therapy* (Boston: Houghton Mifflin, 1951), p. 501.

[11]Maslow, *Motivation and Human Behavior.*

[12]See, for example, David C. McClelland, "Methods of Measuring Human Motivation," in John W. Atkinson, ed., *Motives in Fantasy, Action and Society* (Princeton, N. J.: D. Van Nostrand Company, 1958), pp. 7–42.

[13]See James F. Engel, *How Can I Get Them to Listen?* (Grand Rapids, Mich.: Zondervan, 1977), chs. 4–5.

as the following: "overcoming sexual temptation," "finding effective ways to communicate with my kids when I return from work," "finding others in the church with whom I can really be myself." People then are asked to check whether or not they need help in each area.

In personal conversation, the best approach is to follow Keith Miller's advice to "feel around the rim of the life" until we come to that point of need or hurt. This will require the building of bridges of friendship as well as an ability to listen. Needs are rarely uncovered in the fleeting contact provided by "cold-call evangelism."

The Issue of Felt Need Versus Real Need

An extensive survey of writings on evangelism and missions encompassing such sources as *Practical Anthropology* (now published as *Missiology), Evangelical Missions Quarterly, Christian Communications Spectrum,* and *Journal of the World Association of Christian Communication* disclosed one overriding principle: People will not listen to the gospel message and respond unless it speaks to *felt needs.* There are two basic reasons given.[14] The first reinforces the discussion in Chapter 2, which stressed that perceptual filters close unless a message has pertinence for an individual. Conversely, attention is attracted when content is seen to be relevant. Secondly, Jesus Himself usually followed this principle.

A frequently voiced objection is that felt needs are not real needs, the assumption being that people do not perceive reality in terms of fundamental truth revealed in Scripture. A ministry to felt need, in turn, can be quite superficial and completely overlook the true dimensions underlying a person's situation at any given point in time.

Much of the objection disappears when felt need is viewed as the *starting point for communication.* Few would disagree that attention must be attracted and held and that this most likely will not occur if the gospel is presented as abstract principles. Jesus, for example, did not linger long on felt need but quickly moved to the underlying spiritual dimensions. In the fourth chapter of John, Jesus is recorded as talking with the woman at the well. She was not there for spiritual dialogue but for water. Jesus asked her for a drink, which she provided. He then asked her if she was interested in living

[14]See, for example, Pat Hile, "Communicating the Gospel in Terms of Felt Need," *Missiology,* vol. 5 (October, 1977), pp. 499–506.

water—water that would never dry up and disappear. In rapid succession He asked her questions until she perceived that He was talking about eternal life, and she responded with joy.

But we must be cautious in assuming that felt need is somehow superficial and irrelevant. After all, it is very real to those with the problem, and it must be taken seriously by the communicator.

Let's take as a principle, then, that felt need, in this sense, sets the initial agenda for Christian communication. Now we have an even more disturbing problem: Exactly how does one speak to felt need? The literature is silent on this subject; yet it is a most perplexing question to the communicator.

Assume that a middle-class man in his late thirties says that his greatest concern now is to find meaning and purpose in his job. What is the communicator to say? Some would search for biblical verses that perhaps could be of some help. Others might reply, "I have found peace and purpose in Jesus Christ." This statement is undoubtedly true, but it also has very little meaning for the person with the problem. It comes across as superficial because we have not understood the dimensions of his need. The fact is, we often give shallow answers because we have not probed beneath the surface.

It is important to point out that need-satisfying behavior is always directed by *beliefs* that specify types of activity that presumably will have the best outcomes. The relationship between felt needs and beliefs is spelled out in Figure 5.2:

Some definitions are in order. Beliefs are those things that an individual holds to be true. Values and attitudes specify the extent to which the person feels positively or negatively about those beliefs. Behavior, in turn, is generally consistent with both beliefs and attitudes, and emotional response is an outcome of behavior.

Felt need reflects an emotional feeling. For this reason it is only the tip of the iceberg, and it is imperative to probe more deeply. Now we come to the heart of the matter: *Felt need cannot be ministered to unless underlying belief patterns are changed to bring them into accord with scriptural reality.* This is a widely accepted contemporary principle of counseling,[15] with the exception, of course, that only Christian counselors would add scriptural truth as being the basis of reality.[16]

---

[15]See, for example, Victor Raimy, *Misunderstandings of the Self* (San Francisco: Jossey-Bass Publishers, 1975).

[16]One of the best sources is Lawrence J. Crabb, Jr., *Effective Biblical Counseling* (Grand Rapids, Mich.: Zondervan, 1977).

FIGURE 5. 2.

The Relationship Between Beliefs and Felt Needs

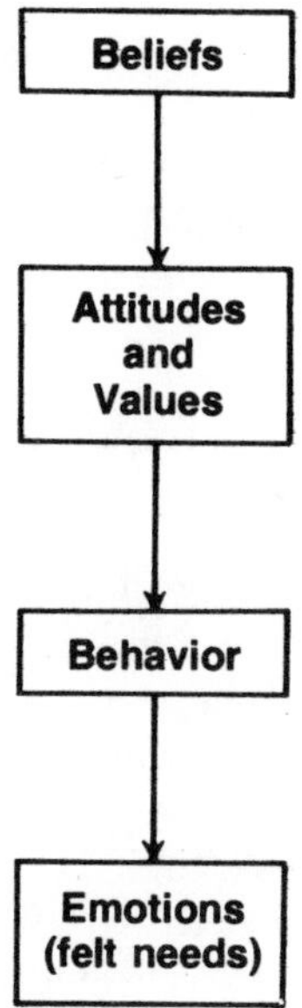

Return now to our friend who is dissatisifed with his job. Assume that deeper probing disclosed this pattern of beliefs:

"I must be a financial success to be significant."

"Financial net worth equals personal worth."

"Everyone must recognize my abilities if I am to be of any significance."

"I must not fail if I am to regard myself as worthwhile."

Now we can move from generalities to some pinpointed use of Scripture. The basic problem is a totally wrong belief about life itself, one which equates financial success and personal achievement with happiness. Jesus might have said to such a person, "Do not store up for yourselves treasures on earth, where moth and rust destroy, and where thieves break in and steal. But store up for yourselves treasures in heaven, where moth and rust do not destroy, and where thieves do not break in and steal. For where your treasure is, there your heart will be also" (Matt. 6:19,20, NIV).

What this boils down to is that erroneous beliefs must be corrected if attitudes and values, behavior, and emotional response (felt need) are ever to be changed. This is a far cry from trying to minister to the tip of the iceberg. Also it may provide the answer to the dichotomy between felt need and real need. The real need, in the final analysis, is to bring beliefs into accord with scriptural reality.

The type of ministry suggested here puts a burden on the communicator to develop an ability to listen, first of all, and then to respond with real empathy. Unfortunately, there are no evangelistic formulae to help in this process.[17]

HUMAN NEED AND THE "FERTILE FIELD THEORY"

Common sense would argue that the best audience target for evangelistic efforts are those who are seeking and looking for change in their lives. Experience at the Wheaton Graduate School shows that people readily acknowledge their striving when this is the case. Filters are open and the probability of some type of movement through the decision process is high if the relevance of the gospel for the underlying need can be effectively communicated. "Seekers," then, represent the fertile field and should receive a greater emphasis in strategy than those who are not so open, all things being equal.

Questionnaire research can readily uncover those who are looking for change in their life-style. But one also should be able to detect such people through sensitivity to changes that occur throughout a lifetime making people more open at some periods than they are at others.

The Effect of Catastrophic Change

Some type of radical change in one's personal situation can lead to a rapid crumbling of values. A good illustration is the effects of land reform on the whole outlook of the Quichua Indians in Ecuador. The reader will recall from Chapter 3 that this factor triggered a widespread re-evaluation of life and opened the door for a Christian "people movement."

Some changes obviously will have more impact than others as the data in Figure 5.3 reveal. Through use of their Social Readjustment

[17]The most helpful book on this subject is Leighton Ford, *Good News Is for Sharing* (Elgin, Ill.: David C. Cook, 1977).

Rating Scale, for example, Holmes and Rahe found that a traffic ticket has little effect on one's outlook toward life, whereas death of a spouse, divorce, or marital separation had an obvious impact.[18] When these more traumatic events occur, it is likely that those most intimately affected will be receptive to the gospel if it is presented lovingly and empathetically.

FIGURE 5.3.

The Effects of Change on Social Readjustment

	LIFE EVENT	MEAN VALUE
1.	Death of a spouse	100
2.	Divorce	73
3.	Marital separation from mate	65
4.	Detention in jail or other institution	63
5.	Death of a close family member	63
6.	Major personal injury or illness	53
7.	Marriage	50
8.	Being fired at work	47
9.	Marital reconciliation with mate	45
10.	Retirement from work	45
11.	Major change in the health or behavior of family member	44
12.	Pregnancy	40
13.	Sexual difficulties	39
14.	Gaining a new family member (e.g., through birth, adoption, oldster moving in, marriage, etc.)	39
15.	Major business readjustment (e.g., merger, reorganization, bankruptcy, etc.)	39
16.	Major change in financial state (e.g., a lot worse off or a lot better off than usual)	38
17.	Death of a close friend	37
18.	Changing to a different line of work	36
19.	Major change in the number of arguments with spouse (e.g., either a lot more or a lot less than usual regarding child rearing, personal habits, etc.)	35
20.	Taking on a mortgage greater than $10,000 (e.g. purchasing a home, business, etc.)	31
21.	Foreclosure on a mortgage or loan	30
22.	Major change in responsibilities at work (e.g. promotion, demotion, lateral transfer)	29
23.	Son or daughter leaving home (e.g. marriage, college)	29
24.	In-law troubles	29
25.	Outstanding personal achievement	28

[18] T.H. Holmes and R.H. Rahe, "The Social Readjustment Rating Scale," *Journal of Psychosomatic Research,* vol. 11 (1967), pp. 213–218.

FIGURE 5.3—Continued

The Effects of Change on Social Readjustment

	LIFE EVENT	MEAN VALUE
26.	Wife beginning or ceasing work outside the home	26
27.	Beginning or ceasing formal schooling	26
28.	Major change in living conditions (e.g. building new home, remodeling, deterioration of home or neighborhood)	25
29.	Revision of personal habits (dress, manners, etc.)	24
30.	Troubles with the boss	23
31.	Major change in working hours or conditions	20
32.	Change in residence	20
33.	Changing to a new school	20
34.	Major change in usual type and/or amount of recreation	19
35.	Major change in church activities (e.g. lot more or less than usual)	19
36.	Major change in social activities (e.g. clubs, movies, dances)	18
37.	Taking on a mortgage or loan less than $10,000 (car, TV)	17
38.	Major change in sleeping habits (e.g a lot more or less than usual, or change in part of day when sleep)	16
39.	Major change in number of family get-togethers (more or less)	15
40.	Major change in eating habits (more or less, or different)	15
41.	Vacation	13
42.	Christmas	12
43.	Minor violations of the law (e.g traffic tickets, jaywalking, disturbing the peace, etc.)	11

Reproduced by special permission from T.H. Homes and R.H. Rahe, "The Social Readjustment Rating Scale, *Journal of Psychosomatic Research,* vol. 11 (New York: Pergamon Press; Ltd., 1967), pp. 213–218.

One must be cautious, however, in assuming that traumatic situations always will lead to psychological distress, because quite the opposite can happen. Reports from the Ohio State University Disaster Research Center show that the majority tend to look upon a natural disaster (such as a devastating storm) as a positive experience.[19] Often disaster can unite people temporarily and lead to high group solidarity and morale.

Changes in Life Cycle

It has long been recognized that one's whole pattern of motivation and outlook toward life changes sharply with maturity, but only

[19]Berta Taylor, "Good News About Disaster," *Psychology Today,* vol. 11 (October, 1977), p. 93ff.

recently has the psychological significance of these "passages" been explored in any depth.[20] The principal researchers all have designated the stages differently, and Figure 5.4 represents an attempt to summarize their efforts.

FIGURE 5.4.

Stages in the "Passage" Through the Life Cycle

1. *Pulling Up Roots.* 18–22. A transition from parent's beliefs to the establishment of new strictly personal beliefs. Often characterized by an identity crisis.
2. *Building the Dream.* 22–30. "Forming the dream" and working one's aspirations through occupational and marital choices. Much importance placed on "doing what we should."
3. *Living Out the Dream.* 30–35. Putting down roots, living out one's aspirations and making them become a reality.
4. *Midlife Transition.* 35–45. Reassessment of the dream and the values which have been internalized. A final casting aside of inappropriate role models. Equilibrium will be restored either through a renewal or a resignation to the realities of life.
5. *Middle Adulthood.* 45–59. Reduced personal striving and more emphasis on living consistently with a clarified code of values placing more importance on personal relationships and individual fulfillment.
6. *Late Adult Transition.* 60–65 and beyond. Diminished active occupational life and eventual retirement. Retirement can either lead to renewal or resignation.

Adapted from Gail Sheehy, *Passages* (New York: Bantam Books, 1976); George Vaillint, "The Climb to Maturity: How the Best and the Brightest Came of Age," *Psychology Today,* vol. 10 (September, 1977), p. 34ff; and Daniel J. Levinson, "Growing Up With a Dream" *Psychology Today,* vol. 11 (January, 1978), p. 22ff.

The age ranges specified in Figure 5.4 probably are arbitrary. They should be viewed as designating the average only, because it is likely that some reach the various stages at different ages. Also, not everyone goes through the stages as described here with exactly

---

[20]The most widely quoted source is Gail Sheehy, *Passages* (New York: Bantam Books, 1976). Of greater significance is the empirical research by Levinson and by Vaillint, both of which will be published in book form. For excerpts, see George E. Vaillint, "The Climb to Maturity: How the Best and the Brightest Came of Age," *Psychology Today,* vol. 10 (September, 1977), p. 34ff; and Daniel J. Levinson, "Growing Up With a Dream," *Psychology Today,* vol. 11 (January, 1978), p. 22ff.

these symptoms. Enough do, however, to give this type of analysis real significance for the Christian communicator.

Stages at Which People Are Most Resistant to Change. Stage 2, "Building the Dream," describes a period in which there usually is not much interest in spiritual things. The dream lies ahead, and life is yet to be tasted. Young adults in Vancouver, Canada, were found, for instance, to be looking for change in life, but little interest was expressed in Christianity or any other religion.[21] Either they were seeking experience in the form of sexual experimentation, new and exotic foods, travel, adventure, and so on, or they were attempting to find various forms of self-expression.

A similar pattern seems to set in around middle adulthood. Once again, values are stabilized and change is resisted. A commitment to Christ usually will come much earlier.

Stages at Which People Are Open to Change. Most people make their initial decision for Christ prior to young adulthood, and the "pulling up roots" period finds many to be highly receptive to the gospel. A survey of high school youth in Quito, Ecuador (ranging between the ages of sixteen and twenty) showed that most were departing from their Catholic background but still were interested in religion.[22] Most of them readily voiced that they were in a stage of relative turmoil over future occupation, political stability in the country, loneliness, self acceptance, and so on. One would have to conclude that there would be a large response to evangelistic efforts. Unfortunately, the Protestant church at that time encompassed only 300 out of the 64,000 high school youth in Quito, and outreach was virtually zero. Moreover, the missions located in the city had made no efforts whatsoever to penetrate this age group, and there has been little effort made as of this writing to capitalize upon this highly receptive segment.

"Midlife transition" is another stage in which values are in flux. Levinson vividly describes what goes on during this period:

> Transition is a time of moderate to severe crises. It evokes tumultuous struggles within the self and between the self and the external world. Every aspect of a man's life comes into question and he is horrified by much that is revealed. He experiences more fully his own mortality and the actual or impending death of others. At the same time he has a strong desire to be more creative: to create products that have values for himself

[21]Wheaton Communications Research Report #56.

[22]Engel, *How Can I Get Them to Listen?*, ch. 9.

and others, join in enterprises that advance human welfare, to contribute more fully to coming generations.[23]

While there is a dramatic reassessment, this does not mean that life during this period is unhappy. In fact, Vaillint found that this was the happiest period in the life of ninety-five men who were studied over their lifetime.[24] The period from twenty-one to thirty-five, on the other hand, was the unhappiest.

Various community surveys at the Wheaton Graduate School verify the upheaval taking place. Those over thirty-five with above average education and income more often than not will express these needs: "strengthening my marriage," "teaching moral and spiritual values to children," "finding satisfaction in my job." Also, there is a growing interest in the Bible and spiritual teaching, even though most are not likely to be active in church. Here, then, is a great opportunity to probe more deeply to the level of underlying beliefs and provide pinpointed Christian answers. Old beliefs are, in effect, "up for grabs," and the church has a great opportunity if it can demonstrate that Christian values indeed will provide a more satisfying direction for life.

The post-retirement stage theoretically should also be a time of values clarification. Most of the surveys undertaken by the author and his colleagues reveal, however, that people are pretty much set in their ways by then. Conversions are few and far between, but this could also be explained by the relative impotence of church outreach to this segment.

THE PROBLEM OF THE "SATISFIED"

Has the reader ever heard a statement from the pulpit that "most people are just waiting to accept Christ if they only knew how"? This sounds very exciting, and it may stir up evangelistic activity for awhile. Unfortunately, it represents a classic case of "armchair quarterbacking," because the reality is quite different.

Surveys of non-Christians in the developed countries almost uniformly reveal that roughly two thirds indicate they are happy with life as it is.[25] Whenever the author makes this point in seminars,

[23]Levinson, "Growing Up With a Dream," p. 89.

[24]Vaillint, "The Climb to Maturity."

[25]For some of the most definitive evidence see Phillip Shaver and Jonathan Freedman, "Your Pursuit of Happiness," *Psychology Today* (August, 1976), p. 26ff. Also see Wheaton Graduate School surveys of Peoria, Ill.; Vancouver, B.C., Canada; Upper Arlington, Ohio; and Rochester, New York.

there are many who rear back in their chairs and ask, "Wait a minute. Do you mean they say they don't have problems?" As Shaver and Freedman have discovered, ". . . happiness is a relative state, based on a comparison with external standards rather than on direct feelings and experiences."[26] Happiness has much to do with accepting and enjoying what one is and maintaining a balance between both expectations and achievements. It certainly does not imply a problem-free life, because those who claim to be most happy also will identify areas of concern such as loneliness.

It should be noted here that the Wheaton surveys disclosing this relative satisfaction with life always encompass a group of related questions. Reply to a single question would be suspect, but identical reactions to six or more stimuli probing this subject cannot be dismissed.

What it boils down to is that people are pretty much satisfied if their life is relatively free from financial problems and outside disturbances. Francis Schaeffer has accurately caught the mood:

> *Personal peace means just to be let alone, not to be troubled by the troubles of other people, whether across the world or across the city—to live one's life with minimal possibilities of being personally disturbed.*[27]

Another contributing factor is the demonstrated tendency to embrace a pleasant and optimistic outlook. This has all been documented by Matlin and Stang who feel that memory processes definitely favor the processing of pleasant information and inhibit the opposite response.[28]

Some object that people cannot be happy without Christ, but such a viewpoint is naive. Remember that happiness is a relative thing—people are happy *given the light that they have.* Furthermore, it will be difficult to convince them to the contrary, because those who are happy and satisfied are a nonresponsive segment with closed filters.

Most people in the Western world, then, are not just "waiting for someone to tell them how to accept Christ," and it is best to recognize that fact. In reality, witness to the "satisfied" is the toughest challenge we face. There are no easy answers here, but there are two possible approaches to follow, remembering that happiness involves a perception of both present circumstances and the ideal state.

---

[26]Shaver and Freedman, "Your Pursuit of Happiness," p. 29.

[27]Francis A. Schaeffer, *How Should We Then Live?* (Old Tappen, N.J.: Fleming H. Revell, 1976), p. 205.

[28]Margaret Matlin and David Stang, "The Pollyanna Principle," *Psychology Today,* vol. 11 (March, 1978), p. 56ff.

Activation of Need

Attacking the Status Quo. Few would be so naive as to shout to the nonbeliever, "Happy! What do you mean you're happy? Nobody can be happy without Christ." But there are ways to stimulate a person gently to re-evaluate the status quo and to trigger some useful thinking. Quite often the mass media are the best way. While there are not great numbers of effective examples, one of the most clever radio spots is reproduced in Figure 5.5 in script form. This is from the famous "Is God Dead?" series produced by Stan Freberg during the 1960s. It is both funny and provocative.

FIGURE 5.5.

Stan Freberg's Attack on the "Satisfied"

Voice one:	So, the point is I'm not saying He's alive and I'm not saying He isn't; it's just that even if I thought He was . . .
Voice two:	Uh huh
Voice one:	My life is pretty full and I don't need any divine (cough)—say, can I get you a drink.
Voice two:	No, thanks.
Voice one:	After all, I got two air-conditioned cars, colored TV, 8 mm camera with a zoom lens. And then I got the boat . . .
Voice two:	How often do you get down to your boat?
Voice one:	Regularly . . . well I haven't been able to get down for about five or six months now, but one of these weekends the wife and I got to get down there, right Baby.
Wife:	Yea, yea.
Voice one:	Now look, Harriet, I'm trying to talk to the man here.
Wife:	You want to do me a favor . . . why don't you stop with all that.
Voice one:	Look I'm trying to explain our lives are very full, so don't start.
Voice two:	Listen, I'm sorry I brought it up. I can see your life is very full.
Voice one:	You bet it's full. We get along perfectly well, thank you, without God.
Voice two:	Right. Just checking.

Radio spot created and produced by Stan Freberg in 1968 for the United Presbyterian Church.

Providing New Light. Many people would come to quite a different evaluation of life in general if some new standards were provided. In effect this requires bringing the new light of the Christian message. Let's be clear on one point: Words alone seldom are sufficient to bring this light. If we claim that our life is somehow different and better than that offered by the world, then the burden of proof is on the Christian. The author and his colleagues have yet to undertake a general audience survey in North America that discloses positive attitudes toward the church and its members (see especially chapter 13). There may be some interest in spiritual matters, but the church usually is looked down upon by the majority. It just does not offer a viable option for life. Our words are tainted by a lack of credibility.

Individuality, achievement, economic success, doing my thing—all of these represent common values of the world. Would unbelievers see different values if they closely examined most of our churches, both corporately and individually? Or would they see a group of humans who have let cultural values contaminate their spiritual life?

Obviously this comes down to the outright necessity of putting true faith into action. The need is to demonstrate love and concern and not just talk about it, showing that materialism is not the only way of life. In the final analysis, there is no alternative to positive, loving action demonstrating a Christian life-style. Perhaps then someone will ask you ". . . to give the reason for the hope you have" (1 Pet. 3:15, NIV), and new light can be given.

CHAPTER 6

Information Search and the Spiritual Decision Process

"A generation in turmoil." These words have been used to describe the nearly 500,000 youth and young adults in Hong Kong between the ages of fifteen and twenty-five. The traditional values of Chinese culture have lost their hold, and the future offers great uncertainty. A sense of rootlessness, doubt, boredom, and monotony characterizes these young lives. Many are openly seeking for answers, but the church, by and large, has not been viewed as a viable option.

Recognizing the extent to which this audience segment has become a "fertile field" for evangelism, a group from within the Fellowship of Evangelical Students envisioned the publication of a hard-hitting magazine distributed through secular channels that would relate the Christian message to the contemporary scene. The result was publication of *Breakthrough.* The first issue was marketed in late 1973 through secular newsstands and bookstores. The cover appears in Figure 6.1. By the end of February, 16,000 copies had been sold, creating a record for the sale of Christian materials in Hong Kong. Succeeding issues have shown steady circulation growth and now *Breakthrough* has become an important part of the publishing scene in this bustling city.

The *Breakthrough* editorial team is all Chinese, and all of the initial financing came from sources in Hong Kong. The magazine has received praise from secular sources for its high degree of professionalism and relevance. From the outset the focus has been on

FIGURE 6.1.

The Cover From the First Edition of *Breakthrough*

audience life-style and needs, with the result that many non-Christians who never would have gone near a church have come to at least an initial understanding of the implications of the gospel for their lives.

Here, then, is a situation in which a large number within an audience segment were living with felt need. Most people with felt needs *actively seek new information* to provide satisfaction once they have discovered that their own values are not sufficient. This is the second stage in their decision process. The key to communication strategy, in turn, is to discover the sources they are turning to and find ways of presenting the Christian message among the other alternatives. In short, we must adapt to their patterns of information search and not expect them to come to us.

This is the first of two chapters on this subject. This chapter centers, first of all, on ways people make use of media sources in their decision process; then we turn to descriptions of the media used in this process. Chapter 7 focuses on the problems of media strategy. It should be recognized at the outset that it is a demanding task to describe the pros and cons of the various media alternatives in one short chapter. Entire volumes have been written about each medium. Furthermore, there are such widespread differences in media availability and use throughout the world that generalizations are impossible.[1] This problem is compounded by the fact that the vast majority of research on this subject is confined to North America, although this situation is rapidly changing. Therefore, the discussion here can only be introductory.

THE SEARCH PROCESS

Much has been written on information search and use in various areas of human activity.[2] It is not possible to generalize from this information to the spiritual decision process, however, since it is unique in many ways. For example, the decision to accept Christ and the decision to buy a new home have only remote similarity because of the working of the Holy Spirit in the process. Unfortunately,

[1]For a general overview of media availability and use in various countries of the world, see Christopher Kolade, "Christian Communication and Third World Societies," *WACC Journal*, vol. 23 (1976), pp. 4–10; *WACC Journal*, vol. 24 (1977), entire issue devoted to media; and Alan Wells, *Mass Communications, a World View* (Palo Alto, Ca.: National Press Books, 1974).

[2]This literature is reviewed in depth in James F. Engel, Roger D. Blackwell, and David T. Kollat, *Consumer Behavior*, 3rd ed. (Hinsdale, Ill.: Dryden Press, 1978), ch. 9.

there have been only a handful of studies that have focused explicitly on the search for information in spiritual decision-making. Nevertheless, some broad preliminary generalizations are possible.

Determining the Importance of Information Sources

There are three dimensions that have proved useful in comparing the relative importance of various sources used in decision-making:[3]

1. Decisive effectiveness: The source was evaluated as being of great importance in arriving at the decision.
2. Contributory effectiveness: The source played a specific role in the process but was not decisive.
3. Ineffective: The person was exposed to the source, but it did not perform any particular role.

The author has been able to uncover only five research projects that come anywhere close to validating these as dimensions of the spiritual quest. Each is briefly described below:

1. *The Scripture Union Study in Great Britain.*[4] The Evangelical Alliance Commission on Evangelism surveyed 4,000 people chosen at random from church rolls in 1968. Questions focused only on decisive effectiveness.
2. *The Japan Multi-Media Evangelism Project.*[5] The Lutheran World Federation Office of Communication in Tokyo surveyed adults who were baptized and confirmed during 1973–74 within four Lutheran church bodies. A total of 438 returned questionnaires covered both contributory and decisive effectiveness. In fact, this project is the most comprehensive of any published to date.
3. *The Costa Rican Conversion Survey.*[6] Through the Institute for In-Depth Evangelization, Sergio Ojeda interviewed 217 Christians in 22 Costa Rican evangelical churches to discover influences on conversion. His questions also covered both contributory and decisive effectiveness.

---

[3]*Ibid.*, pp. 245–246.

[4]*Background to the Task* (Great Britain, Scripture Union, 1968).

[5]*How Japanese Become Christians* (Tokyo, Lutheran World Federation Office of Communication, 1976). Also see Hiroyoshi Okada, "Japan's Multi-Media Evangelism Project," *WACC Journal*, vol. 24 (1977), pp. 21–22.

[6]Paul Pretiz, "An Indepth Study: What Brings People to Christ?" *Latin American Evangelist* (May/June, 1976), pp. 4–5.

4. *Jewish Acceptance of Christ as Messiah.*[7] This was a pilot survey of two small Messianic Jewish congregations in the Chicago area, focusing only on decisive effectiveness.
5. *Wheaton Area Conversion Surveys.* More than two hundred unstructured interviews have been undertaken with Christians in the Wheaton area by students in the author's classes during 1977 and 1978. Generally information was provided on both contributory and decisive effectiveness.

Mass Versus Interpersonal Media

The general principle emerging from decades of communications research is that the mass media generally do not play a *decisive* role in any type of major decision.[8] Rather, their primary effect is *contributory* through the stimulation of awareness and interest and subsequent attitude change. This principle was confirmed for the most part in the above studies. For example, Costa Rican Christians mentioned their exposure to tracts (forty-one percent), a Christian magazine (thirty-two percent), and programs on station TIFC—the evangelical radio station in Costa Rica (twenty-six percent) as having some role in their decision.[9] Christian literary works, on the other hand, were of greater importance in Japan among all age groups, and music and movies also played an important role.[10] The writings of Ayako Miura were mentioned most frequently for the reason that ". . . she is able to describe the kind of living faith for which the people in the actual world long."[11]

Bible reading emerges in all of these studies as being of both contributory and decisive effectiveness. Reading both the New Testament and the Old Testament proved, for example, to be the two most important factors in conversion of Jews.[12]

Some form of personal witness, on the other hand, usually is the

---

[7]"Jewish Evangelism" (a class project at the Wheaton Graduate School completed in February, 1977, under the direction of Dr. Donald Miller. Participating researchers were Lor Cirincione, A.J. Grant, Francie Griffin, and Dan Runyon).

[8]This literature is thoroughly reviewed in Engel, Blackwell, and Kollat, *Consumer Behavior,* ch. 9. Also see Wilbur Schramm, *Mass Media and National Development* (Stanford, Ca.: Stanford University Press, 1964); and Ted Ward, "Fuzzy Fables or Communications That Count," *Christian Communications Spectrum,* vol. 1 (Winter, 1975), p. 10ff.

[9]Pretiz, "What Brings People to Christ?"

[10]*How Japanese Become Christians.*

[11]*Ibid.,* p. 3.

[12]"Jewish Evangelism."

dominant decisive influence, although there are many exceptions to any generalization of this type. Often a church leader or evangelist is mentioned, but witness of friends and relatives is of equal importance. In many instances, this contact was gained through involvement in religious schools or in the church itself prior to the point of conversion. This assumes, of course, that personal influence was credible, and this is by no means always the case.

There is additional evidence that documents the important contributory role of religious radio. In a broad review of studies on radio impact in Great Britain, Dinwiddie concluded that religious broadcasting has succeeded in creating a climate of acceptance of the standards of Christian life and conduct.[13] More recently Anne Ediger completed a survey of those who listen to Back to the Bible III, a Hindi program aired in India.[14] About half indicated that the program had helped them accept Christ as their Savior.

While the mass media occasionally will be decisive in stimulating a conversion, this is not their usual function, with one major exception. There is some anecdotal evidence that Christian radio and other forms of mass media are more likely to perform the decisive role when there is not an active church. Shortwave radio, in particular, appears to have played a more decisive role in the communist countries, although the evidence is far from conclusive.[15]

The Need for Media Integration

To use the analogy of the apostle Paul, the mass media are useful in planting or seed sowing, whereas personal influence is the primary means of watering and reaping (1 Cor. 3). But there is an important implication that may not emerge at first glance: Mass and interpersonal media must be integrated. One without the other will be ineffective. The problem enters because publishers and broadcasters, by and large, are parachurch organizations with only an indirect relationship to the local church. Face-to-face witness, on the other hand, is generally more closely related to the local church. How then are these to be integrated? This is a major subject to be considered in the next chapter.

---

[13]Melville Dinwiddie, *Religion by Radio* (London: George Allen and Unwin, 1968).

[14]"Hindi Programs Strengthen Faith," *Religious Broadcasting,* vol. 19 (December/January, 1978), p. 36ff.

[15]For the most thorough review, see Jane Ellis, "Christian Broadcasting to the U.S.S.R.," *WACC Journal,* vol. 24 (1977), pp. 14–15; and Jane Ellis, "Broadcasting to Russia: How Much is Getting Through?" *Christian Communications Spectrum,* vol. 3 (Winter, 1977–78), p. 22ff.

THE PRINT MEDIA

The printed page is frequently believed to offer greater prestige and believability than other media, perhaps based on the adage that "seeing is believing." There is no convincing research to verify this claim, but it is a generally accepted principle that print induces superior retention of complex factual material as compared with oral presentation. Also many feel that print forces a reader to become deeply involved with the subject matter through striving to understand and to evaluate.[16]

There is the obvious disadvantage, however, that there must be at least a degree of audience literacy present before print can be used. Furthermore, literacy figures can be highly misleading. For example, Søgaard has found that most people in Thailand cannot read, even though literacy is reported as being seventy percent.[17] Imagine what the situation would be in Bangladesh where literacy is far less; in fact, only ten percent of the population can be reached through any type of print medium.[18]

During the 1960s it was widely ballyhooed, following the lead of Marshall McLuhan, that the "Guttenburg era" was dead. The assumption was that print would soon give way to electronic media. But the reported death of print was decidedly premature, as will be demonstrated as we discuss the evangelistic uses of newspapers, magazines, books, and tracts.

Newspapers

Figures released by the United Nations document the widespread use of newspapers throughout the world.[19] Over 8,100 daily papers are published, with a total circulation of nearly 400,000. Of these, over 2,000 are published in Asia; 232 are published in Africa, 1,812 in Europe, and 658 in the Soviet Union. The greatest circulation is in the Soviet Union followed by the United States and Japan.

Characteristics of the Medium. Once again, it should be stressed that media usage varies from one country to the next, and the problem is compounded by the fact that the vast majority of media research has

---

[16]For an excellent review of relevant research, see Joseph T. Klapper, *The Effects of Mass Communication* (Glencoe, Ill.: Free Press, 1960), pp. 110–112.

[17]Viggo B. Søgaard, "Comparative Media Study" (Paper delivered at the Tell Asia Seminar, Hong Kong, October, 1976), p. 13.

[18]*Ibid.*

[19]"Media Throughout the World" (UNESCO Statistical Yearbook, 1975).

been undertaken in the United States and other Western countries. Therefore, what is true in those locations may not be true elsewhere.

Even given this disadvantage, we can learn something of the nature of the newspaper medium from the published research. The newspaper has been found to be a way of life to most Americans, according to a study conducted by the Bureau of Advertising of the American Newspaper Publishers Association. Here are just a few of the findings:[20]

1. Readership is high. Daily coverage includes eighty-seven percent of all households.
2. Well over two thirds claim to read the paper thoroughly. Given this fact, the average page has an eighty-four percent chance of being seen.
3. Reader involvement is shown by the fact that more than half of those surveyed clipped and saved some items, and seventy percent discussed content with others.

At one time, printing quality tended to be low. But recent improvements have allowed sophisticated color and photographic reproduction, and future improvements are imminent.[21]

One of the disadvantages of newspapers in a country such as the United States is the high cost of national coverage. Advertising costs, for example, can be approximately one hundred percent higher than would be the case with radio or television. Furthermore, newspapers are not retained in the home for long periods of time. Thus, there is only limited opportunity for repeat exposure.

Evangelistic Uses. One of the ways newspapers can be utilized in evangelism, of course, is through reporting relevant news. Assuming the church is engaged in activities of interest to the general public, this type of coverage can improve image. There are some cautions, however. As veteran UPI reporter Wesley Pippert makes clear, the function of any news medium is to seek and relate the truth.[22] This point is further affirmed by eight of the leading reli-

[20]*A National Survey of the Content and Readership of the American Newspaper* (New York: American Newspaper Publishers Assn., 1973).

[21]For thorough documentation, see the entire issue of *Advertising Age* (November 17, 1975).

[22]Wesley G. Pippert, "Journalism and the Forgotten Virtues," *Christian Communications Spectrum,* vol. 3 (Winter, 1977), pp. 8–9.

gious reporters in the United States.[23] Any attempt at persuasion violates the fundamental canon of newspaper ethics:

> A journalist who uses his power for any selfish or otherwise unworthy purpose is faithless to a high trust. Partisanship and editorial comment, which knowingly departs from the truth, does violence to the best spirit of American journalism; in the news columns it is subversive of a fundamental principle of the profession.[24]

Placement of advertisements is another possibility. This has been done in various geographic areas with mixed results.[25] Usually some type of coupon or other direct response device will be included. This makes an assumption that the person has reached a point in his or her decision process where there is both some awareness of gospel fundamentals and interest in pursuing Christianity further (–5 or –4 on the model used in Chapter 3). When that is not the situation, the likelihood of response is quite low. On the other hand, the newspaper used appropriately in this fashion provides a logical bridge for person-to-person contact.

Magazines

While there are no reliable worldwide figures to quote, any observer can quickly report that the magazine is an increasingly popular medium. In the decade from January 1964 to December 1973, for instance, 923 new magazines were introduced in the United States market, while 233 ceased publication.[26]

Characteristics of the Medium. As a rule both possession and readership of magazines increase as education and income increase.[27] The greatest advantage offered, however, is the opportunity provided to reach a great variety of audience segments. Special interest publications abound, and it is here that the growth of new magazines is greatest. The more general magazine also provides the opportunity for geographical segmentation, particularly in the

---

[23]Glenn F. Arnold, "Saltless City Rooms?" *Christian Communications Spectrum,* vol. 3 (Winter, 1977), pp. 11–13.

[24]Cited in James L. Johnson, "A Lesson in Ethics," *Christian Communications Spectrum,* vol. 4 (Winter, 1977–78), p. 6.

[25]See, for example, Søgaard, "Comparative Media Study," and "Churches Use Ads in Evangelism," *Action,* vol. 27 (February, 1978), p. 5.

[26]"Compton Media Review," Compton Advertising, January, 1974, p. 25.

[27]See, for example, "The 1970's New Demographics" (New York: Magazine Publisher's Association, undated).

United States. Such magazines as *Time* and *Better Homes and Gardens* offer nearly 150 regional editions. Therefore, the magazine makes it possible to reach a discrete and specialized audience, both geographically and demographically. Furthermore, high quality printing and reproduction is almost always an advantage.

Evangelistic Uses. One of the most obvious evangelistic possibilities offered by magazines is the publication of articles that present a Christian viewpoint on the subject matter covered within a given magazine. Sometimes this can take the form of testimonies, as has been the case frequently in *Sports Illustrated* and other sports publications in North America. At other times the need is for a distinct Christian perspective on world news, science, literature, or other topics, which range from general to specialized interest. Here the demand is for scholarship that approaches the subject with integrity, rather than writing that seeks a platform to present the plan of salvation surreptitiously. Such writing, of course, falls into the category of proclamation and performs the needed function of building understanding of the tenets of the Christian message.

Magazines also accept advertisements. The advantages and disadvantages would be similar to those discussed earlier in regard to newspaper advertising.

Finally, there has been a pronounced growth during the late 1970s in magazines written by Christians for the general market. *Breakthrough,* discussed at the outset of this chapter, is an excellent example. There has been some careful research on such magazines in Africa, and Donald Smith provides useful guidelines both for editorial slant and writing style.[28]

Two other magazines written for non-Christians are worthy of note. *Magalla* was introduced on the newsstands in eleven Arabic countries in 1978 by Middle East Publications in Lebanon. Its target readership is Muslims aged fifteen to twenty-two with a minimum of six years of education. The objectives are to remove misconceptions about Christianity and to communicate Christian truth in the context of felt need. This is a pioneering venture in that part of the world. Of quite a different nature is *Inspiration,* launched during 1978 on the American market. The objective was to sell 250,000 or more copies on the newsstand, and the price was $1.95 per issue.

---

[28]Donald Smith, "Smaller and Better . . . A New Way to Literature Effectiveness," *Africa Pulse* (published by the Evangelical Missions Information Service, Wheaton, Illinois, March, 1978).

The editorial content apparently assumed a person at –4 or –3 in his decision process, however, because copy was quite overtly Christian, in sharp contrast to *Magalla* and *Breakthrough*.

Such publication ventures as *Inspiration* may seem to be quite promising at first glance. In fact, it is reported that several additional magazines will soon appear on the American market. But it must be born in mind that most people in the western world are satisfied with life and indifferent to spiritual issues. The likelihood of picking up such a magazine would appear to be relatively low, with the result that revenue would fall far short of costs. Not surprisingly, *Inspiration* ceased publication after a few issues. Therefore, great caution should be the rule in such publishing decisions. At the very least, there should be a market test before heavy investment is made. In this sense, the *Breakthrough* team in Hong Kong has provided a good publishing example for all who would attempt a similar effort.

Books

The focus here is on books written by Christians for a non-Christian audience. The growth of religious books in the United States is notable. More than 2,000 new titles were introduced in 1977 by evangelical publishers,[29] and this continues the average growth rate of 18.9 percent per year since 1971, compared with a growth of 10.4 percent for religious publishers in general.[30] While there once again are no figures for the world as a whole, a similar growth has been noted in Japan.[31]

Nature of the Medium. Although it is clear that religious book publishing is growing, one must be cautious in interpreting these figures. By far the greatest proportion of these titles are devotional in nature and are not evangelistic. Furthermore, even in the United States religious books are only about six percent of total book sales.[32]

Viewed strictly from the perspective of evangelism, one can do much with a book that is impossible with periodicals or electronic media. In the first place, subject matter can be covered in great depth and intricacy of argument. Books are usually a permanent

---

[29]Norman B. Rohrer, "Religion in Review," no. 27 (Evangelical Press Association, 1977).

[30]Clayton E. Carlson, II, "An 'Evangelical' Publisher? Who Decides?" *Evangelical Christian Publishers Association Newsletter,* vol. 4 (Winter Quarter, 1978), p. 1.

[31]*Action,* no. 21 (July/August, 1977).

[32]Jennifer K. Byron, "What Those National Best Seller Lists Don't Tell Us," *Christian Communications Spectrum,* vol. 2 (Fall, 1976), pp. 23–25.

possession, and the opportunity is provided both for reflective initial reading and frequent re-reading. Apologetics is a particularly appropriate subject matter for books. Also, fiction and autobiographical or biographical stories reach their zenith in book form.

The Christian must face the fact, however, that the publishing industry has become even more secularized over the past few decades. In a very revealing study, Wuthnow referred to UNESCO data on books published in forty countries since 1950 to compare the changes in the percentage that were religious in nature with those that were not.[33] For instance, he found that 11 out of 16 books published in Bulgaria in 1950 were religious, compared with 8 out of 3,318 in 1972. Notice this figure: 6.78 percent of all books published in the United States were religious in 1950, compared with 5.62 percent in 1972! Apparently the boom in evangelical sales has not offset the secularizing trend. Interestingly enough, the smallest differences between the percentage of religious and secular books in 1972 was found in Iran, United Arab Republic, Celon and other non-Christian countries, with the lowest percentage of religious books in Cuba, Bulgaria, and the Soviet Union.

Evangelistic Uses. Decision process studies often will reveal that one or more books were instrumental in a person coming to Christ. The author, for instance, clearly can recall the role David Wilkerson's *The Cross and the Switchblade* played in his decision process. Usually such books are reported as showing the relevance of Christ to an individual's needs at the moment, but seldom are they the specific trigger for the decision or conversion.

The author has had opportunity to visit a large percentage of Christian publishers throughout the world. It has been found, first of all, that most of the books in print are written for Christians, as was already pointed out. Moreover, those intended for the general market usually assume the reader to be at the problem recognition stage (–3) in the decision process. This is revealed by the copious use of Scripture and Christian terms that would be noncomprehensible to those at earlier stages in their decision. With only isolated exceptions, there is a great void in books designed for those who have little or no Christian background. Among the relative handful of writers who are trying to reach such people are Francis Schaeffer, the late

[33]Robert Wuthnow, "A Longitudinal, Cross-National Indicator of Societal Religious Commitment," *Journal for the Scientific Study of Religion,* vol. 16 (1976), pp. 87–99.

C. S. Lewis, James L. Johnson, and others. There are even fewer such writers in the developing countries, because the usual practice (now diminishing we hope) is to translate North American books.

What, then, is the great need? The first unplowed field is the novel. Here and there one can point to Christians who have written novels for the general audience. But, as Gordon Jackson has so clearly pointed out, far too many strip characters of the routine evangelical "taboos" and have a "happily ever after" theme.[34] Such writing is quickly perceived by the non-Christians as being sterile, unrealistic, and downright uninteresting. The need clearly is to be realistic about the Christian life, to present real life people coping with their problems in a Christian way. Fiction can have a powerful effect, and it is not just a frivolous diversion of the writer as some evangelicals seem to feel.

Another need is to develop Christian perspectives on the issues of today. Once again, this is not a call for evangelistic literature in the usual sense but for genuine integration of faith and learning. Do Christians have anything meaningful to say to the non-Christian world on such issues as racial prejudice, materialism, war, and so on? Such literature is beginning to appear, and it is encouraging to note that evangelical scholars are now taking this mandate seriously in increasing numbers.

Next, it is time to declare a virtual moratorium on translated North American books in countries outside the English-speaking world. World views of author and reader usually are too different to permit any kind of realistic communication. There are some notable exceptions to this rule, but the acceptability of a translation within a country must be demonstrated through a market test rather than assumed. There should be a growing recognition of the need to train writers in all countries of the world to prepare books that speak more clearly to the needs of those within their own context.

Finally, the reader will recall that Bible reading is an important factor in the spiritual decision process for most people. Usually the Bible has its greatest impact once initial interest in Christianity has been triggered through other influences. Therefore, house-to-house distribution of Scriptures can be a wasteful practice, especially when one recalls the study cited in Chapter 1 showing that ninety percent of Bibles delivered to prisoners were thrown into the trash

---

[34]Gordon Jackson, "Evangelicals and the Arts: Divorce or Reconciliation?" *Christian Communications Spectrum*, vol. 2 (Summer, 1976), pp. 17–20.

can. The greater need is for use of discretion in distribution of the entire Bible or portions, making sure that there is at least some willingness to examine it and consider its message. What this means, of course, is that one must be very cautious in assuming that simply placing the Bible in someone's home is an effective strategy. The important question is, what happens afterwards?

Tracts and Booklets

Brief tracts, booklets, and other similar forms of literature have been used in evangelism for well over one hundred years. Here and there one can find reports that such literature is both read and responded to positively. This appears to be the case, for instance, in some parts of the Muslim world.[35] But, one must be careful not to assume that such a strategy always will work, especially given the fact that most tracts are simply a summary of the gospel and a call for decision. The assumption obviously is made that the audience is at stage −3 in decision process (problem recognition) and that such literature will be efficacious in triggering a decision. In fact, one group reported during 1978 that all of Delhi, India, was saturated with gospel tracts, and the presumption was that the "Great Commission" had been fulfilled. Such a conclusion is patently absurd! Recall from Chapter 2 that communication is a multi-stage process. Some undoubtedly were exposed to the gospel, but did they read the tract, understand it, and respond as intended? Seldom are these latter questions answered, presumably on the assumption that mere exposure will bring about the desired response.

Tract distribution *can* be an important aid to personal evangelism if content is properly directed to the target audience in terms of their gospel awareness and felt needs. This obviously demands audience research, which rarely, if ever, has been undertaken by those engaged in this type of ministry. Therefore, it is not possible to recommend this type of strategy with any degree of confidence until this very commonsense type of analysis is undertaken. The result otherwise may represent, to use an earlier term, more of a great commotion than the Great Commission.

---

[35]Raymond H. Joyce, "Literature for Muslims," *Muslim World Pulse,* vol. 5 (Published by the Evangelical Missions Information Service, March, 1976).

[36]For an excellent review of world broadcasting research, see Sydney W. Head and Thomas F. Gordon, *World Broadcasting: A Statistical Analysis* (Communications Research Report No. 6, Temple University School of Communications and Theatre, April, 1975).

THE ELECTRONIC MEDIA

Today it is possible to reach almost everyone in the world through some form of the electronic media.[36] There are more than 25,000 radio transmitters in the world, with 7,785 in the United States, 3,304 in the Soviet Union, 1,964 in Italy, 999 in Brazil, 944 in Japan, 668 in Mexico, and 94 in South Korea.[37] The number of radio sets now approaches one billion, or 288 per thousand people. North America has the highest number with 1,667 sets per thousand people, followed by the Soviet Union with 441 per thousand, Europe with 313 per thousand, South America and the Caribbean with 170 per thousand, Asia and the Arab States with about 100 per thousand, and Africa with 42 per thousand.[38]

Television transmission and receiving facilities also have grown rapidly, although many areas of the world are not yet penetrated extensively by this medium. On the average, those living in the developed countries have 200 television sets per thousand people, whereas those in the developing countries have fewer than 15 per thousand—quite a contrast.[39] Japan and the United States have a sharp lead over all other countries in terms of the number of transmission points.

What this means, of course, is that the barriers of literacy have largely been transcended. Truly for the first time in history, there is virtually universal mass media access.

Television

Television, said by many to be the marvel of the electronic age, grew from infancy to maturity in less than twenty years after World War II. In many ways, it is the "glamour medium." Certainly there are some real opportunities offered for evangelism, but the medium itself requires a considerable investment of both cost and professionalism. Therefore, it is not the panacea for world evangelization that some have assumed.

Characteristics of the Medium. It should be readily apparent to the reader that television is best at communicating those things that are seen easily and processed most efficiently by the eye. Visually exciting programs almost always are found to be effective. Moreover,

---

[37]"Media Throughout the World."
[38]*The Asian Messenger,* vol. 2 (Winter, 1976), pp. 2–3.
[39]"Media Throughout the World."

television is an experiential medium. The effective program draws the viewer into an intensive participative experience rather than a passive one.[40] While it is not clear that retention of information is better following television exposure than following exposure to other media, it is reasonable to expect a high degree of emotional involvement with and impact from television viewing.[41]

In most parts of the world, television is valued highly for entertainment and news. In fact, Schramm reports that Americans generally rank television as the one medium they would keep if they had to choose just one,[42] and this preference is most pronounced when it comes to news. Elsewhere in the world, entertainment programming often is less frequent than educational and propagandistic broadcasts.

As has been true of other media, most of the relevant research is confined to the Western countries. Probably the best summary of the research was written by Gary Steiner in 1960.[43] He noted that most people consider television to be the greatest invention for making life enjoyable in the last twenty-five years. Nevertheless, there is a growing sense of disenchantment on two dimensions. First is a backlash, at least in the United States, against the extent of sex and violence portrayed in most programs.[44] In fact, people are turning in growing numbers from the commercial networks to public television.[45] Furthermore, the extent of "Commercial clutter" (not confined to the United States, by the way) is leading many advertisers to conclude that television no longer is the "great salesman" it once was.[46]

Anyone who uses television either for programming or advertising must face the fact that costs both for production and commercial time have shot up astronomically throughout the world. For exam-

---

[40]Glenn T. Sparks, "Christian Television: Programming According to the Medium," *Christian Communications Spectrum,* vol. 4 (Summer, 1977), pp. 18–19.

[41]For an excellent review, see Klapper, *The Effects of Mass Communication.*

[42]Wilbur Schramm, "What Makes a News Medium Credible," *The Asian Messenger,* vol. 3 (Autumn/Winter, 1977), pp. 34–36.

[43]Gary A. Steiner, *The People Look at Television* (New York: Alfred A. Knopf, 1963). Other relevant research is reviewed in James F. Engel, Hugh G. Wales, and Martin R. Warshaw, *Promotional Strategy,* 3rd ed. (Homewood, Ill.: Richard D. Irwin, 1975), pp. 239-253.

[44]See, in particular, Gregg Lewis, *Telegarbage* (Nashville: Thomas Nelson, 1977); and Malcolm Muggeridge, *Christ and the Media* (Grand Rapids, Mich.: Wm. B. Eerdmans, 1978).

[45]Rohrer, "Religion in Review."

[46]Harry W. McMahan, "Television, A Great Salesman, Isn't Working Like it Used To," *Advertising Age* (January 3, 1972), pp. 27–29.

ple, costs of $50,000 or more to produce a thirty-second television commercial are not unusual, and if that commercial is aired during the Super Bowl, costs per commercial minute are about $250,000. This problem is compounded by the fact that television is a technically demanding medium. Technicians, producers, and performers thus have developed a high degree of sophistication, which must be matched by anyone who aspires to use the medium.

Evangelistic Uses. There are at least five ways television can be used for evangelism: (1) evangelistic programs, (2) Christian-owned stations, (3) cable television, (4) television advertising, and (5) satellite transmission.

(1) Evangelistic Programs. There are a few Christian programs that appear to have at least a degree of success in attracting a general audience. "This Is the Life," for example, has been shown in virtually every United States market continually since 1961, and it has received more public service air time than any other religious program. Produced by the Lutheran Church, it is the only religious program to win a secular Emmy Award for excellence. The "700 Club" and the "PTL Club" are both talk show formats and are aired daily in two hundred or more markets. Outside the United States, "Circle Square," produced by Cross Roads Television in Canada, has attracted a substantial following among children.[47] Just one of many examples in the developing countries is "Re-encounter," now aired weekly over twenty-seven stations and 182 booster stations in Brazil, a country which previously would allow no gospel broadcasts on television.[48] These are just a few of a number of examples that could be cited.[49]

The reader should not jump to the conclusion that the television program is a vast frontier for evangelism. First of all, remember that television, by and large, is an entertainment medium. A theory has been put forth that most people are going to watch shows that are evaluated as being most pleasant.[50] This is often cited as the LOP principle (least objectionable program). This means that a situation

---

[47]Ruby Peckford Johnson, "Keys to Successful Television for Children," *Christian Communications Spectrum,* vol. 3 (Winter, 1977–78), pp. 28–29. For a study of the effectiveness of "Circle Square," see "Television and Our Children" (A report of the Alternatives in Children's Broadcasting Project, Hamilton, Ontario, Canada, May, 1976).

[48]Faith Sand Pidcoke, "Breakthrough in Brazil," *Christian Reader* (May, 1978), p. 43.

[49]A useful if somewhat dated source is A. William Bleum, *Religious Television Programs* (New York: Hasting House, 1969).

[50]Bert Wollen, "The Christian and Prime Time TV," *Christian Communications Spectrum,* vol. 1 (Winter, 1975), p. 21ff.

comedy usually will outdraw a serious special on events of world interest. In similar fashion, very few will turn on a preaching program or other form of programming with an obvious religious intent. Billy Graham and Luis Palau do stand as exceptions to this rule, but others have been unable to draw similar audiences.

Let's recognize the fact, to take the most extreme example, that a televised Sunday morning service usually will be watched only by Christians who have stayed home from church that morning. Documentaries on Christian issues and television drama, on the other hand, have produced large audiences on British television, largely because professionally trained Christians have attained responsible positions within the secular industry.[51] Such efforts make no attempt to persuade the viewer to make a decision for Christ. This probably explains their effectiveness.

In short, Christians interested in using television for evangelistic purposes must bear in mind that people are not obligated to listen, a principle stated many times in this book. As Benson has pointed out, it can be quite ego-gratifying to say the words of salvation over the air, on the assumption that this has fulfilled our responsibility to evangelize.[52] But if only Christians are listening, this is nothing more than a waste of scarce resources. The psychology of the viewer must be kept in mind so that programs will both inform and entertain. The British Broadcasting Corporation provides a good illustration for North Americans that responsible Christian professionals can produce acceptable programming that will attract a good audience. Unfortunately, this seems to take a backseat in North America to the televised service and preaching program, both of which usually are distinctly inferior to the documentary or drama.[53]

(2) The Christian-Owned Station. The growing defection of viewers in the United States from commercial to public television can serve as a strong incentive for Christians to open their own stations. In a published debate, Jerry Rose and Ed Steele came down on opposite sides of this issue.[54] Rose argued, with some merit, that quality religious programming probably never will fully penetrate prime-

[51]Andrew Quicke, "Christians and Secular Media, *WACC Journal,* vol. 24 (1977), pp. 8–11.

[52]Dennis C. Benson, *Electric Evangelism* (Nashville: Abingdon Press, 1973).

[53]Benson's book should be required reading for all who are contemplating Christian use of television.

[54]This appeared in the Summer, 1976, issue of *Christian Communications Spectrum,* vol. 2. See Jerry K. Rose, "The Case for Christian Owned Television," pp. 13–14; and Ed Steele, "Can Christian Television Really Deliver?" pp. 15–16.

time commercial television. The alternative is to have a Christian-owned station offering quality fare both for evangelism and edification of the believer, fully recognizing that quality programming can be aired without competing for massive audience and advertiser dollars.

Steele countered Rose's position in the following way:

> Christian television stations, for the most part, I believe lack creative appeal, reflect mediocrity, exploit limited interest, appeal to a very narrow spectrum of viewers and in general fail to either really entertain or instruct.[55]

His objection is that programming is confined mostly to panel and call-in shows that have little audience appeal. He would prefer the airing of quality programs on commercial television.

Probably both are correct in the positions they have taken. It is difficult to place quality programs on general television, and there is merit to the Christian-owned alternative. But, the Christian station must be willing to invest large sums to produce airworthy material if it is to have much impact on secular man. At the moment, this is the exception rather than the rule.

(3) Cable Television. Cable Television (CATV) enables television set owners, mostly in the United States and Canada, to connect their home with a community antenna system, thereby greatly expanding the geographic range from which programs may be received. By July, 1977, cable had reached more than seventeen percent of all television homes in the United States,[56] and it is expected that ten million more homes will be added by 1981, making a total of about twenty-six million out of seventy-two million television homes.[57] CATV offers the advantage of local origination of programming, and it is said that a church or other group can produce and air programs with a total investment not to exceed $10,000.[58] There are between thirty and forty programs produced for this purpose which can be purchased and aired,[59] and Thiessen suggests some other options as well.[60]

---

[55]Steele, "Can Christian Television Really Deliver?" p. 15.

[56]*Television Digest* survey, 1977.

[57]*The Gallagher Report,* vol. 24 (November 29, 1976), p. 1.

[58]Terry F. Phillips, "How to Get Into CATV," *Religious Broadcasting,* vol. 10 (February/March, 1978), pp. 46–48.

[59]*Ibid.*

[60]Abe Theissen, "What's it All About in Cable TV?" *Christian Communications Spectrum,* vol. 1 (Winter, 1975), p. 18ff.

Given what was said above regarding prime-time programming, the very worst strategy imaginable would be for a local group to rush on the air with a church service or something similar. Unfortunately, this very suggestion was made a few years ago in a widely disseminated trade publication, although other writers were more cautious.[61] Always ask the question, "Are viewers interested in what we are airing?" The answer may well be yes, if the focus is clearly on events of local interest, local personalities, and so on. The best advice is to proceed with caution and ask whether or not the investment necessary for success in CATV might not produce greater returns if placed into other forms of evangelism.[62]

(4) Television Advertising. It is always possible to place advertisements on both local or national television. The procedures for time buying and media scheduling demand professional expertise,[63] but the results may justify the effort. The Southern Baptists invested over $1 million in a combination of television and magazine advertising.[64] Although this was thoroughly researched both before and after the campaign, it appears that the results were disappointing.[65] The reasons are not clear as of this writing, but the problem often lies in the fact that too much is expected of television. At the very most, spot advertisements can help create a favorable climate for Christianity and stimulate both gospel awareness and interest. But a failure to utilize personal witness to capitalize upon the seeds that are sown will lead to an ineffective outcome.

(5) Satellite Transmission. The launching of Earlybird, or INTELSAT 1, in 1965 marked the beginning of communication by satellite. By 1974 enough satellites were in orbit to permit coverage of almost the entire world, with the result that communicators began to take this form of television transmission seriously.[66] There are three ways in which the satellite can be used:[67]

---

[61]See the various articles on cable television in *Religious Broadcasting,* (April/May, 1974).

[62]Richard J. Senzig, "Cable May Not Be Able," *Christian Communications Spectrum,* vol. 1 (Fall/Winter, 1975), pp. 28–30.

[63]These details are discussed in Engel, Wales, and Warshaw, *Promotional Strategy.*

[64]For a description, see Harry W. McMahan, "Baptists Researching $1,000,000 'Peace of Mind' TV Campaign," *Advertising Age* (December 15, 1976), p. 98.

[65]*Context* (February 1, 1978), p. 1.

[66]For background see *The Satellite Symposium* (Sponsored by International Christian Broadcasters, 1976); "A Short History of Satellite Communication," *The Asian Messenger,* vol. 1 (Winter, 1975), pp. 22–23; and C. Richard Shumaker, "The Opportunities for Satellite TV," *Christian Communications Spectrum,* vol. 1 (Fall/Winter, 1975), pp. 30–31.

[67]Ithiel De Sola Pool, "Technological Advances in the Future of International Broadcasting," *Studies of Broadcasting,* no. 13 (March, 1977), pp. 17–32.

1. As a substitute for land lines in television networks. INTELSAT is used in this manner today.
2. Transmission to community antennae from a satellite and then directly to homes in the usual fashion. This has been done experimentally in India since 1975 through the sophisticated ATS-6 satellite launched by NASA.[68] This innovative effort, referred to as SITE, has brought television to approximately 2,400 out of more than 500,000 villages that otherwise would be unreached. For the most part, programming has been educational in nature, focusing on such issues as health and nutrition.
3. Direct transmission from satellite to homes. This is now being developed experimentally, and some initial implementation appears imminent. Obviously this raises serious issues of international law,[69] but it is entirely possible for countries to obstruct unwanted communication by satellite through banning distribution of necessary antennae and converters or by jamming with conflicting signals.

Christian broadcasters have been among the early users of satellite. For example, the Christian Broadcasting Network has purchased six years of satellite time to extend its network throughout the United States and ultimately to the world at large.[70] Also Project "Look Up" began in 1977 as an experimental outreach to Latin America.[71] Initial programming included literacy training, personal finance, and Moody Science Films.

As of this writing there is an unresolved controversy surrounding Christian use of satellites. Some are quite enthusiastic,[72] whereas others have some strong reservations.[73] Obviously the advantage is the potential opportunity offered to reach many who now cannot

[68]See Daniel K. Eapen, "Social Implications of Satellite and Instructional Television, *The Asian Messenger,* vol. 1 (1976), pp. 24–30.

[69]See Aldo Armando Cocca, "Consent, Content, Spillover and Participation in Direct Broadcasting From Satellites," *Studies in Broadcasting,* no. 13 (March, 1977), p. 30.

[70]E. Alex Blormeth, "Cutting the Cost of Satellite Receivers," *Religious Broadcasting,* vol. 10 (February/March, 1978), p. 36ff.

[71]For a description, see Jeffrey J. Wiebe, "Outreach by Satellite," *Religious Broadcasting,* vol. 8 (January, 1977), p. 37.

[72]See, for example, the comments by James L. Johnson in "Should We Get Involved With Satellites?" *Christian Communications Spectrum,* vol. 3 (Summer, 1977), p. 27.

[73]See the comments by Phillip Booth in *Ibid.* Also James W. Reapsome, "Are Satellites the Answer?" *Evangelical Missions Quarterly,* vol. 13 (January, 1977), pp. 3–4.

receive television, a luxury available mostly to those in urban areas in the developing countries. One of the disadvantages is the cost. Pool estimates that direct transmission to homes will cost one hundred times more than the use of land lines,[74] to say nothing of the investment required to utilize the satellite itself. Furthermore, it is a mixed blessing that it is now theoretically possible for a worldwide audience to see and hear a speaker at the same time. There is just no way that one evangelistic message can be appropriate for all cultures. In reality, this is nothing more than one-way communication at its worst.

It all comes down to the essential issue of whether or not the results are worth the cost. The author is forced to join those who are cautious dissenters, because we have yet to make truly effective use of television as it presently exists. Moreover, other media such as radio and audio cassettes are much more promising in terms of pinpointed communication with a specific target audience. Therefore, we can only urge those interested in satellite to move with great caution. No panacea is offered for world evangelization.

A Concluding Word. It was mentioned earlier that television is a glamour medium. It offers the communication advantages of sight and sound, but these advantages carry with them the requirement for high professionalism and cost investment. Furthermore, vast areas of the globe are not reached by this medium, and expansion to unreached areas is both costly and slow. Finally, television is viewed most often for entertainment, and evangelistic programming must take this into account. What this means is that other media may offer greater results for the investment of both funds and effort.

Radio

Once considered to be a dying medium in the United States, radio is still alive and remarkably healthy throughout the world.

Characteristics of the Medium. First, and most obvious, radio is truly a *mass* medium. On any given day, ninety percent or more of the total population will listen to radio in such countries as Australia[75] and the United States.[76] Similar figures also are found in the developing countries. A radio set is among the most prized possessions in re-

---

[74]Pool, "Technological Advances in the Future of International Broadcasting."

[75]Alan Nichols, *The Communicators* (Sydney, Australia: Pilgrim Publications, Ltd., 1972), p. 63.

[76]"Radio Reach Is Everywhere—Homes, Autos, Outdoors," *Advertising Age* (November 21, 1973), p. 102.

mote areas, and its popularity often is far greater than the other media. In Haiti, for instance, the average person considers radio to be the most important outside influence in his life, with newspapers a distant second.[77]

In another sense, radio is not a mass medium in the usual manner, because the existence of multiple stations in most major urban areas allows great selectivity in programming and audience reach. This means that a limited segment can be reached without waste coverage.

While the evidence is not unequivocal, there is some basis to the claim that there may be less resistance to persuasion over radio, because many activities are directed by the spoken word.[78] Also, it may bring about greater retention, especially among the least educated.[79] Finally, radio is easy to listen to and produces little psychological resistance.

Another important advantage is minimal cost of mass coverage. The expense required to reach a large audience usually is quite low, especially when compared with television. In addition, the cost of producing acceptable material is lower.

One disadvantage, of course, is that only one sense is appealed to. Furthermore, the impression made is momentary, and there is no opportunity for re-exposure. Finally, radio is not universally available to the Christian. Some countries completely prohibit Christian programming, whereas others allow only a limited amount in certain unpopular time periods.

Evangelistic Uses. Among the options to consider are programs and advertisements on secular stations and programs on Christian stations. In addition, it is necessary to comment briefly on the potential of missionary shortwave broadcasting.

(1) Use of the Secular Station. In the United States, secular commercial radio is most frequently used by the Christian only for placement of advertisements. This is because radio, by and large, offers only a music and news format, although there is a trend toward greater use of broadcast drama. Drama offers a yet untapped potential for the church.[80] Also, radio stations are required to offer a certain amount

---

[77] An unpublished survey of the listening audience in Port-A-Prince conducted in 1975 by David Hartt for Radio Lumiere.

[78] For a summary of relevant research, see Darrell B. Lucas and Steuart H. Britt, *Advertising Psychology and Research* (New York: McGraw-Hill, 1950), p. 209.

[79] Klapper, *The Effects of Mass Communication.*

[80] Myrna Grant, "America's Return to Radio Drama: Will the Church be Left Behind?" *Christian Communications Spectrum,* vol. 1 (Winter, 1975), p. 75ff.

of free air time (Public Service Air or PSA) to nonprofit groups. As a result, there are some weekly teaching programs aired on Sunday mornings or other nonpeak periods. Listenership by non-Christians is quite limited.

Christians have made growing use of radio for pre-evangelistic advertising in recent years.[81] Usually spot advertising is accepted free by the station under the PSA rule, but under this arrangement the sponsor has no say with respect to when it is broadcast. Others circumvent this problem by purchasing air time. Those interested in this latter strategy have a number of well-researched and apparently effective options to select from. The "Choice" series by the Mennonite Church has been demonstrated to be highly effective in stimulating interest in Christianity, to mention just one possibility.

Outside the United States, placement of radio programs is a more viable option because of the broader range of subject matter offered over the air. As was mentioned earlier, the British Broadcasting Corporation has a wide variety of religious dramas and issue-oriented programs prepared and broadcast by Christians.[82] Multimedia Zambia (a Christian organization) produces 2,400 radio programs in English and seven vernacular languages.[83] And The Voice of Peace Studios in Thailand prepare a number of programs for government-controlled radio. Christians are allowed radio access as long as they do not speak negatively of the king, the government, or other religions. Research has shown that more than one third outside the major metropolitan areas are listeners.[84]

It must again be stated that all forms of mass media, including radio, tend to be of most value in pre-evangelism. It usually is inappropriate to call for a decision, unless there is clear evidence that many have reached stage −3 in their spiritual decision process. To expect many decisions in response to radio broadcasts (a common expectation among evangelicals) is to do violence to the medium.

(2) Use of the Christian Station. The United States towers over all other countries in the number of Christian owned and operated radio stations. There are now more than 600 of these stations,[85] with

---

[81] A very useful source on radio spots is Paul N. Stevens, "On the Spot," *International Christian Broadcasters Bulletin* (March, 1970), p. 3ff.

[82] Myrna Grant, "British Broadcasting: What Makes Them Think They Are So Good?" *Christian Communications Spectrum,* vol. 3 (Winter, 1977), p. 20ff.

[83] James W. Carty, Jr., "Religious Journalism on the African Continent," *WACC Journal,* vol. 23 (1976), pp. 8–14.

[84] Søgaard, "Comparative Media Survey," p. 11.

[85] Ben Armstrong, "Let's Turn Up the Volume on Christian Television," *Religious Broadcasting,* vol. 9 (April/May, 1977), pp. 33–35.

one new station opening each week during 1977.[86] More than seventy percent of these stations are affiliated with the National Religious Broadcasters (NRB) founded in 1944.[87]

Most religious stations feature teaching and worship programs designed for the Christian. As a result, listenership by non-Christians is minimal when the majority of program fare is of this nature.[88] There is no way to deny this fact, in spite of the claims of some stations to the contrary. There may be a small non-Christian audience and even some conversions, but this is the exception rather than the rule. So, the conclusion is unmistakable: Do not expect to reach non-Christians in any quantity through the traditional Christian station.

Some stations have broken the usual mold and followed the lead of Phil Butler at KBIQ in Seattle.[89] Format was changed from a steady diet of teaching programs to easy listening and good secular music with only occasional use of pre-evangelistic spot announcements. A large non-Christian audience can be attracted in this way, thus offering an exciting opportunity for outreach.

Christian radio stations also exist outside the United States. For example, it is possible to blanket South America through a cooperative network referred to as DIA (Difusiones InterAmericanas).[90] Many of these stations attract a more general audience than their North American counterparts, however, by a conscious effort to present a balanced schedule of educational, entertainment, news, and religious programs. As a result, properly designed programs or spots will have a much higher potential for success. Some stations, on the other hand, have virtually copied the traditional North American format, and, not surprisingly, non-Christians turn elsewhere.[91]

(3) Missionary Shortwave Radio. The Far East Broadcasting Company, Trans World Radio, the World Radio Missionary Fellowship

---

[86]*Eternity* (May, 1978), p. 14.

[87]For a history of NRB, see Virgil Megill, "The Origins of the NRB," *Religious Broadcasting,* vol. 9 (February/March, 1977), p. 35ff.

[88]See David C. Solt, "Audience Profile for Religious Broadcasts," *International Christian Broadcasters Bulletin* (April, 1971), p. 3ff; Ronald L. Johnstone, "Who Listens to Religious Radio Broadcasts Anymore?" *Journal of Broadcasting* (Winter, 1971–72); and *Family Radio News* (July/August/September, 1974), p. 3.

[89]Phill Butler, "Evangelism Experiment by Radio," *International Christian Broadcasters Bulletin* (October, 1971), p. 6ff.

[90]"25 Years in Latin American Gospel Communications," *Latin America Pulse,* vol. 12 (published by the Evangelical Missions Information Service, July, 1977).

[91]"A Study of Christian Radio in Liberia" (A survey conducted by Daystar Communications in 1970).

(HCJB), and Radio ELWA are the leading Christian organizations making use of the shortwave radio band. Because of its characteristics, shortwave makes it possible to reach people located a great distance from the transmitter. Therefore, these stations are enabled to concentrate programming on people who cannot be reached through any other form of Christian outreach. Earlier it was mentioned that there is some fragmentary evidence documenting the impact such programming has had in communist countries.

These stations tend to offer programming very similar to that of the usual Christian radio station, although there is often a greater attempt made to reach non-Christians through some general air fare.[92] KGEI, a division of Far East Broadcasting Company, is a distinct exception in the unusual variety of programs designed for secular man in Latin America.

The problem of shortwave, first of all, is that not everyone has a receiver, although shortwave ownership is higher throughout the world than it is in North America. Furthermore, it is difficult to reach a distinct audience segment in a different country with truly relevant programming. This is only compounded by the difficulties presented in doing audience research in communist countries. Therefore, it is hard to say with certainty what impact programming is having on a secular audience.

Also it is obvious that airing a steady diet of Christian programs, a not uncommon practice on shortwave, is not likely to attract a large non-Christian audience. Some of the organizations mentioned above have departed from such a rigid format in recent years fortunately, and their audience research usually documents an increase in secular listenership.

A Concluding Word. Many share Søgaard's feeling that radio, all things considered, ranks at the very top of all media in terms of the potential for effective evangelism at the lowest cost per individual reached.[93] While there obviously will be exceptions to any such generalization, the author agrees that radio deserves serious consideration, especially when compared with television. The benefits of widespread listenership, low cost, and relative ease of program preparation should not be disregarded.

---

[92]For more background see James C. King, "A Survey and Analysis of the Major International Evangelical Shortwave Broadcasters" (Ph.D. dissertation, University of Michigan, 1973). Also the entire issue of *Religious Broadcasting,* vol. 9 (August/September, 1977) is devoted to this subject.

[93]Søgaard, "Comparative Media Study," p. 11.

OTHER MEDIA

The reader by now is sensing that this chapter could stretch on endlessly. Fortunately, the remaining media (platform media, group media, and direct mail) can be dealt with more briefly. Brevity of discussion should not be interpreted as lack of importance, however, because each has a significant role in evangelism.

The Platform Media

Included in this category are the mass evangelistic meeting, film, and drama. All share in common the characteristic that an audience assembles at some central point for a presentation given to the group in mass without a direct attempt to stimulate feedback and interaction.

Mass Evangelistic Meetings. As Edward Murphy has made clear, mass evangelism is not obsolete.[94] It is, of course, as old as the gospel itself, because it was a favorite method of both Jesus and the apostle Paul. It has always been used by the church, and its impact in a contemporary world is attested by the popularity of such evangelists as Billy Graham, Leighton Ford, and Luis Palau.

The mass media can serve the purpose of proclamation for many in the audience, but it also has been repeatedly demonstrated to be a useful means of stimulating a decision. A significant percentage of most audiences consists of those in the later stages of their decision processes, and the stimulus of making a public response can be a powerful trigger for conversion.

People as a rule seem to like large meetings. There is something of a festival atmosphere that makes such occasions a popular form of diversion. Therefore, the role for the platform evangelist has not diminished in the least as of this writing.

Film. The film medium offers the advantage of television without its great disadvantages—high costs of airing and difficulty of attracting an audience. Films have long been used in all types of group settings with success both in terms of proclamation and persuasion, depending upon the message.[95] Because the opportunity exists for

---

[94]Edward F. Murphy, "Mass Evangelism Is Not Obsolete," *Christianity Today* (February 28, 1975), pp. 6–10.

[95]See Alex G. Smith, "How to Multiply Churches Through Film Evangelism," *Evangelical Missions Quarterly*, vol. 12, (July, 1976), pp. 167–172; Peter Church, "Films and Evangelism . . . 'Communicating the Gospel by Means of the Film,' " in J. D. Douglas, ed., *Let the Earth Hear His Voice* (Minneapolis: World Wide Publications, 1975), pp. 567–573; and James Grant, "Has 'Hiding Place' Finally Opened the Door?" *Christian Communications Spectrum*, vol. 1 (Fall/Winter, 1975), pp. 16–18.

"fine-tuning the message" to the background and felt needs of the audience, this medium is experiencing a healthy growth. The only problem at the moment is that the need for relevant films throughout the world exceeds the supply.

Drama. Drama is an important part of the life of people throughout the world; yet it ranks as the least developed of the Christian media. It provides an ideal opportunity to utilize indigenous forms to present Christianity in an understandable and emotionally powerful way. The problem is that the evangelical church has tended to be unduly suspicious of these art forms as being somehow "worldly" and thus off limits for the Christian. Uneasiness also may exist because of the fact that the dramatic artist may be quite unorthodox in expression.[96] In fact, James Young even goes so far as to say that the true mystery of Christianity lies beyond the rational and hence demands the use of drama and other art forms.[97] Fortunately, a growing number of Christian professionals in dramatic arts are recognizing this fact and are moving quickly to fill the void that exists.[98]

The Group Media

Group media are defined as those communication activities that involve, "a living presentation and/or experience in which people directly participate."[99] These can include any of the platform media plus the addition of audio and video cassettes, storytelling, poetry, audio visuals, and so on.[100] The objective is to stimulate dialogue, thereby moving away from the usual one-way communication characteristic of the mass media. One of the primary advantages is that literacy is not assumed and many thus are exposed to the Christian message who are beyond most of the other means.[101] Also

---

[96]This point is made by Melvin Lorentzen in "Christian Artists: The Mysterious Ones Among Us," *Christian Communications Spectrum,* vol. 1 (Summer, 1976), pp. 21–22.

[97]James Young, "The Church and the Theatre: An Overdue Marriage," *Christian Communications Spectrum,* vol. 2 (Winter, 1977–78), pp. 25–27.

[98]Nigel Goodwin, "The Arts: Necessity or Luxury?" *Christian Communications Spectrum,* vol. 3 (Winter, 1977–78), pp. 24–25.

[99]Jan Hes, "WACC and the Group Media Concept," *WACC Journal,* vol. 23 (1976), p. 40.

[100]For a more extensive discussion see Don Roper, "What Are Group Media?" *WACC Journal,* vol. 24 (1977), pp. 2–5; Dennis C. Benson, "Key Factors in the Use of Group Media," *WACC Journal,* vol. 24 (1977), pp. 7–9; and Jan Hes, "Group Media—A Challenge to Christian Communication," *WACC Journal,* vol. 24 (1977), pp. 10–11.

[101]Roper, "What Are Group Media?" Also see Richard J. Senzig, "Small Media for a Big Impact," *Evangelical Missions Quarterly,* vol. 13 (October, 1977), pp. 219–224.

they may be tailored to individual groups; in fact the vast majority encompass indigenous forms and are produced within the country where they are used.[102]

Some may object that the audio cassette is not necessarily designed for use with groups. Obviously the cassette can be listened to entirely without discussion in the same manner as a radio program, but Søgaard is quick to point out that this can dilute its primary advantage.[103] One of the best uses is as a stimulus to dialogue between Christian and non-Christian. There are now growing numbers of examples in which cassette players have helped in stimulating a people's movement pattern of conversion as tapes are listened to repeatedly, assimilated, and discussed.[104] Indeed the audio cassette (and perhaps the video cassette once costs of playback units are reduced) has rapidly taken its place as one of the most useful tools in evangelism.

Direct Mail

As an advertising medium, direct mail ranks third behind newspapers and television in the United States.[105] It can be highly personalized, and great flexibility is offered in reaching a desired target audience (assuming a mailing list is available). Some groups have used direct mail in evangelism with response rates ranging between one and fourteen percent.[106] Usually a tract is sent, on the assumption that at least some who receive the mailing are in problem recognition and need to be shown how to receive Christ. This, of course, is a debatable assumption, and the extent of negative responses by those who discard the letter rarely is documented. It could have a decided boomerang effect and condition people to be even less receptive. There is no substitute for pretesting documents to learn what the majority response will be.

CONCLUSION

Some may object that we have not covered all possible media in this chapter. What about outdoor ads and bumper stickers? What about them? Do they *really* have any legitimate evangelistic role? At

[102] Hes, "WACC and the Group Media Concept."

[103] Viggo B. Søgaard, *Everything You Need to Know for a Cassette Ministry* (Minneapolis: Bethany Fellowship, 1975).

[104] Royal W. Colle, "Case Studies in Cassette Communication," *WACC Journal,* vol. 24 (1977), pp. 14–22.

[105] "Direct Mail—'Quiet Medium,'" *Advertising Age* (November 21, 1973) p. 119.

[106] See, for example, the strategy of Acts International based in Adelaide, Australia.

best they can only reinforce a central theme in a few words. There is some value to such media in the world of advertising,[107] but evangelism is not advertising. This is a situation in which the message usually does not fit the medium, and this fact becomes even more apparent once one goes outside of the United States.

This survey has been brief, but the reader now has a general exposure to the pros and cons of the various media. Many footnotes have been provided so that those interested in more detail have a guide to relevant sources. There is one common thread that has run throughout the chapter; no mass medium will prove sufficient as the sole method of evangelism in the absence of face-to-face witness. This point cannot be repeated too often. Once this integration has been achieved and various media are utilized in combination with one another, evangelistic effectiveness can be increased many times over as the next chapter and later chapters will demonstrate.

---

[107]For those interested in these media, see Engel, Wales, and Warshaw, *Promotional Strategy,* pp. 266–268.

CHAPTER 7
And How Shall They Hear?

The United Methodist Church in the United States has quite a distinguished evangelistic history. The church doubled in size from 1840 to 1843, for example. Even as recently as 1944, one hundred pastors were given evangelistic training and deployed throughout the country to teach visitation evangelism. Fifteen months later, ninety-two percent of all churches received training and were successful in winning a million new converts and establishing 806 new churches. This upswing continued into the late 1950s when an average of 400,000 members were united with the church annually through conversion.[1]

The 1970s present quite a different picture, however.[2] Total membership dropped from about 11 million in 1965 to 9.9 million by the end of 1975—a net loss of more than one million even though the general population increased. The problem is not a membership departure through the back door but a sharp decline in those who are uniting with the church. In 1974, for example, thirty-six percent of all Methodist churches did not bring in a single new Christian, and more than two-thirds had four or less. If these statistics are combined with those of the Lutherans, Episcopalians, American Bap-

[1]George Hunter, the Director of Evangelism in the Methodist Church has provided these statistics. See "Can United Methodists Recover Evangelism?" *Church Growth Bulletin,* vol. 13 (March, 1977), pp. 109–118.

[2]These statistics also are given by Hunter (*Ibid.*).

tists, Disciples of Christ, and United Presbyterians, there has been a net membership loss of 2.5 million during the past decade. In large part, this is a result of a theological stance that has deviated from a biblical foundation.

As Hunter sees it, the great need is for recovery of a biblical foundation and of evangelistic zeal, and many would quickly agree. Then the problem becomes one of strategy.[3] *How shall they hear?* The apostle Paul raised the same question in the first century:

> Anyone who calls upon the name of the Lord will be saved. But how shall they ask him to save them unless they believe in him? And how can they believe in him if they have never heard about him? And how can they hear about him unless someone tells them? (Rom. 10:13,14, TLB).

There are two important strategic issues to be faced: (1) the media mix (i.e., the best combination of interpersonal and mass media), and (2) integration of mass media with the local church. So this chapter picks right up where the preceding one left off.

THE MEDIA MIX

We have borrowed a term from the advertising world here, but it is a good one. "Media mix" refers to media combinations, and the basic problem is to discover the best mix for the situation at hand. This subject will be approached, first of all, by a brief review of the findings of more than two decades of research into the way in which people accept innovations. This will give important background on the relationship between mass and interpersonal media. Then the focus will shift to the practical issues of media strategy.

Some Insights From Diffusion Theory

An innovation is defined quite simply as any idea, practice, or product that is perceived by someone to be new.[4] In a very real sense, a grasp of the implications of the gospel and the ultimate acceptance of Christ qualifies as an innovation. For this reason, it is pertinent to scan briefly the generalizations that merge from the more than

---

[3]For a very useful planning guide, see Edward R. Dayton, *Planning Strategies for Evangelism, A Workbook,* 6th ed. (Monrovia, Ca.: MARC, 1978).

[4]This has become the standard definition. See Everett Rogers and F. Floyd Shoemaker, *Communication of Innovations: A Cross-Cultural Approach* (New York: Free Press, 1971).

1,800 publications dealing with the way in which innovations diffuse into a social system and are accepted.[5]

Innovations are not accepted by everyone at once. In fact, there are wide differences in the extent to which people are susceptible to change. In 1962, Rogers classified people into five basic categories as follows:[6]

Innovators	2½ percent
Early adopters	13½ percent
Early majority	34 percent
Late majority	34 percent
Laggards	16 percent

The percentages of those at each stage will probably differ from one category of innovation to the next, but this provides a general guide.

As a rule those who are among the first to accept a new idea or practice are influenced by information sources outside the social system itself, including, of course, the mass media. Those among the later adopters also may have been affected by outside influence, but in addition they have had the chance both to observe and interact with innovators and early adopters. More often than not, this informal face-to-face interaction is the dominant factor in the adoption decision.

What emerges from this stream of research is the fact that some people serve as "influentials" or "opinion leaders," meaning that they play a significant role in the decision of another.[7] Opinion leaders quite often actively share their experiences with others for various reasons:

1. Involvement with the idea or practice—the more interested an individual is in the idea or practice, the more he or she is likely to initiate a conversation about it.
2. Self-involvement—sharing with others often performs the function of gaining attention, showing connoisseurship, suggesting status, giving the impression that "outside information is possessed," and asserting superiority.

[5]For a useful review of this literature see the following: Rogers and Shoemaker (*Ibid.*); Everett M. Rogers, "New Production Adoption and Diffusion," in *Selected Aspects of Consumer Behavior* (Washington, D.C.: National Science Foundation, 1977), pp. 223–238; and James F. Engel, Roger D. Blackwell, and David T. Kollat, *Consumer Behavior,* 3rd ed. (Hinsdale, Ill.: Dryden Press, 1978), ch. 12.

[6]Everett M. Rogers, *Diffusion of Innovations* (New York: Free Press, 1962).

[7]The pertinent literature is summarized in Engel, Blackwell, and Kollat, *Consumer Behavior,* ch. 11.

3. Concern for others.
4. Message involvement—some find it entertaining to talk about mass media messages they have been exposed to, especially those that are unusual or humorous.
5. Dissonance reduction—sharing with others sometimes can serve the function of reducing doubt that acceptance of the innovation in question was a correct choice.

The innovator or early adopter, then, can emerge as an opinion leader and materially affect the decisions of others. Opinion leaders seem to be listened to for at least two reasons. First, the fact that they have gained something through their adoption decision gives them a certain measure of expertise and *credibility*. In fact, it is usually found that word-of-mouth influence is evaluated as being far more credible than the mass media for the simple reason that another person is usually not regarded as having something to gain by sharing. The mass media sponsor does not gain this same degree of acceptance nearly as readily. The second factor is that people are open to personal influence when the decision in question has a high degree of perceived risk (i.e., there is much to be gained or lost depending upon the choice made).

For many years it was accepted uncritically that there is a "two-step flow" in the innovation process. The two-step hypothesis stated that influence and ideas "flow from [the mass media] to opinion leaders and from there to the less active members of the population."[8] In other words, as Figure 7.1 illustrates, the mass media were felt to exert their greatest influence on the opinion leader, who, in turn, influenced others.

More recent research has indicated that there is a multi-step flow of information.[9] First of all, the audience is anything but a passive recipient of information, because up to fifty percent of word-of-mouth communications are initiated by people seeking information.[10] Furthermore, both opinion leader and nonopinion leader are exposed to the mass media as Figure 7.2 indicates, and the "trickle down" effect shown in Figure 7.1 often just does not take place.

---

[8]Paul F. Lazarsfeld, Bernard R. Berelson, and Hazel Gaudet, *The Peoples Choice* (New York: Columbia University Press, 1948), p. 151.

[9]Rogers and Shoemaker, *Communication of Innovations.*

[10]Donald F. Cox, "The Audience as Communicators," in Donald F. Cox, ed., *Risk Taking and Information Handling in Consumer Behavior* (Boston: Harvard University Graduate School of Business, 1967), pp. 172–187.

FIGURE 7.1.

The Two-Step Flow Hypothesis of Communication Influence

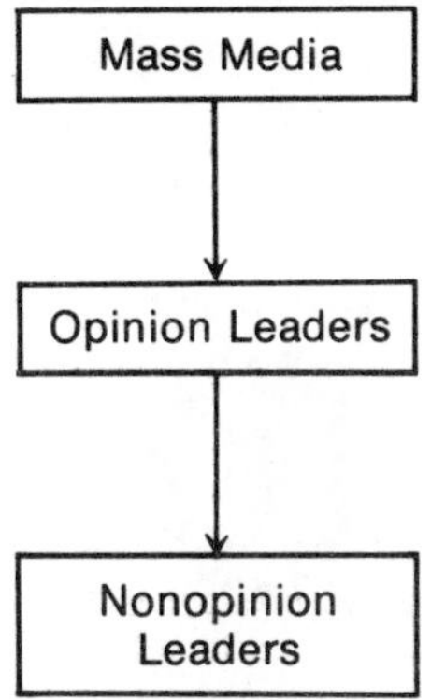

FIGURE 7.2.

The Multi-Step Interaction Model of Communication Influence

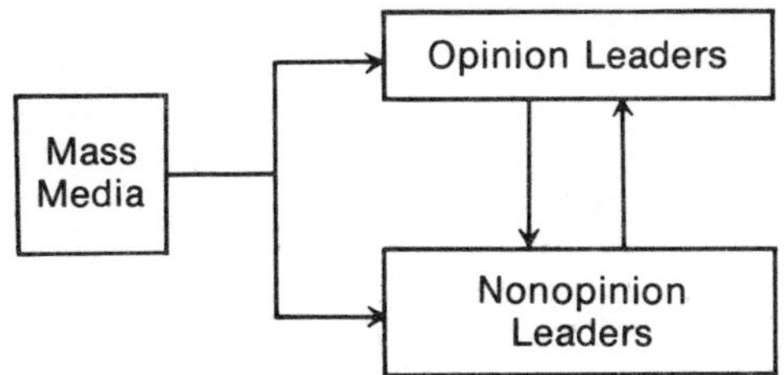

Diffusion research has shown, then, that the mass media can trigger both initial awareness and interest with opinion leader and nonopinion leader alike. This merely reinforces the conclusion reached thus far about the function of the mass media. Word-of-mouth, on the other hand, is usually a more decisive influence.

Obviously, opinion leaders can be an important audience target. The problem is that they can be difficult to isolate and reach with the mass media, although various methods have been developed and tried.[11] The advantage, of course, is that they will greatly accelerate

[11]Engel, Blackwell, and Kollat, *Consumer Behavior,* pp. 281–284.

the whole process of persuasion as they both take the initiative and are sought out by others.

Now, focusing the discussion more directly on evangelism, already existing opinion leaders within a given social structure should serve as the initial target audience, if they can be identified. It should not be assumed without justification that elected leaders, athletes, and others with social visibility will serve as a positive influence in the decision process of others. Unfortunately, the evangelical church seems to have gone overboard in publicizing its parade of so-called Christian celebrities, as if the common man will somehow fall in line. It should be remembered that one person serves as an opinion leader in the life of another only if the latter person has some reason to respect his or her judgment. This can only be verified through research and must not be assumed without evidence.

If opinion leaders can be reached successfully with the gospel, all of the motivations for opinion leadership mentioned earlier no doubt will emerge, and word-of-mouth will be activated. But, notice one thing: The remainder of the audience will respond with interest *only* if the person who is sharing has credibility in their eyes. Evidence of a changed life, in turn, is the best guarantee. So we arrive once again at the unmistakable conclusion that words alone are a mighty insufficient basis for interpersonal influence.

By the way, it is interesting to speculate which of the motivating factors for opinion leadership also underlie personal evangelism. Self-involvement or dissonance reduction could hardly qualify as being sufficient; yet it is probable that such factors as these shape the activities of some of those who are most verbally aggressive. In the final analysis only message involvement (a continuously changing life) and concern for others (love) are truly Christian motivations.

Interpersonal Witness

There are many methods of personal evangelism, most of which train the Christian in a strategy of persuasion. More often than not, the gospel is reduced to the essential points about God, man, and Christ; the person then is trained in how to approach others and encourage them to accept Christ.[12] All who desire to witness effectively should be equipped in this manner as the starting point, as long as they also receive training in how to interact with those who

---

[12]See, for example, James Kennedy, *Evangelism Explosion* (Wheaton, Ill.: Tyndale, 1970).

have not reached the problem recognition stage. Unfortunately, the concept of spiritual decision process still is largely unrecognized, at least insofar as the published manuals on evangelism are concerned. The result is that most Christians are unequipped to cope with the more difficult situations that arise, although there are some useful books for this purpose.[13]

There is considerable emphasis in some quarters of the evangelical church in North America (and to a lesser degree elsewhere) on the necessity of "aggressive evangelism." The author is in cautious agreement with such a philosophy but *only* if the term *aggressive* is defined. Some interpret this to mean turning conversations into evangelistic ventures with virtually everyone with whom there is some form of encounter, even total strangers. In one sense, this is legitimate, because a Christian can do no greater service for another than to introduce that person to Christ. But all too quickly this can be carried to extremes where virtually any pretext is used to introduce Christ's name into a conversation, even if the other person has no interest at all. This is nothing more than impolite manipulation of other people. Christians would be deeply resentful if this were done to them, say, by a used car salesman. Aggressive evangelism of this type thus can become nothing more than rudeness, and it is in marked contrast to the approach of Jesus who showed much greater empathy with people He approached.

Aggressive evangelism, on the other hand, also can denote an attitude of continual personal sensitivity to other people, characterized by a desire to seek the best for them. A personal relationship with Christ *is* the best, and there always will be the prayerful hope that the other person will inquire as to the "hope that is within you." Such openings will not be forced, however, and the sanctity of the other person's privacy is assured. In this sense, every Christian should be aggressive.

It is not necessary to turn this chapter into a handbook on personal evangelism, because it would be a tall order to improve on Leighton Ford's superb volume on this subject.[14] Several methods should be emphasized here, however, including (1) fellowship evangelism, (2) the bridge of friendship, and (3) use of the telephone.

---

[13]See, for example, Paul Little, *How to Give Away Your Faith* (Downers Grove, Ill.: InterVarsity Press, 1966) and Josh McDowell, *Evidence That Demands a Verdict* (Arrowhead Springs, Ca.: Campus Crusade for Christ, International, 1972).

[14]Leighton Ford, *Good News Is for Sharing* (Elgin, Ill.: David C. Cook, 1978).

Fellowship Evangelism.[15] In Acts 20:20, Paul reminded the Christians that he had gone from one house to another to teach them about Christ. The use of the home as an evangelistic center is talked about also in Acts 2:46 and 5:42. In this sense, Christians were being aggressive in evangelism, seeking both to exemplify Christ through their lives and to share verbally. This method rarely appears in any evangelism manual; yet Greenway contends that it holds the key to reaching those living in urban areas in Latin America.[16] Migrants from the rural community soon find themselves cut off from personal and family roots and hence are quite insecure and vulnerable. Greenway stresses that the open arms of a Christian family as well as the neighborhood church (in a sense they become synonymous) meet the basic needs of the transient and provide an ideal atmosphere for evangelism.[17]

Bridges of Friendship. Usually evangelism with total strangers is ineffective. In a very real sense, Christians must earn the right to share with another, and this most commonly means that a friendship must be established. In the final analysis, the power of Christ in day-to-day life cannot be revealed fully in any other way.

Use of the home, of course, is a major bridge of friendship as was mentioned above, but there are other methods as well.[18] Usually it will mean that the Christian must be sufficiently aggressive to take the initiative through such commonplace means as conversation over coffee, joint attendance at sporting events, and so on. Studies of spiritual decision processes by the author and his students frequently show that the most significant influence was someone who cared enough to become a friend.

Use of the Telephone. Most people have telephones in North America (although as many as twenty percent or more have unlisted numbers) with the result that evangelism over the telephone is possible. The percentage of homes with telephones is much lower in other countries, however.

Only one third or less of all homes have telephones in Great Britain, West Germany, Italy, and France.[19] Only the wealthy are

[15]This term is used by George Peters. See "Contemporary Practices of Evangelism," in J. D. Douglas, ed., *Let the Earth Hear His Voice* (Minneapolis: World Wide Publications, 1975), pp. 181–207.

[16]Roger S. Greenway, *An Urban Strategy for Latin America* (Grand Rapids, Mich.: Baker Book House, 1973).

[17]*Ibid.*, p. 102.

[18]Leighton Ford offers some very useful suggestions in *Good News Is for Sharing.* Also see Howard Hendricks, *Say It With Love* (Wheaton, Ill.: Victor Books, 1972).

[19]Paul H. Berent, "International Research Is Different," in Edward M. Mazze, ed., *1975 Combined Proceedings* (Chicago: American Marketing Assn., 1975), p. 295.

likely to have this privilege. Even in such geographic areas, however, telephone evangelism has been surprisingly successful.

Probably the first thing to enter the mind of many readers is the practice in the United States of calling people at random with some type of survey and gospel presentation.[20] Some people may pray to receive Christ (the usual expected response) over the telephone just to get rid of the caller, and other times such a response may be a valid conversion. But what about the many who do not respond? There is a decided backlash against unwanted telephone solicitation by business firms, and this method of evangelism is no different. Such an invasion of privacy by a complete stranger is pretty hard to justify.

Meaningful personal interaction is possible, however, when the other person takes the initiative and calls a publicly listed number. This technique, referred to as the "hotline," has been used by many in various countries of the world. For example, short ads were placed in the personal want ad section of local newspapers in Quito, Ecuador, with such headlines as, "Haunted by Feelings of Guilt? Need Help? Call (a given number)." The caller then would hear a three or four minute recorded message dealing with forgiveness offered by God. If they were interested, a second number then could be dialed for personal counseling. This technique also was used with success through spot ads on FM stations in Quito and Guayaquil.[21] Similar success was found with "Dial a Devotion" in Caracas, Venezuela,[22] and Luis Palau and other evangelists have received a flood of responses when they appear on television on a "call-in" program.[23]

Mass Media Strategy[24]

It is obvious from Chapter 6 that there are numerous mass media possibilities, and the question now is how one proceeds to build a realistic media mix. First we will examine four basic factors in media selection. Discussion then shifts to scheduling.

---

[20]This was a basic method used by Campus Crusade for Christ International in its "Here's Life America" campaign discussed in Chapter 1.

[21]Tom Fulghum, "Telephone Hotline: Hope for Desperate People" *Christian Communications Spectrum,* vol. 2 (Summer, 1976), pp. 11–12.

[22]"Gospel 'Upreach' in Caracas," *Latin America Pulse,* vol. 10 (Published by the Evangelical Missions Information Service, September, 1975).

[23]See the report of Luis Palau's Bolivian crusade in *Christianity Today* (May 5, 1978), p. 43.

[24]This section closely follows the discussion in Chapters 11 and 12 of James F. Engel, Hugh G. Wales, and Martin R. Warshaw, *Promotional Strategy,* 3rd ed. (Homewood, Ill.: Richard D. Irwin, 1975). The reader interested in more detail should turn to this source or any other standard textbook on advertising and promotion.

Media Selection. While there are many things to be taken into account in media selection, four factors are of particular importance in evangelistic strategy: (1) achieving the desired audience, (2) reach versus frequency, (3) cost efficiency, and (4) qualitative considerations.

(1) Achieving the Desired Audience. The basic goal of strategy is to select media vehicles that reach the target audience with a minimum of waste coverage (this is often referred to as *selectivity*). For this to be done, the audience must be specified with precision in such terms as age, geographic location, socioeconomic status, and so on. The next obvious step is to consult data on the audience of various candidate media (assuming such data are available) in these same demographic terms and select those that cover the target with least waste.

Various syndicated audience research services provide data on audience profiles of secular media in the United States, Canada, Western Europe, and some other countries as well. In the United States, for example, A. C. Nielsen and American Research Bureau (ARB) collect data on television audiences; the Target Group Index (TGI) documents magazine readership, and radio audiences are assessed by RADAR (Radio's All Dimension Audience Research) to mention only a few. When such services are not available, the only recourse is to consult the individual medium to determine whether or not audience research is available. Unfortunately, such studies often are highly suspect, for the reason that they are usually undertaken to get advertising.

This type of research has been done by secular media since the late 1920s, but only in the past few years has there been any real interest in audience research among the Christian media. The first to take this step were the magazine publishers who seem to have a degree of sensitivity to audience needs. Also many need to attract advertisers. It still is relatively unusual, however, to find Christian radio stations with accurate measures of listenership, but this situation is changing.

Because valid data are not always available, the author always includes media exposure as one of the categories of information to be collected in community surveys. Often it is possible to analyze data in such a way that insights can be gotten that otherwise are impossible. For example, a syndicated survey, which normally provides only basic demographic information, never could show the media preferences of males over age thirty in Vancouver, Canada, who desire help in the marriage and family situation.

(2) Reach Versus Frequency. Once audience selectivity has been

evaluated, it is important to determine both reach and frequency. *Reach* is defined as the number (or percentage) of *different* homes exposed to the message during a given period of time. Advertisers generally compute reach over four weeks. *Frequency* refers to the number of times that the *average home reached* was exposed during that same period. In advertising circles a summary measure is used, which is referred to as *gross rating points* (GRP). GRP is computed as the product of reach times frequency. It is widely used as an indicator of advertising weight or cumulative impact generated by the media schedule. Unfortunately, this computation requires data on the duplication or overlap between media. To the extent that two or more media reach essentially the same audience, the less the total reach of the media schedule and vice versa. Also it is necessary to have measures of the percentage of the audience exposed to one or more of the media insertions.

In the absence of such data, one is forced to make rough estimates, which usually will prove sufficient. For example, frequency will be enhanced by repetitive use of a limited number of media, whereas reach will be achieved by an opposite strategy. It all depends, of course, on the basic campaign objective.

(3) Cost Considerations. Because budgets are usually limited, space and time costs can become an important factor in media selection. These data either can be procured from the individual medium or from the volumes published by the Standard Rate & Data Service (SRDS) in the United States.

Costs of various media candidates are best compared through use of the cost per thousand (CPM) formula computed as follows:

$$\frac{\text{space or time rate x 1,000}}{\text{audience reached}}$$

In the case of newspapers an alternate computation is used, referred to as the milline rate. Because costs are always quoted per line, it is necessary to use 1,000,000 as the multiplier.

All things being equal, one will select the media vehicles that offer the lowest CPM, but there are some necessary precautions. First, it may be assumed erroneously that costs are *the* dominant factor in media selection. However, the other considerations mentioned thus far can be of greater importance, especially audience selectivity. Furthermore, notice that the denominator in these formulae is gross circulation, readership, or viewership. Unless modifications are made to estimate reach of the target audience, some misleading conclusions may be reached. A CPM of $2.78 could easily be a CPM of $20.00 for the target audience because of lack of media selectivity. Such computations, of course, assume the availability of media audience data.

(5) Qualitative Media Characteristics. Sometimes also referred to as "editorial climate," the term "qualitative" has come to assume several possible meanings. It is confined here to mean the role played by the medium or vehicle in the lives of its audience.

As of this writing there are no continuing data sources used to assess qualitative characteristics across media classes. Rather, the analyst is forced to rely on isolated research reports and on judgment. One interesting study was done by Tigert in which he assessed differences in life-style profiles of the audiences of fifty-three magazines in thirteen related groupings.[25] *Reader's Digest,* for example, was found to be the magazine of the establishment: Readers were interested in their community and showed little understanding of the problems of today's youth. *Newsweek* readers differ from their *Time* counterparts in that they look more for security, worry more about big government and union power, read the Bible more, have somewhat old-fashioned tastes, are more concerned about health, and have a strongly negative attitude toward advertising.

In the absence of such data, judgment can be quite sufficient. Most business firms, for instance, would not advertise laundry detergents in the *Atlantic Monthly.* The basic question is this: Does the medium create the mood for a positive reception of the message? Or is there a real incompatibility? In the preceding chapter, the author stated his opinion that bumper stickers and billboards are inappropriate when used for calling for a decision, and the same could be said for a whole variety of advertising specialties such as T-shirts, pens, balloons, and so on. Evangelism requires more than sloganeering. Some will disagree with this assessment, but the issue becomes even more complicated when one considers the potential use of such magazines as *Playboy* (see Figure 2.5) and television soap operas. Where does one draw the line?

Probably the best general guideline can be gained from the exam-

[25]Douglas Tigert, "A Psychographic Profile of Magazine Audiences: An Investigation of Media's Climate," paper given at the Consumer Research Workshop, The Ohio State University, August 22, 1969.

ple of Jesus. He never seemed to hesitate to go where people congregated who had needs and were receptive to what He had to say, even though the religious authorities of His day raised their eyebrows. Apparently He did not establish any firm limits here. But notice that His primary attention was focused on the likelihood of finding receptive people, and that was the most important factor. He did not very often take advantage of mass public gatherings as He could easily have done. Also, He never employed gimmicks to attract attention, although some might argue that His miracles served that purpose. The display of such slogans as "Solution Spiritual Revolution" is nothing more than gimmickry in the author's opinion, and it may do more for the morale or ego of the one who displays it than it does for anyone else.

(4) Proper Use of the Factors. Most will agree that audience selectivity is the most important factor to be considered. The majority of candidate media will be eliminated as this criterion is employed. The analyst next will probably want to weigh the qualitative considerations of the remaining candidates, and this no doubt will reduce the list even further. Now the selection becomes fine tuned as reach versus frequency is taken into consideration. Finally, cost considerations will be the final determinant.

Media selection, then, cannot be done by formula. The factors given here provide a kind of analysis routine that helps to discipline the thinking of the media planner. There is no such thing as *the* best schedule. Rather, the goal is to arrive at a media mix that is appropriate given the stated objectives for the campaign. Even though the computer is increasingly being used in large advertising agencies, media selection is still much more of an art than it is a science.

Media Scheduling. Once media have been selected it then is necessary to prepare a schedule for the timing and allocation of space and time inserts. This will require scheduling by geographic region, by season, and within a chosen medium (size and location of insertions).

(1) Geographic Scheduling. Business firms go to great lengths to estimate geographical market potential,[26] and media are allocated in proportion to an index of relative sales possibilities on a market-by-market basis. This is nothing more than the fertile field principle discussed elsewhere in this book. The goal always is to assess receptivity first and then, when possible, concentrate efforts where the probability of response is highest.

[26]Engel, Wales, and Warshaw, *Promotional Strategy,* ch. 9.

(2) Seasonal Scheduling. Many consumer products show seasonal variations in demand, and commercial persuasion will be varied throughout the year consistent with this pattern. Is there a similar "demand curve" in terms of response to evangelism? It is likely that religious interest is higher among most people around the conventional holidays of Christmas and Easter. Therefore, there may be merit to a greater evangelistic thrust at such times. Vacation periods, on the other hand, will find large numbers of people away from their homes and scattered elsewhere. Also, major decisions most frequently are deferred during such periods of relaxation. This could call for a decrease or even cessation of efforts during those times, although there has been some success with beach evangelism at holidays.

(3) Scheduling Within a Medium. The first question here is the size or length of the insertion. As a general rule, it has been found that doubling the size of an advertisement does not double readership. In fact, readership increases roughly in proportion to the square root of space increase.[27] Whether such a principle applies outside of space advertising is not known, but it is likely that it reveals a general pattern. The relative advantages of variation in length of television or radio time units defy generalization. The only thing that can be said with certainty is that there are creative advantages to use of longer time, because the greatest problem is always faced when it is necessary to compress a message unduly. It should be noted, however, that advertisers have found that thirty seconds can be too much for some messages and ten seconds more effective.[28] From the point of view of the audience, brevity frequently is a virtue.

In space advertising the general rule is that the message itself is a greater factor in readership and response than is its position within the publication. The only exception is that there is somewhat greater readership if use is made of the covers or the first ten pages, but differences are not especially large.[29] The only general rule in broadcast advertising is that commercials frequently perform better when inserted as part of a regular program as compared with station breaks, which frequently are characterized by undue commercial clutter.

[27]Roger Barton, *Media in Advertising* (New York: McGraw-Hill, 1964), p. 109.

[28]This point was made by Harry W. McMahan, at "Advertising in the Television Age," a seminar sponsored by the Columbus, Ohio, Advertising Club, December 5, 1963.

[29]The evidence is summarized in Engel, Wales, and Warshaw, *Promotional Strategy*, pp. 294–295.

The points mentioned here, of course, are most applicable when advertising media are used; but they also can provide a general guideline to follow when making use of nonadvertising media as well.

The Media Budget

The budget decision is one of the greatest headaches faced in both advertising and sales management. Theoretically, the decision is an easy one, because all one need do is to calculate how much expenditure is needed to produce an *optimum* response. Optimum is defined to be that point at which additional investment does not produce the expected response; expenditure beyond this point soon will generate a diminishing overall return as the graph in Figure 7.3 illustrates. The same principle applies in evangelism.

FIGURE 7.3.

A Hypothetical Response Curve and Optimum Budget Level

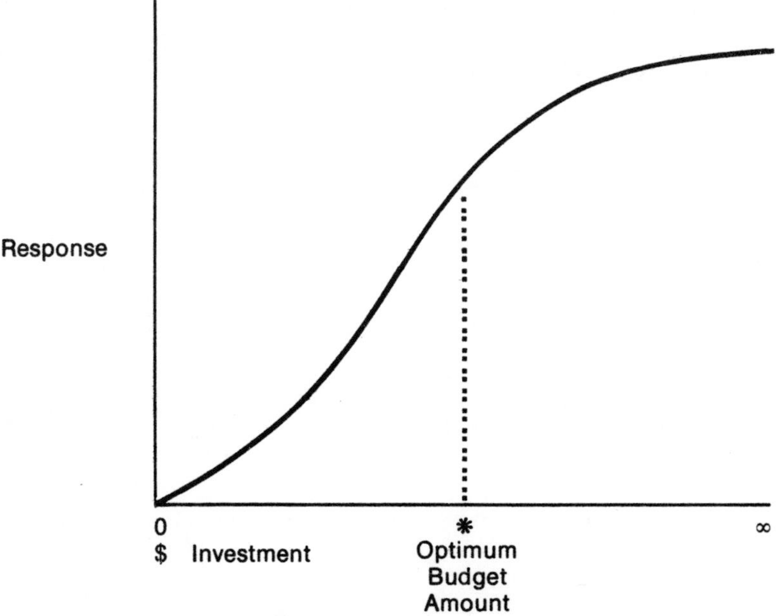

The business firm, of course, would compute the optimum in terms of sales, but in reality this seldom is done. The problem is that extremely costly field research is required to document sales response at various expenditure levels while all other things are held equal. Because of both the research sophistication and investment required for this purpose, only a handful of firms have made the effort. What it boils down to is that the budget decision often reflects guesswork more than anything else.[30]

One common approach is to determine a budgetary limit in advance and then require strategy planners to stay within the determined boundaries. Often the boundaries are dictated by restrictions on available funds. Only by accident will the optimum point be reached in this manner.

A far better approach is to try to approximate the optimum by what is now known as the "build-up method." Given the overall objectives, planners attempt to estimate what is needed in the way of media support and interpersonal efforts. These costs are accumulated into a lump sum that will serve as a proposed budget. Obviously, however, the amount may exceed available funds, with the result that some type of compromise will be required.

In terms of evangelistic planning, it may be perfectly appropriate to determine the budget in advance on the basis of available funds. Usually these will be so limited that there is no danger of expenditures *past* the optimum point. Obviously, this arrangement is far from ideal, but it is a realistic approach. While God is not limited in His resources and will reward the faith of His servants, the financial facts of life must be faced at any point in time.

Yet, if we only follow the "all you can afford" principle outlined in the above paragraph, it should be recognized that it can violate the criteria of good budgeting. Even though funds may be limited, planners should weigh the goals and objectives and follow the build-up method. What are the costs, for example, of evangelistic training, printing, purchase of books and tracts, spot radio commercials, and so on? What, in other words, will it cost if no limits are imposed? This may not arrive at the optimum either, but it will be much closer than if a budget limit is imposed at the outset. If the expenditure arrived at by this method exceeds available funds, then it will be necessary to decide whether or not it is worth the effort to raise this amount. Such an evaluation must be made prayerfully, because the sum arrived at by the build-up approach may reflect what God wants. If so, financial limits quickly can be transcended by prayer.

---

[30]The various methods used are discussed in *ibid.*, ch. 10.

Chapter 13 will include a case example of a strategy developed to equip churches in Rochester, New York, for evangelization as well as a plan for actual outreach itself. This is one of seven different strategies prepared by student teams in a class led by the author. It was interesting to see the extent to which proposed budgets varied. The group of churches in Rochester indicated at the outset that $25,000 was the probable budgetary limit, although they would be willing to exceed that amount if proof could be provided that it was necessary. Some groups simply took this budget as a given, whereas others put serious thought into the build-up approach. The suggested budgets of these latter groups ranged from $14,000 to $31,000! In part, this variation reflected some differences in strategy (for example use or nonuse of television.). But there is the very real possibility that the $25,000 figure was either too high or too low for the stated purpose. In the final analysis, each plan must be studied on its own merit in terms of whether or not the stated strategy will accomplish the objectives.

MASS MEDIA AND THE LOCAL CHURCH

A fundamental theme at various points in this book is that mass and interpersonal media must be integrated into a common strategy. This is of such importance that it is the subject of Chapter 13 where the emphasis is on a unified strategy of outreach. The problem to be addressed here arises from the fact that most of the agencies specializing in mass media and evangelism are parachurch organizations, whereas the church itself is responsible for face-to-face sharing. How can these thrusts be integrated?

One of those who has been most outspoken on this subject is Phill Butler, who sees two issues that must be resolved.[31] First, the parachurch organization tends to view its medium as an end in itself. If the church is to be involved at all, it, by and large, is confined to follow-up of converts. The church, on the other hand, has not done much to help the parachurch organization; so both are at fault.

The only sensible answer is to be found in increased communication between these two entities, accompanied by a genuine commitment to work together. First, the parachurch agency must recognize that the local church bears the primary evangelistic responsibility and that the agency's role, in turn, is to be a servant to the church. As

[31]Phill Butler, "Radio and the Local Church: A Problem of Integration," *Christian Communications Spectrum*, vol. 1 (Winter, 1975), p. 12ff.

we have mentioned before, some parachurch organizations act as if the very reverse of this principle is true. This means that church leaders should be contacted individually and collectively and an assessment made as to how radio, print, or whatever can be used to help in their outreach. Most local churches do very little with the media because of lack of expertise. Many would welcome such initiative. In addition, the parachurch organization may serve as a catalyst to bring local churches together into unified outreach.

The church, in turn, must be open to creative uses of the media, a step some have been quite unwilling to take. Also, it must put aside any tendencies toward separatism that have served as a potent barrier to cooperation. No local church will have all of the talent and resources to function in this way apart from others in the body.

In short, a genuine spirit of Christian cooperation is required if the concept of the media mix is ever to become a reality. The Lausanne Congress marked the turning point, and the climate for cooperation is becoming decidedly favorable throughout the world. There is now good reason to believe that those who have not yet heard *will hear!*

CHAPTER 8

Formation and Change of Beliefs and Attitudes

Robin Graham set out on a most interesting venture—to circle the globe by himself in a small sailboat.[1] Only a teen-ager, Robin accumulated a lifetime of experiences in just a few years. Part of the excitement was meeting Patti in the South Seas and later becoming married.

Robin and Patti described themselves as typical "California pagans." Neither had ever attended a religious meeting that they could remember. Using Robin's words, ". . . if anyone had mentioned God or Jesus we would have walked the other way and been careful to avoid that person in the future."[2] God was at work in Robin's life, however, and he soon began to realize that physical survival in the face of certain death was no accident. He pondered the meaning of the universe on those long days and nights at sea and eventually turned to the Bible. Contemplation of Genesis led to this conclusion: "Genesis sounds a lot better than anything old Darwin wrote."[3]

Clearly Robin was progressing without fully realizing it through a spiritual decision process. God revealed Himself through nature, and Robin's meager Christian awareness began to focus until he had at least some knowledge of the facts of the gospel. Once he began to read the Bible, however, this knowledge galvanized into a belief that

[1]See Robin Lee Graham, *Dove* (New York: Harper & Row, 1972).
[2]*Ibid.*, p. 197.
[3]*Ibid.*, p. 165.

God must be taken seriously. Slowly life began to change until he and Patti finally visited a church in California. There, at long last, they observed people with a living faith. Then, and only then, did they grasp the implications of the gospel for their life, and their attitude toward taking the step of a personal relationship with Christ became positive. Together they took the step of faith and became Christians. As they put it:

> Our belief is simple. It is the belief that so many of our own generation are discovering—a belief that God isn't dead as some of the older generation have told us. In a world that seems to be going crazy we are learning that Jesus showed men the only way they should live—the way we were meant to live.[4]

Robin and Patti's story parallels that of so many others. Both had some fragmentary awareness of biblical truth, but it was of no consequence. When it came to asking them what they believed religiously, there was nothing to say. The events of life itself, however, enabled them to grasp what the gospel really is all about, and mere knowledge changed to firm belief. Belief was followed by a positive attitude toward becoming a Christian. Attitude, in turn, led to an intention to act and an ultimate decision. This is a good illustration of what this chapter is all about—formation and change of beliefs and attitudes.

WE ARE WHAT WE BELIEVE: INSIGHTS FROM ATTITUDE THEORY

Until the 1970s, attitude was probably the single most important variable in the literature of social psychology. Defined in various ways, it always has referred to an *evaluation*, positive or negative, of some person, event, or phenomenon.

Why has this one variable assumed such importance? The answer is that many theorists have postulated that a system of attitudes serves as a person's "map of the world." This map exerts a profound effect on both thinking and behavior. Therefore, the traditional viewpoint still accepted today is that "we are what we believe."

Traditional definitions of attitude encompassed three related dimensions:[5]

---

[4]*Ibid.*, p. 197.

[5]See, for example, W.J. McKeachie and Charlotte L. Doyle, *Psychology* (Reading, Mass.: Addison-Wesley, 1966), p. 560.

1. *Cognitive*—information and beliefs about the object or phenomenon in question.
2. *Affective*—feelings of like or dislike about the attitude object.
3. *Behavioral*—tendencies to act in a manner consistent with both beliefs and positive or negative feelings.

A virtually unlimited variety of measurement methods emerged over the years,[6] and there was no consensus whatsoever until recently just how one should go about attitude research. As might be expected, the literature on this subject became pretty confused and muddled.

Is Attitude Change a Valid Communication Goal?

One of the greatest controversies has centered around the basic promise that a change in attitude will be followed by a change in behavior. The whole theory of persuasion to be discussed later rests squarely on this foundation, and if it is faulty, entire shelves of library books are invalid.

Surprisingly, this critical premise remained completely unverified for years, and two camps were formed. One, of course, took the affirmative, and this has included most of those who undertake research on persuasion. The other group held strongly to the contrary, and some have even dismissed attitude as a "phantom variable."

Those on the positive side of this issue have tended, almost without exception, to come from the applied fields of public opinion or marketing research. They point to a number of studies clearly documenting that a change in attitude through some type of persuasive campaign is usually followed by extensive behavioral change.[7] In fact, many marketing researchers feel that attitude change should be a primary goal of promotional strategy. DuBois summarizes this

---

[6]See, for example, A.N. Oppenheim, *Questionnaire Design and Attitude Measurement* (New York: Basic Books, 1966). Also, M.E. Shaw and J.M. Wright, *Scales for the Measurement of Attitudes* (New York: McGraw-Hill, 1967).

[7]Some of the more useful references are Alvin A. Achenbaum, "Advertising Doesn't Manipulate Consumers," *Journal of Advertising Research,* vol. 12 (April, 1972), pp. 3–14; "Ads Can Change Attitudes, Hike Sales, Effects Are Measurable," *Marketing News* (February 13, 1976), p. 5; and Steven J. Gross and C. Michael Niman, "Attitude-Behavior Consistency; A Review," *Public Opinion Quarterly,* vol. 39 (Fall, 1975), pp. 358–368.

position by stating that the better the level of attitude, the more users you hold and the more nonusers you attract.[8]

On the negative side, researchers, usually in the academic ranks, have not always been so successful in documenting a positive relationship. Deutscher was led to state that "disparities between thought and action are the central methodological problem of the social sciences."[9]

There are three reasons for such a divergence of viewpoint:

1. *Varying definitions.* Fishbein and Ajzen reviewed 750 articles published between 1968 and 1970 and found almost 500 different ways of conceptualizing and measuring attitude.[10]
2. *Varying measurement methods.* Only in recent years have there been any serious attempts to determine which approaches have greatest validity.[11]
3. *Assignment of too much predictive weight to a single variable.* Common sense should indicate that attitude alone cannot fully explain behavior; yet that has been the expectation. There are many other factors such as social pressure, personal financial situation, and so on.

When the author first joined with his colleagues Blackwell and Kollat to write *Consumer Behavior* in 1968, a standard textbook in that field, there was no resolution to this controversy, and the same was true when the 1973 edition was published.[12] Fortunately, the outlook has now changed.

New Light on a Confused Subject

One of the first to suggest some solutions to the blurred link between attitude and behavior was Milton Rosenberg.[13] Taking a

[8]C. DuBois, "Twelve Brands on a Seesaw," in *Proceedings of the 13th Annual Conference* (New York: Advertising Research Foundation, 1968).

[9]L. Deutscher, "Words and Deeds: Social Science and Social Policy," *Social Problems,* vol. 3 (1966), p. 235. Also see Martin Fishbein, "Attitude and the Prediction of Behavior," in M. Fishbein, ed., *Attitude Theory and Measurement,* (New York: Wiley, 1967), p. 477.

[10]Martin Fishbein and Icek Ajzen, "Attitudes and Opinions," in *Annual Review of Psychology,* ed. P.H. Mussen and M.R. Rosenzweig, vol. 23 (Palo Alto, Ca.: Annual Reviews, Inc., 1972), pp. 188–244.

[11]See, for example, Joel N. Axelrod, "Attitude Measurements That Predict Purchases," *Journal of Advertising Research,* vol. 8 (March, 1968), p. 3.

[12]James F. Engel, Roger D. Blackwell, and David T. Kollat, *Consumer Behavior* (New York: Holt, Rinehart and Winston, 1968 and 1973).

[13]Milton J. Rosenberg, "Cognitive Structure and Attitudinal Effect," *Journal of Abnormal and Social Psychology,* vol. 53 (1966), pp. 367–372.

similar perspective, Martin Fishbein and his colleagues have emerged as the leading voices.[14]

Fishbein contends that each of the three dimensions of attitude (cognitive, affective, and behavioral) are variables in themselves. His contribution lies in confining attitude only to the affective dimension (i.e., positive or negative evaluations) and treating the other aspects separately.

Following his lead, the first necessary step is to establish some new definitions as follows:

1. *Belief* (the cognitive dimension): those things that people hold to be true with respect to a given subject matter or action.
2. *Attitude* (the affective dimension): a positive or negative evaluation toward undertaking a given *action* consistent with beliefs in a particular set of circumstances.
3. *Intention* (the behavioral dimension): the subjective probability that beliefs and attitudes will be acted upon.

It is important to note that attitude is defined here in terms of an *action* rather than an *object,* because research has proved that how one feels about something in general does not necessarily lead to consistent actions.[15] Furthermore, behavior is found to be consistent with attitudes only when the research focus is on outcomes in specific situations.[16]

Fishbein goes on to hypothesize quite realistically that both the existence of social pressures and individual motivation to comply with that pressure also must be taken into account when predicting behavior. Figure 8.1 shows how all of these factors fit together, based on research undertaken to date.[17]

Belief is the most important building block in Figure 8.1. Beliefs, of course, are based on knowledge as the diagram shows. Both

---

[14]The most important source is Martin Fishbein and Icek Ajzen, *Belief, Attitude, Intention and Behavior: An Introduction to Theory and Research* (Reading, Mass.: Addison-Wesley, 1975).

[15]This was first shown in a famous study in which attitudes toward those of different races did not predict behavior in specific situations. See R.T. LaPiere, "Attitudes vs. Actions," *Social Forces,* vol. 13 (1934), pp. 230–237. Also see Martin Fishbein, "Attitude, Attitude Change, and Behavior: A Theoretical Overview," in Philip Levine, ed., *Attitude Research Bridges the Atlantic,* (Chicago: American Marketing Assn., 1975), p. 12.

[16]Milton Rokeach, "Attitude Change and Behavioral Change," *Public Opinion Quarterly,* vol. 30 (1966–67), pp. 529–550.

[17]See Fishbein and Ajzen, *Belief, Attitude, Intention and Behavior.* Also an extensive body of research is summarized in James F. Engel, Roger D. Blackwell, and David T. Kollat, *Consumer Behavior,* 3rd ed. (Hinsdale, Ill.: Dryden Press, 1978), ch. 15.

FIGURE 8. 1.

The Relation Between Knowledge, Belief, Attitude, Intention, and Behavior

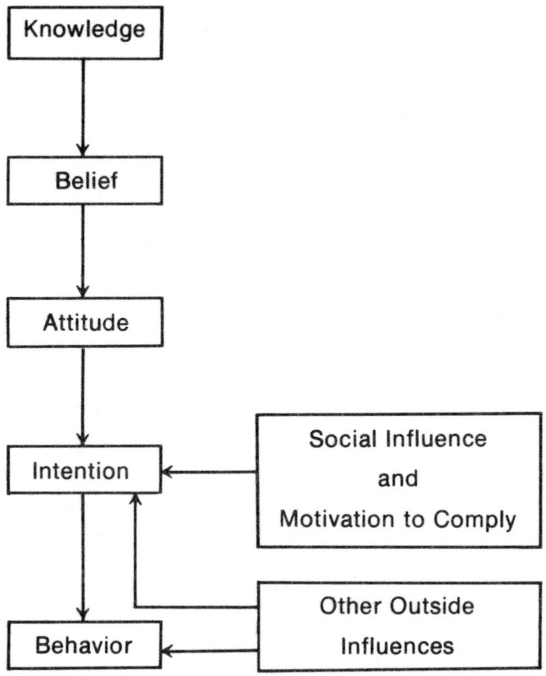

attitude and intention are outcomes of belief—attitude being one's evaluation of what one holds to be true and intention being the likelihood one will act on those beliefs. Therefore, all things being equal, *a change in belief will lead to changes in both attitude and intention as well as behavior itself.* All things may not be equal of course, if social norms oppose such behavior and the individual is motivated to comply with those norms.

Figure 8.1 also shows that there can be other influences from the environment that can either enhance or inhibit both intention to act as well as behavior. While this has been verified by research,[18] it simply represents common sense.

Figure 8.1 (excluding "other outside influences") has come to be

[18] J.N. Sheth, "An Investigation of Relationships Among Evaluative Beliefs, Affect, Behavioral Intention, and Behavior," unpublished paper (Urbana, Ill.: University of Illinois, 1970).

known as the *extended Fishbein Model.*[19] It has rapidly become the theoretical foundation for attitude research in such practical settings as business and politics. There are some rather precise measurement procedures which still are undergoing modification;[20] but the most important contribution is the clarification of the attitude-behavior link. Again, we now can say with some certainty that a change in attitude will lead to a corresponding change in behavior, as long as other influences on behavior also are taken into account, Furthermore, attitudes are changed by changing the underlying belief structure. This means that beliefs must be studied as a variable in their own right.

BELIEFS, ATTITUDES, AND THE SPIRITUAL DECISION PROCESS

The reader now may begin to see some of the theoretical rationale of the spiritual decision process first described in Chapter 3 and repeated in part in Figure 8. 2.

FIGURE 8.2.

Beliefs, Attitudes, Intentions, and the Spiritual Decision Process

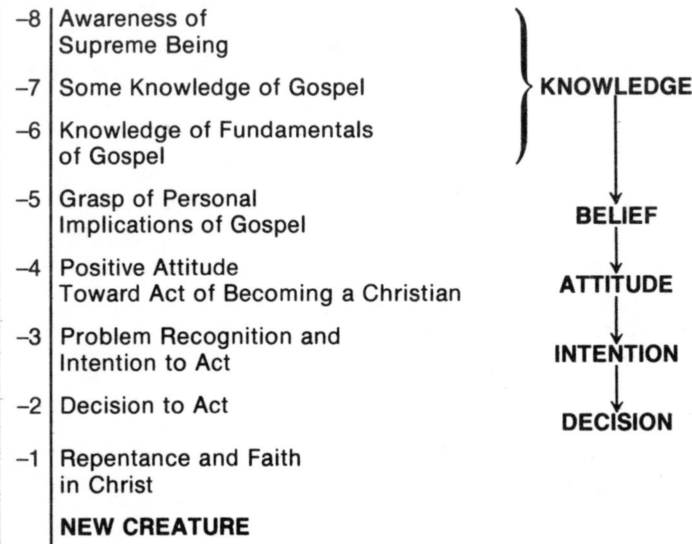

[19]This is described most fully in Fishbein and Ajzen.

[20]Those interested in such details should consult Fishbein and Ajzen, *Belief, Attitude, Intention, Behavior.* Also Engel, Blackwell, and Kollat, *Consumer Behavior,* pp. 399–405.

It was stated earlier that there is a minimum of knowledge necessary if one is to make a valid and lasting decision for Christ, and this falls into five categories:

1. There is one God, Creator, who actually exists in space and time.
2. Man has become imprisoned by a self-seeking existence with no possibility of restoring communication with God by his own action.
3. Jesus Christ provided through His death and resurrection the only way for mankind to be restored to fellowship with God.
4. The Bible is a valid witness to spiritual truth.
5. Restoration of fellowship between God and man requires that man accept God's free gift on the terms that God has provided.

This is the knowledge acquired as the individual moves from stages –8 to –6. It is difficult to state the exact amount of understanding that must be gained, because people differ in their willingness to undertake action with limited information. Also, spiritual truth never is fully discerned until one has become regenerated by an act of the Holy Spirit (1 Cor. 3).

The mere possession of religious knowledge, however, does not imply that the individual actually believes it. Beliefs are established once biblical truth is discerned in the context of basic motivations and needs (stage –5). Belief, then, is more than just intellectual assent. Beliefs are those aspects of one's world view that determine the way in which an individual looks at life itself.[21] Beliefs are said to be *salient,* in turn, when they are closely related to one's self concept. This means, of course, that intellectual understanding also will be accompanied by motivation to act. This merely underscores the essential fact that grasp of gospel implications is a most crucial stage in the process.

---

[21]This point has been made by many authorities. For example, *belief* corresponds to Schaeffer's use of the term *presupposition.* See Francis A. Schaeffer, *How Should We Then Live?* (Old Tappen, N.J.: Fleming H. Revell, 1976), p. 19; Also see Charles Y. Glock and Rodney Stark, *Religion and Society in Tension* (Chicago: Rand-McNally, 1965), ch. 1; Richard R. Clayton and James W. Gladden, "The Five Dimensions of Religiosity; Toward Demythologizing a Sacred Artifact," *Journal for the Scientific Study of Religion,* vol. 13 (June, 1974), pp. 135–143; Paul W. Pruyser, *Between Belief and Unbelief* (New York: Harper & Row, 1974), p. 80; Geoffrey E. W. Scobie, *Psychology of Religion* (New York: Wiley, 1975), ch. 1; and Donald Wiebe, "Is Religious Belief Problematic?" *Christian Scholar's Review,* vol. 7 (1977), pp. 23–25.

A positive attitude toward the act of accepting Christ (–4) and intention to act (–3) will follow the establishment of belief, and this is quite consistent with the Fishbein model. What this says, of course, is that the establishment of new beliefs and changes of existing beliefs are an important trigger to an ultimate spiritual decision.

Studies of Religious Knowledge and Belief

Figure 8.3 provides a summary of a number of surveys that have focused on aspects of religious knowledge and belief. Each used a somewhat different questioning procedure, and not all followed the same information categories when designing questions. Therefore, there are some gaps here and there, and direct comparison is difficult. Nevertheless, it is possible to make some generalizations.

It is quite obvious that most people in North America believe in God. This, of course, is consistent with Paul's statements in Romans 1 that God clearly makes Himself known to everyone through conscience and nature. But these same people probably also believe in motherhood, their national flag, in the sun coming up every morning, and so on. Therefore, this does not say very much about the religious life of people.

Unfortunately, most of these surveys have not clearly zeroed in on what people feel about the nature of man. The question to ask is this: "Is man morally neutral or not?" If so, then people can be changed through education and personal effort. If not, then there must be help from some source outside the individual. One thing that does emerge from Figure 8.3 is that people in North America apparently do not have much faith in the educational system's ability to provide answers to mankind's basic dilemmas. The adults in Vancouver even went so far as to indicate overwhelmingly that change must start with the individual. This is the basic Christian premise, of course, but it is doubtful that most of those giving this answer see the solution in Christianity. Nevertheless, it is encouraging to see that many at least look internally to discover the ultimate problem.

So far so good—the data show at least some understanding of the Christian faith. But the situation rapidly changes once one examines peoples' conceptions of Jesus Christ. Half or less are aware that He claimed divinity, and one suspects that this answer is given much more frequently by Christians than by non-Christians. That was indeed found to be the case in several of the projects when these two groups were separated. What this means is that most people simply do not grasp what Jesus was saying about Himself and His ministry,

FIGURE 8.3.

Research Studies of Religious Knowledge and Belief

Information Category	Research Study							
	U.S. Adults[1]	U.S. Women[2]	Upper Arlington, Ohio Adults	Peoria, Illinois Adults	Rochester, New York Adults	Vancouver, B.C. Canada Adults	Vancouver, B.C. Canada Teens	Quito, Eucador Teens
Belief in existence of God	94%	90%	76%	87%	83%	73%	57%	80%
Nature of Man								
Man is the cause of all problems						84%		
Education has the answers			23%		37%	30%		
Jesus Christ								
Jesus is God	64%			56%		45%	38%	45%
Jesus is just a man			11%		16%			
The Bible is God's Word	38%		56%	44%	61%	30%	40%	

Religion								
Religion is of some personal importance	56%			60%	50%	60%	43%	23%
Church has personal significance	38%	6%			31%	28%		
God can be found by logic			20%		20%			
Belief in life after death	69%	80%		93%				
Ten Commandments are a good rule for life					71%	81%		

Source: Unless otherwise noted, these studies were carried out through the Research and Services Division of the Communication Department, Wheaton Graduate School. All are available as part of the Wheaton Communication Research Reports series.

[1]George Gallup, Jr., "Religion in Moderation?" (Address given at the 65th General Convention of the Episcopalian Church, September 21, 1976). Additional data from "Survey of the Unchurched American," 1978.

[2]A survey of 60,000 readers of *McCall's* magazine during 1977, as reported in the *Christian Inquirer,* May, 1978, p. 1.

and certainly they cannot have an understanding of the implications for their life. Hence, the majority can only be said to have some knowledge of the gospel (–7), not an awareness of its fundamentals. It is here that most of our communication must begin.

We also encounter difficulty with respect to the Bible. Probably Gallup's data are the most helpful here, because he clearly asked whether people accepted the Bible as being valid without error. This was not always the wording in questions in the other surveys. Only a minority accept this position. Given doubts about biblical veracity, quoting of Bible verses becomes a pretty doubtful strategy. In fact, biblical veracity will have to be established at some point before spiritual belief is established. Questions on this subject are not to be brushed aside as being "satanic sidetracks" as one teacher of personal evangelism alleges.

It is interesting that half or more (with the exception of Catholic Quito) have at least some interest in religion. But notice that this is largely at the periphery of life. The Rochester study, for example, disclosed that few ever would turn to the church in times of real personal problems. It seems to be a paradox that interest in religion is accompanied by skepticism about the church, but this is a fact nonetheless. There are ways that religion can be expressed other than through a formal church experience, and this is what people seem to be saying.

Most people still believe in the basic teaching of the Ten Commandments, and those in other surveys cited here did note that there is such a thing as "right and wrong." Therefore, subjectivism has not yet won the day. Most do not understand the Christian basis for right and wrong, however, which led theologian Elton Trueblood to claim many years ago that we live like cut flowers—with Christian blooms but no roots.

Finally, there is widespread belief in life after death. Just what this means to the individual is not clear. Perhaps it is just wishful thinking.

The Implications for Christian Communication

Most people in the Western world are at –7 or perhaps –6 in their decision process. The goal always is to move them close to decision as God, through the ministry of conviction, gives understanding and motivation through the Christian's witness. There clearly is no need to establish the existence of only one God, a fact which would not be true in the polytheistic world of Asia.[22] Those who have some background in Christianity by and large accept this point. Furthermore, most seem to grasp that the world will change only as people change. But how will this take place? Apparently faith has been shaken in education (and also in governmental action according to many published polls). It all comes down to the individual. So, will the answers be found in meditation, psychiatry, Christianity, or what?

It is the task of the communicator to show that all means of self change apart from Christianity ultimately are fruitless, even though they may be helpful for a period of time. Many surveys have shown, for instance, that the recovery rate of those who undergo psychiatric treatment does not differ much from the rate experienced by those who do not have treatment. The necessity is to explore the options, assess their premises and outcomes, and show that there is no real promise of lasting change apart from a personal relationship with Jesus Christ.

Now this brings us to the whole question of Jesus and His uniqueness. Most are fuzzy on this point, but it will not suffice just to launch into a prolonged apologetic on this subject. Certainly the historic facts about Christ and His life must be established, but it is more important to show how He and He alone is relevant to basic needs and motivations. This point was made in Chapter 5. Remember that existing beliefs must be challenged and shown to be in error in light of Christianity. Happiness does not come through accumulation of wealth, for example. Such a belief is out of accord with biblical reality, and that needs to be made clear. The best way to do this, in turn, is through personal testimony, because credibility is always enhanced when truth can be observed in another's life. The conclusion, then, is that change ". . . occurs when faulty ideas or beliefs are modified or illuminated."[23]

We receive further evidence that true religious belief is not held by most people through lack of religious behavior. While religion may have some conceptual importance, it is not demonstrated by practice. This simply verifies Stark and Glock's point that knowledge or understanding in and of itself says little about the saliency of belief.

---

[22]Viggo Søgaard has provided helpful insights into witness practices under polytheism. See *Everything You Need to Know for a Cassette Ministry* (Minneapolis: Bethany Fellowship, 1975), chs. 3 and 6.

[23]Victory Raimy, *Misunderstandings of the Self* (San Francisco: Jossey-Bass, 1975), p. 4.

Saliency is verified through evidence of religious practice, experience, and effects in daily life.[24]

Once beliefs have been changed, attitude toward the act of accepting Christ should shift positively. If it does not, then it is clear that the individual has yet to grasp the implications of the gospel. Intention to act can also be helped by the encouragement of personal evangelism, but, ultimately only God can activate intention through the ministry of conviction. It is here that we must patiently allow God to perform this role and not to encourage a premature decision. More will be said about this in a later section of the chapter.

CHANGING BELIEFS AND ATTITUDES

Now that the general principles have been established, what strategies can be followed to change beliefs which, in turn, should lead to corresponding changes in attitude, intention, and behavior? The starting point is the determination of objectives. Then it is possible to discuss strategies, and, for this purpose, it will be necessary to delve into the literature on persuasion. This literature, by the way, is enormous. McGuire cited over 800 studies in his review of the evidence published up until 1967,[25] and Fishbein and Ajzen reviewed 790 articles published between 1968 and 1970.[26] Fortunately, there has been less interest in this field since that high-water mark,[27] but the scope of relevant material still is staggering.

Rather than review the evidence in great detail, we can exercise wise selectivity. First of all, there are good reviews of the available literature for the interested reader.[28] Even more important, the author's colleague at Wheaton, Em Griffin, has written a superb little volume on the subject of persuasion entitled *The Mind Changers.*[29] It would be a tall order to improve on what Griffin has done, so we will only highlight some of the principles that appear to have the greatest application in Christian communication.

---

[24]Glock and Stark, *Religion and Society in Tension.*

[25]William J. McGuire, "The Nature of Attitudes and Attitude Change," in Gardner Lindsey and Eliot Aronsen, eds., *Handbook of Social Psychology* (Reading, Mass.: Addison-Wesley, 1968), pp. 136-314.

[26]Fishbein and Ajzen, *Belief, Attitude, Intention, Behavior.*

[27]See Charles A. Kiesler and Paul A. Munson, "Attitudes and Opinions," in *Annual Review of Psychology,* ed. M.R. Rosenzweig and Lyman Porter, vol. 26 (Palo Alto, Ca.: Annual Reviews Inc., 1975), pp. 415-456.

[28]For example, see Engel, Blackwell, and Kollat, *Consumer Behavior,* ch. 16.

[29]Em Griffin, *The Mind Changers* (Wheaton, Ill.: Tyndale, 1976).

Setting Communication Goals

The purpose here is not to specify the number who will accept Christ, join the church, or engage in any other terminal act in the decision process. Rather, it is to state the form and content of communication goals—i.e., those goals pertaining to changes in beliefs and attitudes.

The most important thing is to describe in specific terms what will happen in the life of the other person if communication goals have been reached. In other words, what will he or she be able to say and do after exposure to a message or a series of messages?[30]

Assume that forty-five percent of those surveyed agreed that Jesus Christ was more than a mere man and that He was God. Obviously, it would be desirable to increase this percentage. Probably it becomes arbitrary to state an exact quantitative change, but here is an example of a well-stated goal:

> To increase the number of those who agree that Jesus is God in response to a questionnaire from forty-five percent to sixty-five percent.

Such a goal makes quite clear what is to be done, and it presents a *measurable* target. The usual tendency is to state goals with such fuzziness that no one ever can be sure that they have been attained. Here is just one example: "to make people aware of the divinity of Jesus Christ." How many were aware of this truth at the outset? How will we know if we have been successful? How much change is felt to be desirable?

Goals arise quite naturally, then, from research on knowledge and beliefs. When these levels are found to be deficient in such areas as Jesus and His message and the authenticity of the Bible, it is here that communication should be targeted. The amount of change one can expect varies, depending upon receptivity of the audience. Also, the larger the available finances, the greater the effort that can be put forth. But there is no easy formula to follow in determining how much change should result from a given level of effort.

Goals also should be set for each area of verified felt need. Referring to Chapter 5, the general intent is to change the belief structure underlying a statement of need so that beliefs are brought into

[30]An excellent source is Robert F. Mager, *Preparing Instructional Objectives* (Belmont, Ca.: Fearon Publishers, 1972). Also see James F. Engel, Hugh G. Wales, and Martin R. Warshaw, *Promotional Strategy*, 3rd ed. (Homewood, Ill.: Richard D. Irwin, 1975), ch. 9.

accord with biblical reality. Assume that one target audience is made up of those over thirty-five who are in the midst of mid-life crisis manifested through such stated needs as "finding purpose on my job," "learning to communicate with my kids," "restoring romance to my marriage," and so on. It will be necessary to pry beneath the surface to find the underlying belief. Perhaps marriage is felt to be a problem because of the erroneous belief that sexual love will provide a permanent marriage bond. Here the communicator has the obligation to relate the truth of Christian love (agape love) in the context of marriage and show that real marital happiness is not possible without a relationship with Christ. Such a goal might be stated in this way:

> After a period of six months, thirty percent of those in the target audience will be able to articulate the meaning of Christian love when asked by a questionnaire and state that the acceptance of Christ is a viable answer to marriage problems.

The purpose is to relate a Christian answer to the problem in such a way that it is both grasped and articulated by those within the target audience. By the way, it is an impossibility to achieve this result with everyone; therefore, it always will be only a portion of the total who can be reached in this way.

Further discussion of goal setting is reserved for Chapter 13, at which time an example of a complete evangelistic and discipleship program will be presented. But this brief discussion at least provides the reader with a grasp of the principles to be followed.

Determination of the Message

Now it makes sense to examine some possible strategies to follow in message design. Before jumping in too deeply, however, it is necessary to state one of the most well established communication principles: *The probability of change in beliefs is directly proportional to the credibility of the source or sender.*[31] What this says, of course, is that Christians can make use of satellites, network television, gospel blimps, door-to-door visitation of every home, literature saturation, or any other conceivable strategy and *totally fail* if people lack confidence in their credibility.

Credibility is not determined by words—it is determined by the

[31] Literally hundreds of citations could be given. For example, see Alice Tybout, "Relative Effectiveness of Three Behavioral Influence Strategies as Supplements to Persuasion in a Marketing Context," *Journal of Marketing Research*, vol. 15 (May, 1978), pp. 229–242.

life we live individually and corporately. If people do not see the church as being a viable alternative for their life-style, it will do little good to argue to the contrary. Rather, the church will have to demonstrate that viability. This is a foundational rationale for the emphasis in this book on the need for church revitalization prior to grand schemes of evangelistic strategy. What more can be said than to repeat this point again and again? To borrow an advertising principle: No amount of promotion will ever succeed in building repeat purchase of a product that people for some reason do not want. The strategy starts with product change.

Overcoming Resistance to Persuasion. It has been well established in earlier chapters that people resist change in strongly held beliefs. A frontal attack on their beliefs is a virtual guarantee of a closed filter. Two distinct areas of research in social psychology shed some light on this problem.

Jack Brehm has said some very practical things in his writings on the theory of psychological reactance.[32] The theory is a simple one based on the concept of free choice. If someone restricts our freedom of action, we react negatively, and lost alternatives become even more attractive. This negative response is referred to as reactance, and it has been found to increase in proportion to the extent of free behavior that is being eliminated.

The relevance of this theory for persuasion lies in the fact that it calls the *hard sell* strategy into question. Some leaders train would-be evangelists to counter every objection that might be expressed with just another biblical appeal. How is this different from a high pressure pitch of a used car salesman who won't take no for an answer? Most of us resent being trapped in this way, and such an approach certainly does not represent love for another person. In reality it is nothing more than spiritual brainwashing. As Joe Bayly said, Jesus always presented His case but was willing to let the other person go without manipulation.[33]

Now, shifting gears slightly, what happens when we encounter someone who does not appear to be open to the gospel and, in effect, hit that person over the head with the message anyway? Some writers steeped in another psychological school of thought, the theory of cognitive dissonance, advocate this as the best approach.[34]

---

[32]Jack W. Brehm, *A Theory of Psychological Reactance* (New York: Academic Press, 1966).

[33] Joe Bayly, *Out of My Mind* (Wheaton, Ill.: Tyndale, 1970), pp. 86–89.

[34]See Jack W. Brehm, and Arthur R. Cohen, *Explorations in Cognitive Dissonance* (New York: Wiley, 1962).

The argument is that a confrontational approach will bring about a state of conflict or dissonance between a person's beliefs and message content, and the assumption is that the only option is to change the belief to restore a sense of balance. In other words, the more the message deviates from the individual's present belief, the greater the probability of change.[35]

Now this can be very appealing to some evangelists. If the person disagrees with the gospel message, their theory is to let him have it with both barrels. They show him that the consequence of rejection is eternal damnation, and they do it in the most dogmatic of terms. Now this is not to say that eternal consequences should not be stressed; the question lies in how it should be done. The confrontational approach will work under certain circumstances, but carefully note the prerequisite conditions: (1) the person must not be ego-involved with his or her present belief,[36] and (2) the person sending the message must have high credibility.[37] If, on the other hand, the recipient feels strongly about present beliefs and the evangelist is not perceived as trustworthy, the best choice is to run for the door and hope it is open. It is doubtful that anything positive will happen.

Sherif and his colleagues have suggested a winsome alternative to confrontation.[38] It is their theory that the extent of ego involvement is indicated by the degree to which a person will tolerate or accept a position on an issue that is different from his own along a scale of belief. This range of acceptable positions is referred to as the *latitude of acceptance,* and those felt to be unacceptable fall into the *latitude of rejection.* To the extent that ego involvement and corresponding resistance to change is present, the latitude of rejection will be large and the latitude of acceptance small.

The meaning of all this for communication strategy lies in the finding that beliefs change only when the message is designed in such a way that it falls at the outer edge of the latitude of accep-

[35]See, for example, Philip Zimbardo, "Involvement and Communication Discrepancy as Determinants of Opinion Conformity," *Journal of Abnormal and Social Psychology,* vol. 60 (1960), pp. 86–94.

[36]For a pertinent illustration see Frederick W.F. Winter, "A Laboratory Experiment of Individual Attitude Response to Advertising Exposure," *Journal of Marketing Research,* vol. 10 (May, 1973), pp. 130–140.

[37]This literature is thoroughly reviewed in Brian Sternthal, "Persuasion and the Mass Communication Process," (Ph.D. dissertation, Ohio State University, 1972), ch. 4.

[38]C.W. Sherif, M. Sherif, and R.E. Nebergall, *Attitude and Attitude Change* (New Haven, Conn.: Yale University Press, 1961).

tance.[39] If this is exceeded, then we have stepped over into confrontation once again with all the negative responses that usually will result.

Here is a possible example of how this might be applied. Let it be assumed that there are eight possible viewpoints one might take with respect to Jesus Christ that fall on a scale as follows:

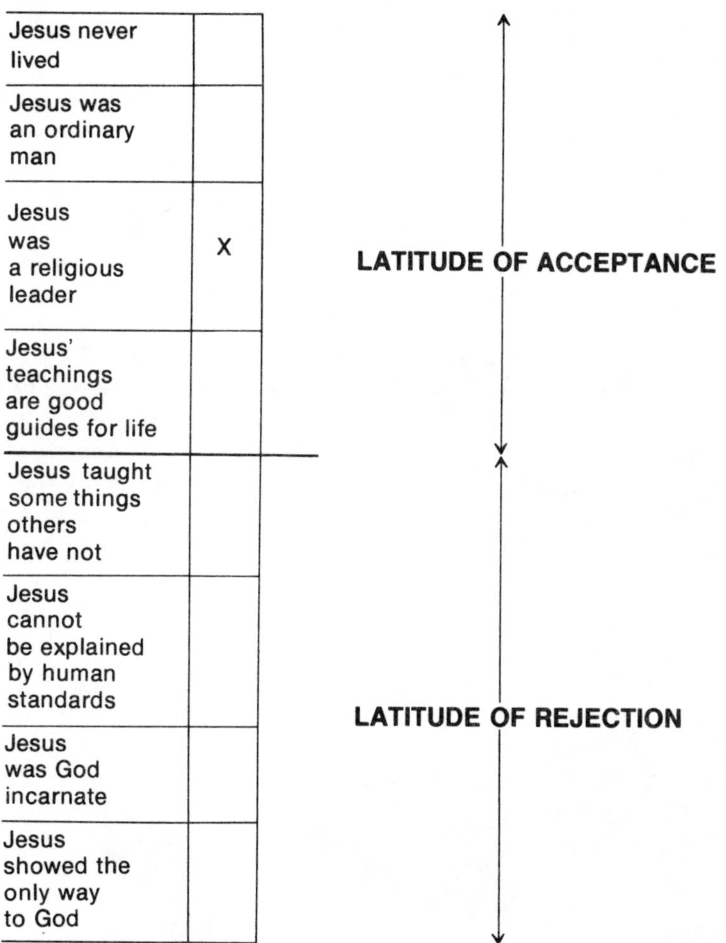

[39]This is the basic tenet of belief change stressed by Fishbein and Ajzen, *Belief, Attitude, Intention and Behavior*, ch. 11. Also see H. Johnson, "Some Effects of Discrepancy Level on Responses to Negative Information About One's Self," *Sociometry*, vol. 29 (1966), pp. 52–66; and J. Whittaker, "Opinion Change as a Function of Communication-Attitude Discrepancy," *Psychological Reports*, vol. 13 (1963), pp. 763–772.

Notice that the person believes that Jesus was a religious leader and also seems receptive to the claim that Jesus gave some teachings that are useful guides for life. Anything beyond that position, however, falls into the latitude of rejection and will be screened out. Therefore, the message should reaffirm that Jesus did offer useful teachings. The hope is that the individual will change his or her belief to that position on the scale. Later, the latitudes of acceptance and rejection may shift again in the direction of accepting the truth that Jesus is the only way to God.

This type of strategy demands an extended time perspective. It recognizes that people often do not change all at once but in discrete steps over time. Therefore, the communicator is content to bring about a small change today and at future points in the expectation that patience will pay off in ultimate acceptance of the full truth.

What this comes down to is that hard sell and confrontation are dangerous strategies. Usually a much better approach is to start with genuine empathy for other persons, even if they are wrong in what they believe. Be content to identify with them where they are and move from there patiently, realizing that change often is slow. The final outcome, however, is likely to be much more positive.

Variations in Message Content and Structure. There are various strategies that might be followed in message design, and it is helpful to review research on use of (1) humor, (2) guilt, (3) fear, (4) statement of a conclusion, and (5) repetition.

(1) Humor. During the 1950s and 1960s commercial persuaders were reluctant to make much use of humor on the pretext that it can overwhelm the main message.[40] For example, recall tests often show that the humor is remembered while the central point is missed entirely. While this always is a danger, there has been less reluctance in recent years.

In the first place, the humorous message really can excel in terms of attention attraction.[41] It can break through the "noise level," so to speak, and that is a real benefit. Furthermore, humor has been found to enhance source credibility, something the religious communicator certainly can benefit from.

[40]See, for example, David Ogilvy, "Raise Your Sights! 97 Tips for Copywriters, Art Directors and TV Producers—Mostly Derived From Research" (internal publication, Ogilvy & Mather, Inc.).

[41]The literature on humor is reviewed by Brian Sternthal and C. Samuel Craig, "Humor in Advertising," *Journal of Marketing*, vol. 37 (October, 1973), pp. 12–18.

Here are some clues to the successful use of humor:

1. Make sure it is not directed against the audience. Rather it should poke fun at the communicator or at some neutral object.[42]
2. The main point of the message must be made clear at the very outset, or there is the danger that humor will overwhelm that point.[43]
3. The type of humor makes a difference. Subtlety is more effective than the bizarre.
4. Humor must be relevant to the central idea, because both recall and persuasive effect are diminished when this link is not established. For a particularly appropriate use of humor in this sense, refer to the Stan Freeburg radio spot in Figure 5.2.

Just one more thing should be said. From more than twenty years of experience, the author has found that students and others with little practical background are too prone to use humor. It takes great skill to make something really funny without detracting from the main point. For the most part, it should be utilized with considerable caution.

(2) Guilt. It should come as no surprise to learn that research has documented the role that appeal to guilt can have in stimulating people to do what they normally would not do.[44] This can lead the more extreme evangelists to have a field day. "You are a no good sinner!" "Keep up your filthy ways and you will end up in hell!" And away we go.

Certainly the eternal consequences of refusing to accept Christ are crystal clear, and no presentation of the gospel can avoid that truth. But should this be the main appeal? There are several dangers. First, it can bring about surface compliance without real inner commitment. Yes, there may be some type of external act, such as stating a prayer, but a real internal change is something else again. Furthermore, it can seriously damage personal relationships. Most of us avoid someone who has made us defensive, and that is exactly what

---

[42]Griffin, *The Mind Changers,* pp. 54–57.

[43]Harold L. Ross, Jr., "How to Create Effective Humorous Commercials, Yielding Above Average Brand Preference Changes," *Marketing News* (March 26, 1976), p. 4.

[44]See Griffin, *The Mind Changers,* ch. 5. Also, J.E. Carlsmith and A.E. Gross, "Some Effects of Guilt on Compliance," *Journal of Personality and Social Psychology,* vol. 11 (1969), pp. 232–239.

guilt can do. The possibility of continued witness, then, can be jeopardized.

On the whole, the message of the gospel is a positive one. The core truth is that God loves us and that He sent His Son not to condemn the world but to point the way to eternal life. Begin with the positive, and the long run prospects of successful communication are greatly enhanced. Then the cost of rejection of the gospel can be stressed without raising undue barriers.

(3) Fear. Em Griffin vividly relates the story of how Jonathan Edwards scared people in his famous sermon entitled "Sinners in the Hands of an Angry God":

> Edwards pictured his eighteenth-century hearers as writhing spiders, dangling over the fiery pit of hell. God would contemptuously crush them under his feet so that their blood would splatter against the walls of the pit. To say that people felt fear is an understatement. Edwards literally scared them into heaven.[45]

This is a classic example of the "fear appeal," an approach to persuasion that has received more research than any other since it first was investigated seriously in 1953.[46] Sometimes this approach works spectacularly as it did with Edwards, and other times just the opposite occurs. What are the factors at work here?

First of all, and probably most important, a fear appeal works *only* in the hands of a highly credible communicator.[47] Jonathan Edwards was the great Christian scholar of his day, and his fame was widespread. The Christian who tells the person seated next to him on an airplane that he or she is going to go to hell unless he or she accepts Jesus Christ usually will not be regarded so highly, and the Christian is likely to be greeted by a stony stare or something more violent. This fact, in itself, should cause most of us to go easy.

Research to date also shows that both too little and too much fear lack persuasive impact; the measure of fear should fall somewhere in between these extremes. If danger is understated, the recipient

---

[45]Griffin, *The Mind Changers,* p. 67.

[46]There have been some really useful reviews of this literature. See K. Higbeen, "Fifteen Years of Fear Arousal: Research on Threat Appeals: 1953–1968," *Psychological Bulletin,* vol. 72 (1960), pp. 426–444; I. Janis, *The Contours of Fear* (New York: John Wiley & Sons, 1968); and Brian Sternthal and C. Samuel Craig, "Fear Appeals: Revisited and Revised," *Journal of Consumer Research,* vol. 1 (December, 1974), pp. 22–34.

[47]The studies on fear and source credibility are reviewed in Sternthal, "Persuasion and the Mass Communication Process," ch. 5.

will fail to grasp the impact. If it is stated too strongly, on the other hand, the response can be either one of avoidance or of fright, which generates virtual inaction. Also, fear may fail to have the desired effect if the other person does not see the personal consequences for his or her life.

Griffin suggests that fear of eternal separation from God can be a potent motivation if the person has already had knowledge of and some involvement with the person of Jesus Christ.[48] Otherwise it is pretty much an empty threat. In other words, the person must see that the consequences being threatened have a good chance of coming true and are undesirable. Therefore, this type of fear appeal, if it is to be used at all, is most appropriate for those at stages –4 or –3 in their decision process. Prior to that point, the message stands a good chance of being screened out as lacking both in credibility and personal applicability. But Griffin wisely raises the caution flag once again:

> As Christians . . . we need to use this persuasive technique carefully. We don't want to call men to Christ only to have them live in perpetual fear. "For God did not give us a spirit of timidity, but a spirit of power and love and self-control" (2 Timothy 1:7).[49]

(4) Statement of a Conclusion. With a sophisticated audience, it is sometimes best to design a message in such a way that the conclusion is stated only implicitly. Often such an approach achieves superior effects over time.[50] This really goes back to the reactance theory discussed earlier. Recall that Brehm and others have found that many people react negatively if they feel "fenced in." When this happens, initial beliefs may be solidified.[51] So there are times when it is best to let the audience come to its own conclusion after the issues have been clearly presented.

(5) Repetition. The benefits of repetition is a fundamental tenet of learning theory. Most authorities agree that it is beneficial to repeat a persuasive message on the assumption that the effect will be cumulative.[52] But a point can be reached where too much repetition leads to

---

[48]Griffin, *The Mind Changers,* p. 73.

[49]*Ibid.,* p. 77.

[50]See, for example, Arthur Cohen, *Attitude Change and Social Influence* (New York: Basic Books, 1964), p. 10.

[51]Brehm, ch. 6.

[52]For an excellent review see Andrew A. Mitchell and Jerry C. Olson, "Cognitive Effects of Advertising Repetition" (Working Paper, no. 49, College of Business Administration, Pennsylvania State University, October, 1976). Also Engel, Blackwell, and Kollat, *Consumer Behavior,* pp. 427–435.

a boomerang effect referred to as *semantic satiation.*[53] Here are some of the main implications of research on this subject:[54]

1. Repetition aids learning and hence is useful at the start of a new message campaign.
2. A pool or group of messages should not wear out (lose effectiveness or satiate) as quickly as a single message.
3. Whenever possible, introduce variations into message structure.
4. A message with humor or a single point wears out more quickly.
5. The greater the time span between repetition, the longer a message can be run.
6. Message wearout on television is greatest among heavy viewers.
7. When budgets are limited, a single message spread out over a period of time may produce greater learning than a pool of messages.
8. Only a good message wears out—those that are ineffective to begin with lose nothing.

The reader should be cautioned that most of the research on this subject centers on the learning of a slogan, nonsense syllable, or some other short message. Under such conditions, repetition can help. However, can repetition be an effective evangelistic strategy? Perhaps it might be if the gospel is reduced to slogans, but the author's disdain for such approaches has been made clear earlier. Perhaps the best conclusion is that a single exposure may not produce the desired effect. Repetition, then, can be helpful. But to move toward a highly repetitive campaign on television or other media centering on one Christian slogan or theme lowers media evangelism to the level of promotional campaigns for detergents or packaged drugs.

Changes in Beliefs and Attitudes Following Decision. While it is valid to undertake communication strategy to change behavior through changed beliefs and attitudes, the reverse also can take place.[55] In

[53]Harriett Amster, "Semantic Satiation and Generation: Learning? Adaptation?" *Psychological Bulletin,* vol. 62 (1964), pp. 273–286.

[54]A. Greenberg and C. Suttoni, "Television Commercial Wearout," *Journal of Advertising Research,* vol. 13 (1973), p. 53.

[55]See Judson Mills, "Changes in Moral Attitudes Following Temptation," *Journal of Personality,* vol. 26 (1958), pp. 517–531; and Ted Ward, "Fuzzy Fables or Communications That Count," *Christian Communications Spectrum,* vol. 1 (1975), p. 10ff.

fact, a true grasp of Christian doctrine is an impossibility until one has received Christ (1 Cor. 3). Furthermore, one would expect attitude toward the act of accepting Christ to become even more positive following experience of the new birth. This is pointed out here only to affirm that changes in belief and attitudes can either precede or follow behavior.

The Quest for Decision Rules. Some readers may be disappointed that no formulae have been presented in this chapter. The reason for that lies in the fact that the state of knowledge on persuasion in general and Christian communication in particular makes it impossible to advance ironclad generalizations. Consider Fishbein's assessment of the state of the art:

> . . . at this time despite an incredible amount of research on this problem, we are still in the position of almost total ignorance. There is not a single generalization that can be made about the influence of source, message, channel, or audience effects on persuasion . . . the traditional approach to communication has also been more harmful than helpful.[56]

There is truth in this assessment, but such a negative outlook is not warranted. Even though definitive decision rules are not available, the evidence such as that cited here gives insights into *certain approaches that might work under certain circumstances.* This is most worthwhile in and of itself.

It is doubtful that there ever will be definitive rules of persuasion, because when so-called rules become established, someone comes along and successfully breaks them.[57] Consider the words of the eminent advertising analyst Harry W. McMahan in this context:

> Examples can help. Guidelines can help. But rules often lead the advertising novice astray. In our 20,000 commercials we can disprove almost any "rule." Why? Because, for one thing, different product fields require different handling in communication and persuasion. . . . It is this difference in market position and the difference in product fields that make most "rules" inapplicable to all advertising.[58]

Decisions are always made on three bases: (1) experience, (2) intuition and creativity, and (3) research. None is sufficient by itself.

---

[56]Fishbein, "Attitude, Attitude Change, and Behavior," in Levine, *Attitude Research,* p. 10.

[57]For one recent example, see Arthur Bellaire, "Bellaire Survey IV Finds Trend Away From Tried-and-True in TV Commercial Techniques," *Advertising Age* (January 2, 1978), pp. 17–18.

[58]Harry W. McMahan, "Advertising: Some Things You Can't Teach—and Some You Can," *Advertising Age* (November 8, 1976), p. 56.

A blind reliance on so-called rules would short-circuit any expression of creativity, to say nothing of the leadership of the Holy Spirit, and would lead to rejection of sound research data.

What this all comes down to, of course, is that evangelism is not done by formula. The sooner the church grasps this fact and moves away from its reliance on rigid methods, the better. Perhaps a good starting point is to declare a moratorium on all methods until they have been shown, through valid research, to produce the intended effects on the audience. The days of unverified assumption have long since departed.

A WORD ON SPIRITUAL BRAINWASHING

One cannot complete a discussion of methods of persuasion without raising the very real danger that the methods used will have a manipulative effect on the audience. Manipulation occurs when use is made of *"Any persuasive effort which restricts another's freedom to choose for or against Jesus Christ."*[59]

One form of manipulation, and a disturbingly common one, is the use of outright deception. That's right—deception is not the exclusive property of the advertiser or salesman. What about evangelists who present only the positive side of the gospel without articulating the moral and ethical demands? "Accept Jesus and You Will Be Happy," so the refrain goes. In and of itself, such a claim is not false, but it is only a half truth. People are attracted to the Savior for the wrong reasons, and it is small wonder that North American churches seem to be full of relatively contented believers, going on with the "American way of life" as usual. They have never really heard anything to the contrary. False and misleading advertising is governed by the Federal Trade Commission and state regulatory agencies. Who ever raises a voice against false and misleading evangelism?

Another form of manipulation lies in the whole set of devices employed to induce someone to "come forward" or undertake some other type of coerced overt behavior. The choir sings "Just as I Am" for the fourteenth time; the evangelist says, "This may be the last chance you have"; counselors rise in large numbers giving the impression of a mass movement; friends use subtle pressure on the

---

[59]Griffin, *The Mind Changers,* p. 28.

nonbeliever, and so on. Yes, people can be induced to act, but what does it all mean in the long run if this is an action they would not have taken of their own free will without the use of such devices?

Every reader could give glaring examples of methods used, to be quite frank, to "close the sale." We would scream quite loudly if business were to do the same thing, but somehow the end presumably justifies such means in evangelism. Or does it? We had better consider the words of the apostle Paul on this point:

> . . . we use no clever tricks, no dishonest manipulation of the Word of God. We speak the plain truth. . . . For it is Christ Jesus as Lord whom we preach, not ourselves; we are your servants for Jesus' sake. . . . This priceless treasure we hold, so to speak, in common earthenware—to show that the splendid power of it belongs to God and not us (2 Cor. 4:2–7, Phillips).

To cite Paul's words once again, ". . . our exhortation does not come from error or impurity or by way of deceit; but just as we have been approved by God to be entrusted with the gospel, so we speak, not as pleasing men but God . . ." (1 Thess. 2:3,4, NASB).

We are justified to make use of any insight from the behavioral sciences, persuasion, advertising, and so on; but every action will be judged by these rigorous biblical standards. The end clearly does not justify audience manipulation when God's Word is used as the guideline.

CHAPTER 9
Decision

He is referred to as a "soul-winning phenomenon." Having "led" over 8,000 to Christ in just a few years, this Christian dynamo (we'll just refer to him as Dick) has been written up in several Christian magazines. His methods are interesting, to say the least. For example, he claims to witness as often as he can when he is stopped at a red light, and he reports seeing as many as three people in one car pray to receive Christ before the light turns green. There even have been times when he has led as many as 200 to Christ in a given day through all kinds of methods.

One could argue, with some justification, that the church needs more people like Dick who care enough to share the good news aggressively. But many readers are feeling some uneasiness right now. First of all, most of us will never see such results because we do not have the gift of evangelism. But, more seriously, the thoughtful reader cannot help questioning just what these so-called "decisions" really mean in light of our emphasis on spiritual decision process. Do people really become born again when a total stranger in the car next to them explains the gospel, through traffic noise, in about thirty seconds? What about Dick's keeping such detailed statistics. How does this differ from a salesman's call report?

The purpose here certainly is not to disparage Dick and others like him but rather to examine in depth the real meaning of the last stage in the decision process—acceptance of Christ through repentance and faith. We are assuming, of course, that the process has taken its normal course through need activation, search for information, and formation and change of beliefs and attitudes—those stages discussed in the preceding chapters in this unit.

The focus, then, is on audience response from stages –3 to –1 in the decision model reproduced once again in Figure 9.1. There now is a wealth of research on conversion undertaken by specialists from a variety of academic perspectives, but it will soon become apparent that all of this evidence has only added marginally to the teachings of Scripture, which are crystal clear on this subject. The issue of greatest importance is the appropriateness of evangelistic strategies such as those described above. What is the role of Christian witness at this culminating phase of the process? Most of those who have taken evangelism seriously will agree that it is time for some rethinking.

Next, the very fact that a decision has been made gives rise to the critical question of the outcomes of that decision. What happens once the person has time to reflect on the step taken (stage +1)? What are the proofs that this decision was valid? The factors to be examined in this context are incorporation into the church (stage +2) and the onset of conceptual and behavioral growth (stage +3).

RESEARCH ON RELIGIOUS CONVERSION

Religious conversion has become quite a popular subject among social scientists in the past decade in particular, and the journals bulge with research on this topic.[1] No one has ever really improved on the definition given by William James at the turn of the century:

> . . . the process, gradual or sudden, by which the self hitherto divided and consciously wrong, inferior and unhappy becomes unified and consciously right, superior and happy in consequence of its firmer hold upon religious realities.[2]

One of the very first empirical studies was undertaken at about that same time by Starbuck who centered his inquiry on a whole series of

[1]Among the most useful sources are Jacques Waardenburg, *Classical Approaches to the Study of Religion: Aims, Methods, and Theories of Research* (The Hague: Moeton, vol. 1 published in 1973 and vol. 2 in 1974); J.E. Dittes, "Psychology of Religion," in Gardner Lindzey and Eliot Aronsen, eds., *Handbook of Social Psychology,* vol. 5 (Reading, Mass.: Addison-Wesley, 1969), pp. 602–659; and Geoffrey E.W. Scobie, *Psychology of Religion* (New York: Wiley, 1975).

[2]William James, *The Varieties of Religious Experience* (London: Longmans, 1902), p. 114.

FIGURE 9.1.

The Spiritual Decision Process With Focus on Stages −3 to +3

	−8	Awareness of Supreme Being
Proclamation ↓	−7	Some Knowledge of Gospel
	−6	Knowledge of Fundamentals of Gospel
	−5	Grasp of Personal Implications of Gospel
	−4	Positive Attitude Toward Act of Becoming a Christian
Call for Decision ↓	−3	Problem Recognition and Intention to Act
	−2	Decision to Act
	−1	Repentance and Faith in Christ
		NEW CREATURE
Follow Up ↓	+1	Post-Decision Evaluation
	+2	Incorporation Into Church
	+3	Conceptual and Behavioral Growth

changes in character ranging from "evil to goodness, from sinfulness to righteousness, and from indifference to spiritual insight and activity."[3]

Most of the research falls into three broad categories: (1) psychological, (2) sociological, and (3) physiological. Virtually without exception, attempts are made to explain conversion by natural processes in complete disregard of the supernatural. Therefore, it is

[3]E.D. Starbuck, *The Psychology of Religion* (New York: Charles Scribner and Sons, 1901).

vitally important to conclude this brief review by restating what Scripture has to say on the subject, a source considered to be irrelevant by most behavioral scientists.

The Psychological Perspective

Psychologists have put forth several basic reasons why people turn to religion. The first reason, and probably the most important, is to overcome some type of deprivation.[4] In other words, something is missing and religion compensates for it. Physical or economic threat is often found to be the underlying factor.[5] In other cases psychological need is the determining consideration, such as turning to religion to reduce the traumatic effects of high manifest anxiety[6] or to find happiness.[7]

Others have found that religion helps in the process of personality integration. Conversion, for example, has been found to strengthen a weak ego.[8] Others seem to feel that this is a normal part of the maturation process in which the individual is striving to establish a viable world view[9] and to reaffirm and integrate existing values.[10]

One of the most perplexing explanations centers around resolution of an oedipus complex. According to this perspective, conversion presumably alters perception of one's actual father as being weak or ineffective by supplying a strong and principled substitute parental figure with clear values and firm judgments.[11] Religion thus will serve as an aid in adolescence by countering longings to retain or reestablish a union with the maternal figure. Well, moving right on. . . .

---

[4]This seems to be the perspective of Glock and Stark in their important survey studies. See Charles Y. Glock and Rodney Stark, *Religion and Society in Tension* (Chicago: Rand McNally, 1965).

[5]Stephen M. Sales, "Economic Threat as a Determinant of Conversion Rates in Authoritarian and Non-Authoritarian Churches," *Journal of Personality and Social Psychology,* vol. 23 (1972), pp. 420–428.

[6]Charles M. Spellman, Glen D. Baskett, and Donn Byrne, "Manifest Anxiety as a Contributing Factor in Religious Conversion," *Journal of Consulting Clinical Psychology,* vol. 36 (April, 1971), pp. 245–247.

[7]W.P. Wilson, "Mental Health Benefits of Religious Salvation," *Diseases of the Nervous System,* vol. 33 (1972), pp. 382–386.

[8]Gerda E. Allison, "Psychiatric Implications of Religious Conversion," *Canadian Psychiatric Association Journal,* vol. 12 (1967), pp. 55–61.

[9]This is the position taken by Starbuck, *The Psychology of Religion,* p. 73.

[10]Ronald C. Wimberley, Thomas C. Hood, C.M. Lipsey, Donald Clelland, and Marguerite Hay, "Conversion in a Billy Graham Crusade: Spontaneous Event or Ritual Performance?" *Sociological Quarterly,* vol. 16 (Spring, 1975), pp. 162–170.

[11]Joel Allison, "Adaptive Regression and Intensive Religious Experiences," *Journal of Nervous Mental Disease,* vol. 145 (1967), pp. 452–463.

Decision

Coming down from those psychiatric heavenlies, it is interesting to note that the many research efforts attempting to document a relationship between religious belief and personality have largely been fruitless.[12] One of the leaders in this inquiry was forced to the conclusion that religious belief is largely a cognitive activity acquired and sustained by social influences but independent of personality.[13]

The Sociological Perspective

Religious behavior never is solely explained by psychological factors, because religion also is a social activity. Acceptance of a particular set of beliefs may be a totally normal part of the socialization process. Church membership is sought, therefore, just because this is the usual behavior of most people.[14]

A second very common reason is accommodation to social pressure.[15] In some cases, friends or relatives may exert conformity pressure, and religion is adopted to avoid being viewed as a deviant.[16] In other cases, friends or relatives are viewed in a sense as opinion leaders, and they play a major role in stimulating at least a positive viewpoint toward the religious action in question. It is interesting in this context to note that the great majority of those who made a response of some type at Billy Graham's Seattle Crusade in 1976 were brought to the meeting by someone else.[17]

The legitimacy of these explanations is affirmed by the common phenomenon of conversion in the form of a "people movement" or group conversion mentioned in earlier chapters.[18] Perhaps even a better term is "multi-individual conversion." Social factors coincide in such a way that a large number make an individual commitment at about the same time for largely the same reasons, and group consen-

---

[12]This research is reviewed in Scobie, *Psychology of Religion,* ch. 5.

[13]L.B. Brown, "The Structure of Religious Belief," *Journal for the Study of Religion,* vol. 15 (1966), pp. 259-272.

[14]Milton Yinger, *The Scientific Study of Religion* (New York: MacMillan, 1970). Also David O. Moberg, *The Church as a Social Institution* (Englewood Cliffs, N.J.: Prentice Hall, 1962).

[15]Michael Argyle and Benjamin Bert-Hallahmi, *The Social Psychology of Religion* (Boston: Routledge and Kegan Paul, 1975), p. 40; and Reginald W. Bibby and Murlen B. Brinkerhoff, "Sources of Religious Involvement: Issues for Future Empirical Investigation," *Review of Religious Research,* vol. 13 (Winter, 1974), pp. 71–78.

[16]Bibby and Brinkerhof, "Sources of Religious Involvement."

[17]Win Arn, "Mass Evangelism—The Bottom Line," *Church Growth: America* (January/February, 1978).

[18]A particularly useful source here is Eugene A. Nida, *Message in Mission* (New York: Harper & Brothers, 1960), ch. 6.

sus is an important consideration. This, of course, is largely seen outside a North American setting.

The Physiological Perspective

Sargant puts forth the theory that normal man is suggestible and can be induced to adopt a nonsensible belief in two ways.[19] The first is to overexcite the nervous system through music, repetition, and so on. The second means is sensory deprivation through mystic contemplation where one idea is in focus in exclusion of others. Both allegedly alter brain function. Sargant apparently would pointedly exclude anything valid in such decisions.

A Biblical Perspective on Conversion

If the reader finds some of the above theorizing a bit difficult to take, consider the dilemma of the author who pored over the output of a computerized search of *Psychological Abstracts* and many other sources as well. Some of these explanations, of course, are relevant, especially the deprivation hypothesis and the sociological theories. They do explain certain aspects of conversion, but it is mostly done in human terms without reference to any divine intervention in the process. The Bible states flatly that this anti-supernatural bias is grossly in error, "For it is by grace you have been saved, through faith—and this not from yourselves, it is the gift of God—not by works, so that no one can boast. For we are God's workmanship . . ." (Eph. 2:8–10, NIV).

Deprivation, psychological integration, and social influence all help explain why people turn to religion in the first place and, with specific reference to Christianity, shed some light on why people arrive at a positive attitude toward the act of accepting Christ. But no light is shed whatsoever on the remaining steps in the process. It is important to note that becoming a Christian is vastly different from becoming a member of other religious bodies, because man, by himself, cannot take this step. Christ has made this perfectly clear. He said, "You did not choose me, but I chose you . . ." (John 15:16, NIV). Mankind, in short, is chosen and called by God according to His sovereign will (Eph. 1:11–13).

Next, problem recognition and intention to act (stage –3) cannot occur without the ministry of the Holy Spirit who ". . . will convict

[19]William Sargant, "The Physiology of Faith," *British Journal of Psychiatry,* vol. 115 (1969), pp. 505–518.

the world concerning sin, and righteousness, and judgment" (John 16:8, NASB). Problem recognition is a sense of intolerable discomfort that compels the individual to make a choice. He or she has sufficient Christian understanding to grasp that Christ must be taken seriously when He claims that He is, ". . . the way—and the truth and the life," and that "No one comes to the Father except through me" (John 14:6, NIV). The Holy Spirit works to intensify the perceived gap between what is and what might be, thus leading to a firm intention to act one way or another with respect to Christ. No human persuasion enters into this process.

The individual now has the option to accept Christ or to reject Him. While there are some varying theological perspectives on whether or not mankind ultimately is autonomous with respect to choice, free will *does* exist at the point of decision. Those who act positively must first of all, take the step of repentance. This requires an agreement with God's Word that he or she is a sinner (Rom. 3:23), a person imprisoned to self-seeking who can never be pleasing to God and who will ultimately experience spiritual death (Rom. 6:23). Repentance also implies a willingness to seek the ultimate solution to this spiritual dilemma through an act of the will to accept salvation through Jesus Christ (John 3:16).

Once there is agreement with God's assessment of each person's spiritual status, the next step is one of belief. In the words of the apostle Paul, ". . . if you confess with your mouth, 'Jesus is Lord,' and believe in your heart that God raised him from the dead, you will be saved. For it is with your heart that you believe and are justified, and it is with your mouth that you confess and are saved" (Rom 10:9,10, NIV). Belief in this context is more than cognitive assent; it has the connotation of "betting one's life" on the gospel message. This is the sense in which reference is made to the heart, because belief must penetrate to the very core of one's being. A public testimony is verification of the commitment that has been made.

Conversion, then, requires both the motivation and calling of God through the Holy Spirit and an individual act of decision. A person could accept any other religion by his or her own individual choice without this divine intervention. In that sense religious choice, in general, is no different from choice decisions studied in such areas as political science and consumer psychology. It is this broader context in which the research cited earlier must be interpreted, and obviously it is of only limited value in understanding Christian conversion.

CONVERSION AND EVANGELISTIC STRATEGY

Evangelistic strategy as discussed in the previous chapters has centered on proclamation as the only appropriate form of witness at earlier stages of the decision process. Strategy shifts to a call for decision, however, once those in the audience are discovered to be at the stage of problem recognition (–3 in Figure 9.1). Now the great need is to communicate how a spiritual decision is made and to provide gentle encouragement to take that step. This, of course, is evangelism as it is traditionally taught in most orthodox circles. As was mentioned previously, the assumption is made that "people are just waiting to receive Christ if they only knew how." This assumption is true *only* when someone has reached this stage. But once they have, various methods can be employed to "lead that person to Christ."

Leighton Ford has provided an excellent review of the standard evangelistic techniques (examples are the Four Spiritual Laws and the Romans Road). All contain these essential elements in one form or another: (1) God's purpose, (2) man's need, (3) Christ's provision, and (4) man's response.[20] The first three points, of course, summarize the essence of the gospel to verify that the other person truly understands the implications of the action being taken. These have been discussed sufficiently in earlier chapters, but little has been said about the manner in which the response is to be made. Must there be recitation of the so-called "sinner's prayer?" This is an important and controversial question requiring further discussion. Also, it is necessary in this context to examine two additional issues: (1) the motivation for witness and (2) the evangelistic gift.

The Issue of the "Sinner's Prayer"

The author once was conducting a seminar for church leaders from a number of Asian countries. This question was put forth: "How does someone become a Christian?" The answer from one member of the audience was, "You must invite Jesus into your heart." But there was an immediate objection from a member of the contingent from Laos: "No, you must invite Christ into your liver."

Now we had a real dilemma. Probing more deeply the author

[20]Leighton Ford, *Good News Is for Sharing* (Elgin, Ill.: David C. Cook, 1977), ch. 11.

turned back to the one who responded initially and asked why Christ must be invited into the heart. The answer was, "Because it says so in Revelation 3:20." The next question then was, "How do we get Christ into the heart?" "Why through a prayer asking him to come in, of course." Is it heresy, then, to make reference to the liver rather than to the heart? Things almost degenerated to a discussion of human anatomy.

The problem here has its roots in a North American evangelistic strategy that says that some type of overt response is required for another person to accept Christ. Most evangelistic methods dutifully cite Revelation 3:20 as the proof text; this verse says, "Behold, I stand at the door, and knock: if any man hear my voice, and open the door, I will come in to him . . ." (KJV). The necessary response then is to pray a prayer that says, in effect, "Lord Jesus, come into my heart."

The problem with this approach is that it does gross violence to the biblical text. Revelation 3:20 is written to *Christians* only, and Christ is giving an invitation for a degenerate church in Laodicea to be restored to His grace. It says nothing whatsoever to the non-Christian!

Furthermore, there is nothing in Scripture that makes reference to any type of sinner's prayer. Repentance and faith are called for, and nothing else. How one takes this final step is not clearly specified, except for the necessity of the public testimony as mentioned in Romans 10.

Now we can begin to see how absurd the heart and liver issue really is. In a sense, the tribal people in Laos are closer to the truth in what they said, because the liver is viewed by them as the seat of the emotions and will. Therefore, conversion demands a total commitment from within, and it is best expressed in terms of the liver in their context.

Revelation 3:20 and the resultant sinner's prayer probably crept into evangelistic strategy because of the fact that most North Americans are activistic and need to take some overt step. Therefore, a prayer of commitment is valid for many people *living in that context.* The author prayed such a prayer himself in 1965 as did his wife, and we have seen many others come to faith in Christ through that means. *But it is not a biblically normative strategy.*

The real danger enters through the unverified assumption that some type of overt act is necessary if one is to be saved. Yet, the author has found that great numbers of Christians cannot recall a point in time at which they went forward in a meeting, prayed a prayer, and so on. Does this mean they have not been saved? Some might say so, but such an evaluation is unwarranted in light of what has been said here. The important issue is not *how* repentance and saving faith were expressed but rather the fact that this did take place as verified by present life-style and actions. What right do we have to require an action that is not required in Scripture?

The problem becomes compounded by the all-too-common tendency to count those who "prayed" or went forward as being Christian converts. This was the error made in Japan, of course, in the evangelistic crusade cited at the outset of Chapter 3. This may be our friend Dick's error when he evangelizes at the stop light and elsewhere. Notice again the precision of his records all based on the number who responded as he intended. Nothing is said, of course, about what happened afterward.

It is now becoming painfully obvious that our proclivity to measure overt actions in this manner is leading to some downright erroneous conclusions. People can be induced to pray such a prayer for many reasons—as an act of courtesy, as an act of desperation to get rid of us, as a desire to curry our favor and gain some advantage through this means, and so on. Yet, evangelistic organizations cite such statistics with seeming abandon, and some have even declared the Great Commission to be "fulfilled" in some geographic areas on such a basis. Frankly, the author has now reached the point where such claims are completely discounted until there is evidence at a much later time that these supposed converts are united with the church and living under the lordship of Christ. We would do well to follow the example of Billy Graham and other reputable evangelists who carefully label those who undertake these types of overt action as "inquirers" and nothing more.

What, then, is the role of evangelistic strategy at this stage? First, summarize the gospel message, and second, make clear that repentance and faith are necessary. It may be perfectly appropriate to suggest some type of prayer in which the other person acknowledges his or her need for salvation and makes a commitment to follow Christ, based on the belief as Paul said in Romans 10 that Jesus is Lord and that He has been raised from the dead. The validity of such a prayer depends on the cultural context. There will be times when many will make such a decision simultaneously in the form of a people's movement. The exact form really does not matter.

The author has found through many years of personal evangelism that the ultimate response is between the individual and God. There was a time in which he functioned much as Dick, doing everything in his power to encourage another person to invite Christ verbally into his or her heart. These responses then were duly noted as decisions, and it certainly did brighten a day when someone took this step. Then it began to become known in the halls of the Business School at Ohio State University that the best way to get an "A" from Engel was to come in and pray with him. This was not true, of course; the grading system was in no way connected with the spiritual status of students. Nevertheless, some strategic changes were needed. From then on sharing was done with more discretion, and the other person always was encouraged to think it over and count the costs before the great step of commitment was taken. The percentage who evidenced a valid commitment seemed to increase sharply after that point.

Let's be perfectly clear that it is not the task of the evangelist to "close the sale." Some evangelistic training, frankly, is no different from that used to sell a product in a business firm. The evangelist is not a persuader, and the badge of honor sometimes awarded to those with the most "decisions" is far more secular than it is Christian. Gentle friendly encouragement is the extent of our task; the persuasion is up to God and God alone.

Evangelistic Motivation

There was a time when the author both lived by and taught this rule to others: "Show me a person who is not leading people to Christ and I will show you a defeated Christian." There is quite a measure of truth to this in that the Christian life must have an outlet to the world if we take the mandates of the kingdom of God seriously. But, there are some serious negative consequences to such thinking that must be met head on.

First, this rule, advocated by many in evangelistic training, has no basis in Scripture. One can search in vain to find any teaching where God ties the spirituality of the Christian to evangelistic output. Rather, it smacks more of the kind of sloganeering designed to motivate salesmen to "conquer the territory." Furthermore, it focuses undue attention on the kind of evangelism practiced by Dick and downgrades proclamation, which, more often than not, is required for those at earlier stages of the decision process. Finally, and perhaps most seriously, it motivates evangelism out of a sense of duty and obligation, thereby representing nothing more than an extreme form of legalism. It may succeed in cranking up the "Great Commission machinery," but it does so in violation of scriptural teaching that all forms of outreach are to be motivated by genuine love as the Christian views another through the eyes of Christ.[21]

Another inadequate motivation is an appeal to a false sense of eschatological urgency. "The world is falling apart around us and Christians are doing little more than 'straightening the pictures on the wall' while the house is burning down." And on we go. Once again, there is real truth to such an appeal given moral deterioration on the world scene and Christ's teaching on the stewardship of the believer. But some have even gone so far as to set dates specifying when the "task is to be finished," presumably on the assumption that the end is imminent. The unfortunate outcome is that Christians, motivated by fear, disregard the common sense of audience analysis and proper planning and pull out all stops for world evangelization. But who sets such dates, man or God? Christ Himself said that the eternal timetable is only known to God the Father (Mark 13:32).

Of course, the church should respond with greater urgency as world conditions deteriorate. This is quite consistent with the teaching of Jesus that we should keep watch, each performing his assigned task in anticipation of His return (Mark 13:32–37). Yet urgency never demands that the "great commotion" replace the Great Commission. We all can benefit from the example of Martin Luther who reportedly gave this answer to a question asking what he would do if he knew Christ were to return tomorrow: "I would plant a tree."

What does God ask of the church? He asks for *faithfulness, obedience,* and *trust* in the leadership of Christ as head of His church. Jesus always motivates in a quiet, gentle way, asking simply that we follow Him. Guilt, legalism, fear have no place here. In the final analysis such appeals manufactured by men can swamp the voice of God and produce a response of frenzy rather than genuine obedience.

The Evangelistic Gift

The question of motivation is further sharpened by recognition that there is such a thing as the gift of evangelism. This means that some will have special obligations for this reason alone, not shared by other members of the body. Consider Peter Wagner's penetrating insights:

---

[21] This point is made quite strongly by Leighton Ford (*Ibid.*). See especially chs. 1–3.

> It's a matter of structured versus casual witness. Every one of us should take opportunities to witness for Christ when God provides the occasion, but only those with the gift of evangelism ought to be expected to be working at it in special, structured ways. Too many Christians are gloomy and frustrated because they do not have the gift of evangelism yet are being told that it is expected of them. The result is a debilitating guilt complex.[22]

It is Wagner's contention that no more than ten percent of those in the church have this gift and that others are equipped for ministries of teaching, administration, helps, and so on to build a healthy body enabled to have a vital outreach.[23]

Those who contend that Christian vitality is commensurate with individual evangelistic output are guilty of trying to make everyone into an eye or an ear. In short, they are assuming, in violation of Scripture, that all are to do the work of an evangelist. Not only does this build an enormous load of guilt as Wagner points out, but it also leads to neglect of the other spiritual gifts. It is small wonder that the church is bogged down in the institutional mire rather than functioning as an organism. Furthermore, a reverse theorem may hold here: Christian vitality is dampened when believers are forced into activities in contradiction to spiritual gifts. Growing numbers are finding true fulfillment only when they are making use of their spiritual gift(s) because of the unmistakable evidence of the presence of God in their lives through His supernatural power.

Are all to be evangelists? The answer must be no, but all *are* to be witnesses, ready and willing to give a reason for the hope that is within them (1 Pet. 3:15).

There is one more thing that should be said in this context. It is interesting to observe how some churches are packed with new believers, even though there is little overt emphasis on evangelism by the individual believer. The key seems to lie in the fact that the body is healthy and growing as intended, without evangelistic frenzy.[24] In such situations, the body itself, collectively rather than individually, is having a distinct evangelistic result. This appears to be far closer to the scriptural norm for the church than some of the grand strategies of outreach being practiced today.

---

[22]Cited in an interview with C. Peter Wagner and Arthur Johnson entitled "Intensity of Belief: A Pragmatic Concern for Church Growth," *Christianity Today* (January 7, 1977), p. 14.

[23]C. Peter Wagner, *Your Church Can Grow* (Glendale, Ca.: Regal, 1976), pp. 72–76.

[24]This is an important point made by Howard A. Snyder in *The Community of the King* (Downers Grove, Ill.: InterVarsity Press, 1977), ch. 7.

POST-DECISION CONSEQUENCES

A person decides to follow Christ through repentence and faith, regeneration occurs, and all heaven rejoices! (Luke 15:7). Now what? The reader will recall from Chapter 3 that the new convert has become a disciple in one sense, but the *process* of discipleship has only begun as he or she is conformed to the image of Christ. One of the very first outcomes often is a stage of post-decision evaluation, at which time the decision must be solidified and grounded on a basis of faith through follow-up. Then, and only then, will the validity of the decision be affirmed through two important types of evidence: (1) uniting with a local church and (2) the onset of conceptual and behavioral growth.

Post-Decision Evaluation

The acceptance of Christ is the most important decision a person will make in his or her lifetime. With any type of major decision there can be two types of immediate outcomes: (1) satisfaction and (2) dissonance. Satisfaction, the first of these, is defined as an evaluation that the decision made is consistent with prior beliefs with respect to Christianity and its effects on motivation and life-style. Beliefs thus function as a type of hypothesis regarding the consequences of an action, and post-decision results serve either to confirm or to reject these hypotheses. If confirmed, beliefs are further strengthened. If disconfirmed, the outcome may be highly unfavorable. This argues, of course, for immediate follow-up of the new believer to verify that the beliefs held are consonant with biblical reality. It is especially necessary to reaffirm that the entire decision was based on faith in an unchanging God.

Dissonance, the second type of outcome, is post-decision doubt motivated by awareness that one action was taken and the existence of beliefs that unchosen alternatives also have desirable consequences.[25] Often the individual is quite motivated to search for additional information to reaffirm the choice and thereby reduce doubts. Frankly, the moral and ethical demands of Christianity are

[25]James F. Engel, Roger D. Blackwell, and David T. Kollat, *Consumer Behavior* (Hinsdale, Ill.: Dryden Press, 1978), p. 495. This builds on the theory of cognitive dissonance. See Leon Festinger, *A Theory of Cognitive Dissonance* (Evanston, Ill.: Row, Peterson, 1957).

stringent and can lead to some wrenching changes in previously desirable aspects of life-style. Follow-up performs the important function, first of all, of reaffirming the desirable features that attracted the individual to Christianity in the first place—God's love and unconditional acceptance, the promise of power to overcome felt need and shortcomings, and so on. Next, it helps the individual to evaluate the old life in light of the new, stressing especially the power that is derived through prayer, Bible reading, worship, and praise.

The evangelist has a responsibility to help the new believer over these hurdles. The author was having dinner once with a veteran evangelist who quickly shared Christ with a waitress and persuaded her to pray the sinner's prayer on the spot. He turned to another colleague without batting an eye and said, "See to it that somebody gives her a Bible or something, will you?" That was that and conversation resumed. He might have been successful in "winning" yet another soul, but he did not care enough to help her become grounded in the faith. Not surprisingly she pointedly avoided us during the following days.

Uniting With a Local Church

The cardinal principle of church growth theory discussed at so many points throughout this book is that church membership is absolutely essential for the new convert. In fact, the act of uniting with other believers is a proof that the decision was valid in the first place, because those who did not truly express repentance and faith are unlikely to take this step.

The author has been in countless communities throughout North America and the rest of the world in which an evangelistic campaign of some type has not been followed by church growth. This always is a danger sign, because it implies that many who supposedly received Christ probably were not truly converted. Therefore, the statistics cited can be quite misleading. It also may say something negative about follow-up efforts, because it is entirely possible that new converts are left pretty much to themselves. If this is the case, Christian growth will not occur as it should any more than a plant will grow properly in a dark room.

---

[26]See, for example, C. Peter Wagner, "Does Church Growth Really Work?" *Church Growth Bulletin,* vol. 10 (September, 1973), pp. 47–51.

In this very important sense, church growth theory has had a profoundly positive effect on evangelistic strategy. It has correctly recognized that the church is God's primary agent for world evangelization, and it also affirms the scriptural fact that spiritual growth occurs within that setting. Finally, its advocates have motivated churches to set evangelistic goals in church growth terms, and there have been some remarkable increases in size as evangelism is intensified with new vision.[26] The reader should also recall, however, that growth per se is never a valid goal for a church built on the institutional model.

The Onset of Christian Growth

The mere act of joining a church, while a necessary step, is not a final guarantee that the person has made a valid spiritual decision. This is one of the dangers for emphasizing church growth to the exclusion of the quality of individual and corporate life in the church.

At the end of his fruitful ministry, the apostle John reflected on the attributes of the true believer and boiled them down to three essentials, which are found in 1 John 2 (NASB). First, "Keep His commandments" (2:3), that is, obedience. Next, love will be in evidence: "The one who loves his brother abides in the light and there is no cause for stumbling in him" (2:10). Finally, there will not be conformity to the world: "For all that is in the world, the lust of the flesh and the lust of the eyes and the boastful pride of life, is not from the Father, but is from the world" (2:16). If these three qualities do not begin to become apparent after a reasonable period of time, it might be well to verify that there was a valid conversion. In the final analysis, this is the most definitive proof of the validity of what took place.

PART III
THE PROCESS OF MOTIVATING SPIRITUAL GROWTH

It has been stressed repeatedly that the act of making disciples in all nations merely has begun once a person has been converted. The great need from that point forward is to unite the convert with a church and to encourage growth toward maturity as he or she becomes increasingly conformed to the image of Jesus Christ over a lifetime.

The fact that only two chapters are devoted to this subject should not be taken as an indication that the subject matter is less important than evangelism. Bear in mind that evangelism will not take place without a vital church, and a vital church, in turn, is the end product of believers who, individually and collectively, take the mandates of the kingdom of God seriously. Much that has been said in previous chapters provides important background for the subject matter covered here.

Chapter 10 explores in depth the whole meaning of spiritual maturity and puts forth the conceptual foundation then built upon in Chapter 11, which focuses more directly on the strategy of cultivation.

CHAPTER 10
Freedom in Christ

Watching an automobile assembly line is an interesting experience. It moves along slowly, never stopping unless there is a crisis of some type. At the outset the automobile is only a collection of nonrelated parts. But soon it begins to take shape as one part is added here and another is added there. After only a few minutes, a finished product emerges at the end, identical in every detail to the one that preceded it and the one that will follow.

At the end of a plant tour, two Christians were overheard talking. "You know, that assembly line is pretty much like my church. We produce just one standard model, and those that don't fit the mold are treated as rejects and sent back for further work."

If the church is just a great assembly line producing standardized products, then Paul is guilty of an empty statement when he said, "It is for freedom that Christ has set us free. Stand firm, then, and do not let yourselves be burdened again by a yoke of slavery" (Gal. 5:1, NIV). The new believer is set free from self striving once he or she accepts Christ, but the Christian assembly line imposes yet another form of bondage.

Fortunately, this is not what is meant by freedom. True freedom is the process of being conformed to the image of Christ (Phil. 1:6), and this is the essence of Christian growth.

All that was said in Chapters 5–9 really has only served to provide the basis for Christian growth and discipleship. The individual has become regenerated, but growth now begins as he or she is baptized and taught to obey everything Christ has commanded (Matt. 28:19,20). As the Holy Spirit performs the work of sanctification, the Christian communicator has the obligation of cultivation of the new believer and encouragement of growth in three dimensions: (1) communion with God through prayer and worship, (2) stewardship of all personal resources, and (3) reproduction of the life of Christ both in the church and in the world through use of spiritual gifts and various forms of outreach. Maturity is a gradual process as Figure 10.1 indicates, culminating only when the believer is physically united with Christ after this life.

This chapter is not intended as a manual on discipleship. Frankly, the author has yet to find any such manual (aside from the Bible) that he could recommend with much confidence. Rather, the intent is to uncover the dynamics of the process and to provide clues for a biblical strategy of cultivation.

RESEARCH ON RELIGIOUS BEHAVIOR

Now we jump headlong into quite a sizeable amount of literature. As was mentioned previously, religion has become quite a popular arena for the behavioral scientist who usually operates from a perspective that denies the supernatural. The focus of research in this context is on what has come to be known as *religiosity*. The primary concern is, first of all, to distinguish the religious from the nonreligious and next to find correlates of religious behavior. In other words, what traits and types of behavior make the religious person different from his or her counterpart?

Religiosity Scales

Most readers are not especially interested in the details of research instruments, but the methods used to measure religiosity are widely quoted. Therefore, the reader should have at least a minimal understanding of how this is done. Only those scales that have received the most citation in the published literature are mentioned here.

The Glock and Stark 5–D Scale. Charles Glock and Rodney Stark

[1]There are two especially useful sources for an overall review of the evidence. See J.E. Dittes, "Psychology of Religion," in Gardner Lindzey and Elliot Aronsen, eds., *Handbook of Social Psychology*, vol. 5 (Reading, Mass.: Addison-Wesley, 1969); and Geoffrey E.W. Scobie, *Psychology of Religion* (New York: Wiley, 1975).

FIGURE 10.1.

The Complete Spiritual Decision Process

GOD'S ROLE	COMMUNICATOR'S ROLE		MAN'S RESPONSE
General Revelation		−8	Awareness of Supreme Being
Conviction ↓	Proclamation ↓	−7	Some Knowledge of Gospel
		−6	Knowledge of Fundamentals of Gospel
		−5	Grasp of Personal Implications of Gospel
		−4	Positive Attitude Toward Act of Becoming a Christian
	Call for Decision ↓	−3	Problem Recognition and Intention to Act
		−2	Decision to Act
		−1	Repentance and Faith in Christ
REGENERATION			**NEW CREATURE**
Sanctification ↓	Follow Up ↓	+1	Post Decision Evaluation
		+2	Incorporation Into Church
	Cultivation ↓	+3	Conceptual and Behavioral Growth • Communion With God • Stewardship • Internal Reproduction • External Reproduction
		•	
		•	
		•	
		Eternity	

have led the way for research on religiosity in the past two decades.[2] They divide religious experience into five dimensions:[3]

1. Ideological—those tenants of religion that a person holds to be true (beliefs)
2. Ritualistic—religious practices such as acts of worship and devotion
3. Experiential—feelings and direct subjective knowledge of ultimate reality through contact with the supernatural
4. Intellectual—knowledge of the basic tenants of the faith and its rights
5. Consequential—effects of religious belief, practice, experience, and knowledge on day-to-day life

This typology has been operationalized into a twenty-three-item scale by Faulkner and Jong.[4]

Much research has been undertaken using the 5-D scale.[5] There has been some disagreement, however, regarding the hypothesis that each of the five dimensions is a separate and distinct factor. Nudelman, for example, reanalyzed the Stark and Glock data from a major study of Protestant and Catholic church members and found devotion and practice to be the most important components of religiosity.[6] Clayton and Gladden, on the other hand, found ideological commitment to dominate all other considerations.[7] But Davidson in a major study of members of Baptist and Methodist churches strongly affirms the validity of the assumptions underlying the 5-D scale, although he argues that much more research is needed before the issue is settled.[8]

[2]Much of this pioneering research has appeared in two important books. See Charles Y. Glock and Rodney Stark, *Religion and Society in Tension* (Chicago: Rand-McNally & Co., 1965); and Rodney Stark and Charles Y. Glock, *American Piety: The Nature of Religious Commitment* (Berkeley, Ca.: University of California Press, 1968)

[3]*Ibid.*

[4]Joseph L. Faulkner and Gordon E. Jong, "Religiosity in 5-D: An Empirical Analysis," *Social Forces,* vol. 45 (1966), pp. 246–254.

[5]For a helpful review, see Arthur E. Nudelman, "Dimensions of Religiosity: A Factor-Analytic View of Protestants, Catholics, and Christian Scientists," *Review of Religious Research,* vol. 13 (Fall, 1971), pp. 42-54; and Richard R. Clayton and James W. Gladden, "The Five Dimensions of Religiosity: Toward Demythologizing a Sacred Artifact," *Journal for the Scientific Study of Religion,* vol. 13 (June, 1974), pp. 135-143.

[6]Nudelman, "Dimensions of Religiosity."

[7]Clayton and Gladden, "The Five Dimensions of Religiosity."

[8]James D. Davidson, "Glock's Model of Religious Commitment: Assessing Some Different Approaches and Results," *Review of Religious Research,* vol. 16 (Winter, 1975), pp. 83–93.

The Allport Scale. From the Allport, Vernon, Lindzey study of values,[9] a scale has been abstracted that focuses directly on religiosity.[10] Two dimensions have been isolated, the intrinsic and the extrinsic. The intrinsic refers to personal devotion and religious experience, whereas the extrinsic refers much more to the institutionalized and outward behavioral aspect. From the original twenty-one-item scale devised by Allport, Feagin has devised a more compact and apparently more valid scale.[11]

Yinger's Scale of Nondoctrinal Religion. Yinger feels that most religiosity scales focus too much on beliefs and behavior with respect to the institutional church. It is his contention that all religions are based on a common structure, and he devised a seven point scale that avoided an institutional orientation.[12] Others have found, however, that there are several factors implicit within this scale. First, Nelson, *et. al.,* have found that the two implicit factors are acceptance of belief and order in the universe and affirmation of the value of suffering.[13] Roof and his colleagues have a different conclusion in that their data suggested three factors: (1) the value of religious efforts, (2) value of difficult experiences, and (3) belief in order and pattern.[14] In turn, the Yinger scale was found to correlate quite positively with other more conventional measures of religiosity.

Correlates of Religiosity

How do those scoring high on a scale of religiosity differ from those who do not? Here are some of the most important relationships that have been found:

1. Females are more religious than males. This is a consistent finding reported across a great number of studies.[15]

---

[9]G.W. Allport, P.E. Vernon, and G. Lindzey, *Manual for the Study of Values,* 3rd ed. (Boston: Houghton Mifflin, 1960).

[10]See Gordon W. Allport, "Behavioral Science, Religion, and Mental Health," *Journal of Religion and Health,* vol. 2 (1963), pp. 187–197. Also Gordon W. Allport, "Religious Context of Prejudice," *Journal for the Scientific Study of Religion,* vol. 5 (1966), pp. 447-457.

[11]J.R. Feagin, "Prejudice and Religious Types: A Focused Study of Southern Fundamentalists," *Journal for the Scientific Study of Religion,* vol. 4 (1964), pp. 3–13.

[12]J. Milton Yinger, "A Comparative Study of the Substructures of Religion," *Journal for the Scientific Study of Religion,* vol. 16 (1977), p. 67.

[13]Hart M. Nelson *et. al.,* "A Test of Yinger's Measure of Non-Doctrinal Religion: Implications for Invisible Religion as a Belief System," *Journal for the Scientific Study of Religion,* vol. 16 (1976), p. 265.

[14]Wade Roof *et. al.,* "Yinger's Measure of Non-Doctrinal Religion: A Northeastern Test," *Journal for the Scientific Study of Religion,* vol. 16 (1977), p. 403.

[15]Scobie and Nudelman both review this literature.

2. Contrary to orthodox Marxism, members of lower economic classes are not more religious than their higher-class counterparts.[16] Education rather than socioeconomic status seems to be the determining factor; there is a direct correlation between education and religious participation.
3. Religiosity and church participation are greatest among those with orthodox religious beliefs.[17]
4. There is no correlation between the existence of strong religious beliefs and social and community action.[18] It seems that religion is more a private matter providing comfort and support than it is anything else.
5. Contrary to the findings of some,[19] there is no consistent relationship between religiosity and political and economic conservatism. Wuthnow reviewed 266 efforts to examine this relationship, and the great majority show either no correlation or a negative correlation.[20] The only exception emerges when measures of religious orthodoxy are combined with fundamentalistic views.
6. There is a pretty consistent finding that the conventionally religious are the most racially prejudiced.[21] It seems that sustained in-group relationships tend to lead to intolerance and ethnocentrism.[22] Fortunately there also is some evidence that the genuinely devout are less prejudiced than those who confine their religion to such conventional activities as church attendance.[23]
7. Those who report a devout personal faith are much more likely

---

[16]Stan Gaede, "Religious Participation, Socio-Economic Status, and Belief in Orthodoxy," *Journal for the Scientific Study of Religion,* vol. 16 (1977), pp. 245–253.

[17]*Ibid.*

[18]James B. Davidson, "Religious Belief as an Independent Variable," paper presented at the 1969 Annual Meeting of the Religious Research Assn. This finding also has been reported by Glock and Stark in 1965.

[19]Richard J. Stellway, "The Correspondence Between Religious Orientation and Socio-Political Liberalism and Conservatism," *Sociological Quarterly,* vol. 14 (1973), pp. 340-349.

[20]Robert Wuthnow, "Religious Commitment and Conservatism: In Search of an Illusive Relationship," in Charles Y. Glock, ed., *Religion in Sociological Perspective: Essays in the Empirical Study of Religion* (Belmont, Ca.: Wadsworth Publishing Co., 1973), pp. 117–132.

[21]This literature is reviewed in Scobie, *Psychology of Religion,* ch. 7.

[22]Wuthnow, "Religious Commitment and Conservatism."

[23]J.G. Keloy, J.E. Person, and W.J. Holtzman, "The Measurement of Attitudes Toward the Negro in the South," *Journal of Social Psychology,* vol. 48 (1958), pp. 305–317.

to have mystical religious experiences than those whose primary commitment is to the institution.[24]

8. Religious students view their families as being more happy, warm, and accepting than nonreligious students.[25]
9. There has been no consistent success in relating personality and religiosity.[26] In fact, as was also mentioned in Chapter 9, the evidence shows that religious belief is primarily a cognitive activity acquired and sustained by social influences, and it appears to be independent of personality.[27]

About all one can say from this evidence is that religious people, on the whole, are unconcerned about social action in its various forms and also are more likely to be racially prejudiced than people in general. Not a very favorable picture, is it? If one's knowledge of religion were based only on this data, it certainly would not present an appealing life-style.

A Biblical Perspective

The first thing we must do is drop the term "religiosity." All too often it is defined in various scales as activities and beliefs, which are not necessarily Christian. After all, Jesus could refer to the Pharisees as being religious. A far better term is "maturity," viewed in the context of the extent to which the believer has become conformed to the image of Christ.

Probably the clearest exposition on Christian maturity appears in the Book of 1 John, and there are three tests: (1) theological, (2) social, and (3) moral.[28] (The following references are from the New International Version.)

The Theological Standard. The bedrock of Christian belief is confession that Jesus is Christ. "This is how you can recognize the Spirit of God: Every spirit that acknowledges that Jesus Christ has come in the flesh is from God, but every spirit that does not acknowledge

---

[24]Ralph W. Hood, Jr., "Forms of Religious Commitment: An Intense Religious Experience," *Review of Religious Research,* vol. 15 (1963), pp. 29–36.

[25]Martin A. Johnson, "Family Life and Religious Commitment," *Review of Religious Research,* vol. 14 (1973), pp. 144–151.

[26]Scobie, *Psychology of Religion,* ch. 5.

[27]L.B. Brown, "The Structure of Religious Belief," *Journal for the Study of Religion,* vol. 5 (1966), pp. 259–272.

[28]The author is indebted to Dr. Glen Barker, Provost of the Fuller Theological Seminary, for this exposition of 1 John presented at the Evangelical Roundtable at Palm Springs, California, March, 1978.

Jesus is not from God . . ." (4:2,3). Moreover, "Everyone who believes that Jesus is the Christ is born of God, and everyone who loves the father loves his child as well" (5:1,2).

This belief in Christ demands far more than acquiescence to a theological statement, and John is very specific about how the Christian should live as a result:

1. Jesus is not a silent partner; rather His goals and those of the believer intermingle as they live in fellowship (1:3).
2. The Christian abides with Christ on a moment-by-moment basis; in fact the word "abide" is used twenty-five times in 1 John.
3. There is consistent acceptance of His grace through prayer (3:22).

The Social Standard. The basic criterion of the Christian life in this context is love for the brethren. Love is considered by John to be basic to the Christian faith, and reference is made to the initial commandment given by Jesus (2:7) and reported in John 13 and 15. It is understood in terms of the love that we have received as children of God (3:1), and it is viewed as the very essence of all that we do (4:7,8).

John provides these tests of love (3:10–18):

1. Do we hate any brethren? If so, this is no different from an outright act of murder.
2. Are we willing to make the most severe personal sacrifices for a fellow believer, even to the point of death if need be?
3. Are we willing to share our material wealth with those in need?

The Moral Standard. Here the focus is on the outward actions of the Christian life, and the tests provided once again are stringent:

1. Do we walk in darkness? "If we claim to have fellowship with him yet walk in the darkness, we lie and do not put the truth into practice" (1:6). This refers to such behavior as problem solving based on expediency rather than faith, ignoring world need with a "business as usual" attitude, and living without the love and power that God alone can provide.
2. Do we confess our sin, especially to one another in the body of Christ? (1:8–10).
3. Do we keep Christ's commandments? "The man who says, 'I

know him,' but does not do what he commands is a liar, and the truth is not in him" (2:4). Notice that this passage is in the context of the command to love fellow Christians.

4. Do we esteem power, prestige, reputation, and other "things of the world" more than we do Christ and His commandments? "Do not love the world or anything in the world. If anyone loves the world, the love of the Father is not in him" (2:15).

Religiosity Compared With Christian Maturity

The criteria of Christian maturity are a far cry from the dimensions of religiosity contained in most of the scales used for measurement. If the focus were on maturity, there is no way that prejudice, ethnocentrism, and lack of social concern would emerge. Instead, the focus is on conventional religion rather than the standards defined by Christ. While we probably can learn something from research on religiosity, it sheds little or no light on the true meaning of freedom in Christ. In fact, it might be more misleading than anything else.

SETTING THE CHRISTIAN FREE[29]

We have now established that conformity to the image of Christ over a lifetime is the essence of Christian maturity. But what exactly does this mean? This question, of course, defines the continuing dilemma faced by the church ever since the first century, and there never has been an answer leading to consensus. There are some insights, however, from the field of psychological counseling, which have shed needed light; and one simple principle emerges: *Right thinking leads to right behavior.* Therefore, it is useful to define Christian maturity as the process whereby an individual's beliefs are modified so as to enhance his or her uniqueness as created in the image of God and to reflect revealed scriptural truth.

The Importance of Right Thinking

For many years the author has been troubled with depression. It never has been sufficiently serious to prove incapacitating, but it can function to take the "edge off of life." It proved quite disturbing that this problem lingered without relief after conversion to Christianity. Is this what is meant by the "abundant life"?

[29]The author gratefully acknowledges the contributions to this section made by his friend and colleague at the Wheaton Graduate School, Dr. Frances White.

Over the years many solutions have been tried. One friend, who bills himself as a Christian psychologist, suggested that there must be some unconfessed sin. Therefore, introspection was resorted to and all sorts of things confessed, but there was no lasting relief. Another suggested that the key is to "reckon yourself dead to the problem" (following Romans 6 but missing the point of what Paul was saying). That too proved fruitless, and on it went. Finally, a book was published on this subject which has become a best seller. It was eagerly procured in the expectation that help at last would be forthcoming. What was the remedy proposed? Be filled with the Spirit. At that point the book was tossed into the trash heap in disgust, because the necessity to be filled with the Spirit had become a way of life with the author many years before and the problem still persisted.

Finally, healing began following discussion and prayer with others in a house fellowship. It became apparent that two beliefs had become dominant: (1) God does not really accept me as I am with all my failures, and (2) Christian activity and busyness is the key to spirituality. These beliefs were not consciously recognized, but they surfaced through some careful questioning by Christian friends. Soon it became apparent that life had become rooted on an erroneous foundation. Goal attainment, in turn, had become frustrated, and this failure led to a deep inward sense of anger directed at times both to God and self. Anger, then, found expression in one of its most common forms—depression.[30] After a period of prayer and reflection, the assurance of God's acceptance without a frenzy of activity led to a more positive Christian self-image and to a gradual but nonetheless very real reduction in both the incidence and the frequency of depression.

This personal example was related for a very important reason: All too often we treat only the symptoms while ignoring the real problem—a belief structure that deviates from reality. As was stressed in Chapter 5, this is now a widely accepted principle of counseling,[31] but only those with a Christian perspective see reality as lying in biblical truth.[32]

Figure 5.2 depicted the relationship between beliefs and felt

---

[30]For an important discussion on this subject, see Jack Birnbaum, *Cry Anger* (Don Mills, Ontario, Canada: General Publishing Co., Ltd., 1973).

[31]See Victor Raimy, *Misunderstandings of the Self* (San Francisco: Jossey-Bass Publishers, 1975).

[32]Probably the leading proponent of this point of view is Lawrence J. Crabb, Jr., *Effective Biblical Counseling* (Grand Rapids, Mich.: Zondervan, 1977).

needs, and this model is of sufficient importance to warrant its reproduction here (Figure 10.2). Felt needs and problems such as depression find their expression in the emotions. As such, they are only the tip of the iceberg, so to speak. Treatment at this level focuses only on symptoms and leaves the real problems untouched. Needs are not to be ignored, but it must be recognized that need-satisfying behavior has its origins in the mind. A person behaves in a manner consistent with beliefs—those things that he or she holds to be true and hence values positively. Therefore, a permanent change can only come when beliefs are modified.

FIGURE 10.2.

The Relationship Between Beliefs and Felt Needs

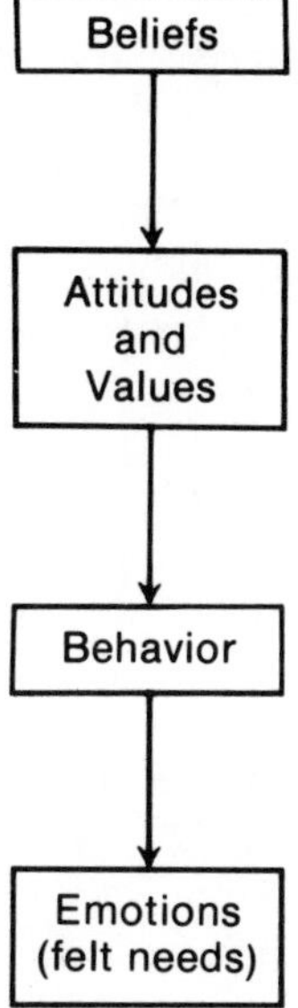

How Beliefs Are Formed

Proponents of the theory of transactional analysis have clarified the process of belief formation.[33] They have modified traditional

[33]One of the most useful sources is the self-study manual by Muriel James and Dorothy Jongeward, *Born to Win: Transactional Analysis With Gestalt Experiments* (Reading, Mass.: Addison-Wesley, 1973).

Freudian theory in some significant ways and have suggested that there are three ego states in personality, with an ego state being defined as persistent patterns of feelings, experience, and beliefs related to corresponding behavior patterns. These three ego states are described as parent, adult, and child.

The *parent* ego state incorporates attitudes and behavior of those who have been emotionally significant people and hence have served as "parent figures." It is the means whereby external standards find their way into beliefs. The *child* is the seat of emotions and response patterns that come naturally to an infant. The *adult* deals objectively with reality and is influenced by education and experience. It functions to collect and organize information, predict consequences of actions, and make decisions.

The healthy individual lives in the adult ego state, making use of the parent and child when appropriate but not being dominated by either of these to the point that adaptation to reality is impaired. To determine how these ego states are functioning, use is made of what has come to be known as "script analysis." The assumption is that everyone begins to develop at birth a lifescript that is learned, rehearsed, and acted out. It contains the input of family, culture, and other influences, and it is based on these three questions: (1) Who am I? (2) What am I doing here? and (3) Who are all these others? Lifescripts, then, really are belief statements. Pathology is created to the extent that they deviate from reality.

Most erroneous beliefs are seated in the parent. "The important thing in life is to succeed and be happy." "The more money you make, the happier you will be." "To be a good person you must do this and not do that." Teachings of the church also find their way into the parent, and they can be equally nonadaptive as the next section of this chapter will show.

Once lifescripts have been uncovered (this is not an easy task), it is then possible to throw off inappropriate beliefs and behavior patterns. What it boils down to is a decontamination of the adult ego state so that it can evaluate reality with greater clarity. Soon this is reflected in greater spontaneity as the adult is equipped to choose from the spectrum of both parent and child behavior and feelings.

The perceptive reader will by now begin to sense that this is striking very close to the meaning of freedom in Christ. Lifescripts are modified as nonfunctional beliefs from the parent are discarded and childish ways of thinking and behaving are put aside. Biblical truth, of course, becomes the new foundation, and the individual is now freed to cope in an altogether new way through the adult ego state. This is the bedrock of the theory of Christian growth put forth in this book, and more is said later on the practical issues of discipleship.

Before moving on, it should be pointed out that the child ego state is not to be regarded as irrelevant or nonfunctional. It can become that only when it dominates in inappropriate ways. The child functions to bring about much of the real joy and fun in life, and it is created by God to play an important role in the life of the believer. There are some writers and teachers who imply that everything in life must be "spiritual." "A spiritual person doesn't resort to such frivolities as television, non-Christian books, secular music, and so on." To those who would try to lay such thinking on others, the author joins Steve Board in calling for a change:

> Christian discipleship does not call us to be always taut as a violin string with pious passion. Young Christians often think so and begrudge themselves the leisure, the hobbies, the humor that would make them seem more human and more real.[34]

Erroneous Beliefs: Dead Ends to Spiritual Growth

The church itself can implant some beliefs that, if unchallenged, can have some decidedly negative consequences and hence serve as dead ends to growth. Those that have some of the most devastating consequences fall into the categories of (1) self worth, (2) legalism, and (3) cultural syncretism.

Self Worth. One Sunday in church the author was shocked suddenly into the awareness that most of the input he was receiving was a put down of his self worth. The first hymn talked about mankind (Christians included) as being little more than "worms" (yes that term was used) and of no value at all to God. The prayer of petition confessed the manifest unholiness of all in attendance. The sermon was the capstone as it stressed repeatedly our failure to live up to God's standards.

Is this how God views the Christian? In other words, does He see us only as being useless and of no worth? If so, then our present standing with God is on very shaky ground. A surprising number of Christians have told the author in recent years that they have shared his own problem of self-image. Yes, we can know we are saved

[34]Editorial by Steve Board in *His* (May, 1974), p. 32.

through the grace of Jesus Christ and that our eternal destiny is secure, but what about the present time? Our natural tendency is to struggle to earn His acceptance through our actions, but this is never possible if the human is viewed as being without any intrinsic merit. The consequence is a warped self concept and impaired potential for spiritual growth.

Crabb has affirmed the essential point that the very foundation of spiritual health is the assurance of our total acceptance as believers.[35] Any belief that deviates from this standard is out of accord with scriptural reality. It is worthwhile stressing the scriptural basis of this doctrine. When a person believes in Jesus Christ, he or she enters into a vital union with Jesus Christ (1 Cor. 12:13; Gal. 3:27). As a result, we are declared righteous (Rom. 3:21–26; Rom. 5:1); all sins are forgiven—past, present, and future (Col. 2:13,14; Eph. 1:7; Isa. 43:25); there is total acceptance by God (Rom. 5:1,2; Eph. 1:6; Eph. 4:30); there is no longer any condemnation (Rom. 8:1, 31–34); and the believer has a perfect, unchanging access to God (Heb. 10:19–22).

What this says, of course, is that the believer is anything but a "useless worm" or any of the other similarly graphic phrases we hear used to describe unworthiness. While no one attains sinless perfection, we are declared acceptable in the eyes of God. That gives a solid rock for a positive self concept, and there no longer needs to be a life of works under the erroneous concept that God will somehow become mad otherwise. In reality, good works should be a consequence of our standing with God and the power He gives to meet His standards.

Legalism. Pete Gillquist has captured vividly another related aspect of Christianity that is robbing the church of vitality:

> So much of the typical Christian emphasis concerns what we *do* rather than what we *are*. The church as a whole has become impotent and listless as a result. Instead of getting back to the essentials of what it is that changes a person, many Christian spokesmen are preaching a work-centered, achievement-based, quasi-Christianity. We hear "get involved," "redouble your efforts," "give more," "sin less," "love your neighbor," "why have you not been more faithful?" until we are numb.[36]

Spirituality, then, is reduced to a few rules based upon external standards. In part, this reflects a faulty understanding of the be-

[35]Crabb, *Effective Biblical Counseling,* p. 61.

[36]Peter E. Gillquist, *Fresh New Insight Into Love Is Now* (Grand Rapids, Mich.: Zondervan, 1978), pp. 23–24.

liever's acceptance by God as was stressed above. Perhaps more often, rules are put forth to generate a well-trained and disciplined "Christian army."

Legalism may bring about conformity and the external appearance of spirituality, but the long run consequences are tragic. As Webber clearly states,

> . . . it reduces spiritual responsibility to readily defined limits, both in terms of what a person may do, and with whom a person may associate. This, in turn, helps to create an individualistic, personalistic spirituality which cannot come to grips with the expanded spiritual responsibilities of the Christian to culture and to thought.[37]

A doctrine of works is a return to law, and law was given not to produce righteousness but to prove the guilt and condemnation of the unbeliever (Rom. 9:30–10:4; 2 Cor. 3). Law makes acceptance become based on performance (Deut. 28:2) and produces a fear motivation (Deut. 28:15). The opposite of law is grace, which emphasizes faith (Gal. 3:11,12), love as a motivation (Gal. 5:6), and acceptance based on the finished work of Christ (Eph. 1:6). Law and grace are mutually exclusive. If the two are mixed as is done so frequently today, there is no freedom in Christ. Once again wrong thinking leads to wrong behavior.

Cultural Syncretism. In all cultures, but particularly in North America, there is a strong pull toward accommodating Christianity with prevailing cultural norms and practices. As Webber puts it:

> . . . we interpret our faith through the glasses of the culture in which we find ourselves. We tend then to impose these cultural categories of thought on the faith, articulate our faith through these categories, and create an expression of Christianity peculiar to those cultural forms. Consequently the faith becomes inextricably interwoven with a particular view of life, or method.[38]

In North America Christianity has tended to take on the stance that it is quite proper to be a professing Christian while, at the same time, enjoying the fruits of materialism. One does not have to look far to uncover testimony, popular books, or radio or television preaching in which it is stated, quite overtly, that becoming a Chris-

---

[37]Robert E. Webber, *Common Roots* (Grand Rapids, Mich.: Zondervan, 1978), p. 221.

[38]*Ibid.*, p. 143.

tian is the key to success. As Kinzie has lamented, "It is as if living in one kingdom, the earthly state, and enjoying its benefits, we want to enjoy as well the benefits of the other kingdom, the kingdom of God."[39]

Christ does not allow the option of living with a foot in both kingdoms, "For where your treasure is, there your heart will be also" (Matt. 6:21, NIV). Equating material success with Christian victory is yet another instance of an all too common belief that does not square with Scripture, but its consequences are especially far-reaching. Spokesmen from all ranks of evangelicalism ranging from President Hudson Armerding of Wheaton College[40] to Richard Quebedeaux[41] have deplored the trend toward such syncretism. Quebedeaux has gone so far as to introduce the term "worldly evangelicals," and his warnings are worthy of note:

> Christ demands that his followers take up their cross and travel a narrow way that can never be popular. In many ways that demand challenges almost all of the values of the wider culture that Christians often take up as a *compromise* because the way of the cross is just too hard.[42]

Quebedeaux goes on to ask this searching question: ". . . what will we do with the cross? Wear it, or bear it?"[43]

The Ministry of Cultivation

It is the job of the church to help the believer grow in the faith and approach maturity, but how is this to be done? Specific strategies of cultivation are the subject of the next chapter, but there are three principles that should be discussed first: (1) the "end product" (desired belief and behavior patterns) must be specified; (2) felt need is a clue to strategy; and (3) the church must function as a healing community.

Specification of the "End Product." No one responsible for helping another to grow spiritually can proceed until they have in mind a model of the outcome of their efforts. What beliefs and behavior patterns will be evidenced? Usually this model is not made suffi-

---

[39]Charles E. Kinzie, "The Absorbed Church," *Sojourners,* vol. 7 (July, 1978), p. 23.

[40]Hudson T. Armerding, Baccalaureate address to Wheaton Graduates, May 21, 1978.

[41]Richard Quebedeaux, *The Worldly Evangelicals* (New York: Harper & Row, 1978).

[42]*Ibid.,* p. 168.

[43]*Ibid.,* p. 79.

ciently explicit that measurable goals can be set and progress assessed. As a result there is a plethora of teaching and discipling programs, most of which have never been conclusively validated in these terms.

It is not the intent of this book to spell out what this end product should be. Indeed, that is a separate book in its own right. But several broad suggestions can be advanced.

First, and clearly most important, the outcomes specified must be firmly rooted in Scripture. Saying this and making it become reality, however, can be two very different things. Obviously, Scripture lends itself to differing interpretations as is attested to by the endless variety of theological schemes. So, which interpretation is valid? Without delving into hermeneutical principles, there is a very helpful criterion: Does the interpretation agree with apostolic tradition? Webber in his influential book, *Common Roots,* contends that, ". . . the modern individualistic approach to the interpretation of Scripture should give way to the authority of what the church has always believed, taught, and passed down in history."[44] The reason for this is that theological interpretation is always conditioned by time, location, and culture. Therefore, recourse must always be made to the core of truth found in the historic creeds. Application must, of course, be made to the contemporary scene, but this provides an essential safeguard against misuse of revealed truth.

Next, legalism must be resisted. Reference is not made here strictly to the traditional list of "dos and don'ts." Legalism also enters when a Christian doctrine is taken out of context and given distorted emphasis. A tendency referred to many times throughout the book, for example, is to make evangelism the overriding criterion of spirituality. When it is distorted in this fashion, it has been labeled as "Great Commissionitis." At all costs this "evangelical assembly line" mentality mentioned at the outset of the chapter must be avoided.

The end product also must embody the essence of the doctrine of the kingdom of God. The kingdom, of course, is merely inaugurated by believers in the present age, and its chief expression lies in manifestation of the lordship of Christ over all phases of life. As such, it is the very antithesis of cultural syncretism. Once again there can be a large disparity between the statement of principle and working it out in practice. Theologians have always disagreed on the stand that Christians must take with respect to culture and social

[44]Webber, *Common Roots,* p. 249.

responsibility, but there may be some common ground to build upon.[45] First, because of God's act of creation the Christian has no choice but to identify with the world and view it as the arena for redemptive activity. But separation is to be practiced in the sense that the believer is not to live by its standards. Finally, redeemed people are to influence culture and bring change where possible to stimulate greater equity and justice.

The specified end product must, in addition, preserve each Christian's uniqueness and affirm that individuality is the very essence of God's creation. It is here that the standard model Christian concept becomes so offensive. It may create a measure of surface conformity, but it also may destroy, or at the very least dampen, the divine spark within each person. Bruce Larson's prophetic warning is worthy of careful note:

> Now if God made each person to be unique, a one and only version of that life, then sin is expressed when internal and external forces cause us to lose our uniqueness and become a carbon copy, and usually a poor one, of another person or group. So the change that God offers is one that helps a person to find his true identity, his true personhood, and to become "the one and only you."[46]

Felt Need as the Clue to Strategy. Christian growth is anything but a smooth upward pattern. Rather it always will be characterized by ups and downs. The fairly common teaching that a mature Christian will not have problems lays an unwarranted load of guilt upon those who take it to heart because *growth comes through failure.* What this means is that every dedicated believer who takes his or her faith seriously will, at times, fall quite short. Furthermore, while the root cause sometimes lies in unconfessed sin, it is more likely that God is using this means to focus concern on shortcomings and thereby motivate the individual to do something about them.

When perceived consciously, these shortcomings become *felt need.* Therefore, the presence of felt need in the life of the believer must be taken seriously, because it is the major symptom of an underlying problem. The strategy, of course, will demand probing to the level of belief where the real problem usually lies.

Felt needs are a legitimate determinant of the teaching and discipling agenda of the church. All too frequently doctrine is dished out in abstract fashion not touching life where it is, and this is a sure way

---

[45]*Ibid.,* pp. 199–211.

[46]Bruce Larson, *The One and Only You* (Waco, Texas: Word Books, 1973), p. 38.

to have the church perceived as irrelevant by its members. It is no accident that most of the rapidly growing churches are characterized by a need-centered ministry.

Once again it is worth stressing that treatment of the symptom is a dead end. One popular theory of counseling attests that the best strategy is to attack a believer's problem by identifying sin and exhorting behavioral change. Unfortunately, this can leave the underlying belief completely untouched. Crabb dismisses this as, ". . . a simplistic approach which fails to reflect the essential dynamic of Christianity,"[47] and the author completely agrees.

The Church as a Healing Community. It was stressed in Chapter 4 that a proper view of the church embodies a spirit of *community* or koinonia in which the horizontal ministry of believer to believer is given primacy. The type of cultivation ministry suggested in these pages is virtually impossible in the institutional church characterized by one-way communication. Symptoms must be probed until underlying problems surface. This can only take place in an atmosphere encouraging free and open expression and where genuine concern is manifested without judgment or condemnation. The small group is especially important in this ministry of healing.

Even the healing community is limited, however, in dealing with all situations. Some needs and problems require professional counseling. For this reason, trained counselors are beginning to make their appearance on church staffs. This is a welcome trend indeed.

FREEDOM AS THE HALLMARK OF THE CHRISTIAN

A believer on the way to becoming that "one and only you" characterized by a growing conformity to the image of Christ in beliefs and actions indeed has a message for the world. His or her life stands in sharp contrast to that of the non-Christian imprisoned to self-seeking. While both believer and nonbeliever can find a measure of happiness in this life, the latter person still lacks the assurance of a *place to stand,* to use Elton Trueblood's words. This essential quality is the very essence of the Christian message.

---

[47]Crabb, *Effective Biblical Counseling,* p. 47.

CHAPTER 11

The Strategy of Cultivation

Maturity has been defined as the process whereby an individual's beliefs are modified so as to enhance his or her uniqueness as created in the image of God and to reflect revealed scriptural truth. Now the question is this: How can Christians be helped to grow through the ministry of the church and the parachurch organization? To find the answers, it is necessary first of all to examine the steps in a successful strategy of cultivation and then to review the various media alternatives and the ways in which they can be utilized.

THE STEPS IN SUCCESSFUL STRATEGY

The term "successful" can be misleading and smack of Madison Avenue thinking. That is not the intent at all, because success can only be defined by the extent to which the methods used to help the Christian grow in the faith have enabled that person to become conformed to the image of Christ in thought and action. Furthermore, there is no guarantee that the principles suggested here will result in a packed out church, because true Christianity always has been viewed as a "narrow way." With this word of caution, let's proceed.

Specify the Desired End Product

This starting point of strategy was made quite clear in Chapter 10, but it cannot be emphasized too frequently. Often this step is omitted entirely and everything that follows is built on a mighty flimsy base. Furthermore, the tendency is to give vague but very spiritual sounding statements such as, "Our desire is to see our people live Christlike lives." This is all well and good, but what beliefs and behavior patterns will be evidenced if people are living in this way?

Find the Pulse of the Audience

Back in the seventeenth century Francois Fenelon wrote these insightful words:

> Only pastors should as a rule be allowed to preach. This would be the way to restore to the pulpit the simplicity and authority that it ought to have; for pastors who had experience in doing work and in guiding souls, and who combined that with a knowledge of Scripture, would speak in a way much more suited to the needs of their hearers; whereas the preachers who only have theoretical knowledge deal much less with their hearer's difficulties, hardly ever adjust themselves to their hearer's statement of mind, and speak in the vaguest of terms.[1]

This only serves to reinforce what has been said earlier: Audience needs are a legitimate determinant of the discipleship agenda within the local church. But a warning also should be stated at this point. A ministry to audience needs does not justify a strictly experience-centered ministry that shies away from anything controversial. The demands of discipleship, especially those stated by Jesus, may sound quite radical; there will be times when their proclamation results in a strong rebuke to current Christian behavior. Avoiding the controversial may fill churches, as some well-known pastors have found, but popularity might well be coming at the expense of biblical fidelity. The implications of the lordship of Christ over all phases of life are not likely to be appealing to those who have fallen prey to cultural syncretism, but they must be put forth nonetheless. What is needed is balance—a focus on audience needs on the one hand without forsaking a prophetic use of the Word of God.

There are three important categories of audience information needed to determine a strategy of cultivation: (1) doctrinal beliefs, (2) felt needs, and (3) behavior. The first, of course, reveals the foundation on which the Christian life is built, and if it is faulty, remedial action must be taken. The second is merely a clue that something has gone wrong and that healing is needed. Information on behavior may be more difficult to interpret, however, because a life based on legalism can look very Christian. In other words,

---

[1]F. Fenelon, *Dialogues on Eloquence* (Princeton, N.J.: Princeton University Press, 1951), p. 136.

correct behavior can mask some erroneous beliefs. Nevertheless, it is helpful to document, if only in a rough manner, the extent to which people actually are carrying out in practice what they say they believe.

Information of this type can be difficult to collect because of the ever-present "Christian mask." This describes the outward posture that says, "I am a happy, extroverted, Bible-believing, witnessing Christian; and I have no problems." Some churches, quite frankly, have encouraged their members to wear this type of mask because of the gossip and finger pointing activated once someone admits some problems. The author well remembers a critical incident in his life when he asked a well-known Christian leader for help on the depression problem mentioned in the last chapter. His response? "Spirit-filled Christians don't have problems like that." What a putdown! You can be sure that a mask was worn in his presence after that point, but this man's advice also served to make the author skeptical of what he had to say thereafter. It is difficult to identify with someone who lives so far up in the "heavenlies."

The mask is worn for yet another reason. Most of us hesitate to open ourselves in this manner unless we are in an atmosphere characterized by genuine love and trust. As a result, we tend to hold back.

The problem of the mask means that sensitive observation, the leader's most utilized research tool, may disclose nothing whatsoever. Nonetheless, observation by a sensitive interpreter should always be used, because it can, at times, reveal a great deal.

The small group also can be a useful tool for purposes of research. People often drop their masks in this type of atmosphere, and church leaders can learn much if they attend such meetings on occasion as supportive participants.

Many have found, however, that observation and the small group fall short. Therefore, increasing numbers are making use of surveys administered anonymously from time to time. Opportunity is given for some searching questions, and the mask is likely to be lowered as long as anonymity is guaranteed. The author has helped church leaders around the world use this method, and the insights gained often can be quite astonishing.[2] Unless there are cultural factors that

---

[2]The author has written extensively on this subject elsewhere. For a discussion of the ways in which research can be used in the local church see James F. Engel and H. Wilbert Norton, *What's Gone Wrong With the Harvest?* (Grand Rapids, Mich.: Zondervan, 1975). For a review of techniques of research applicable to the Christian world, See James F. Engel, *How Can I Get Them to Listen?* (Grand Rapids, Mich.: Zondervan, 1977).

make surveying impractical, there really is no substitute for this method.

Set Measurable Goals

It now will be assumed that the desired end product has been specified and data have been collected to reveal the extent to which people approach this ideal in terms of beliefs and behavior. This is the point at which strategic thinking should begin and not before. The usual tendency is to design the discipleship program and charge ahead without any indication of where people are at the outset. This is nothing more than an extreme form of program orientation, and the odds of success are low indeed.

There is an old saying that if you don't know where you are going you will never know if you hit it. Pure and simple, this is the reason for a statement of goals. This statement should specify precisely what is expected to happen within a given period of time. In other words, what will the outcomes be in terms of shifts in belief and behavior if the program is successful? Vague terminology will not do; these outcomes should be put in quantitative terms insofar as possible.

Let's assume that there is good reason within a church to begin a period of teaching on contemporary witness. Here is one possible statement of goals:

1. Ninety percent will have completed the assigned reading (a combination of Bible passages and, we hope, portions of this book).
2. Ninety percent will be able to articulate the spiritual decision process by describing the manner in which a friend came to Christ.
3. Seventy-five percent will have talked with at least one neighbor and will be able both to pinpoint where that person falls in the spiritual decision process and to identify important felt needs.
4. Fifty percent will have taken steps to initiate bridges of friendship with at least one person that they did not know well prior to the start of this class.

Obviously this is quite sketchy and should be viewed as illustrative.

It is always difficult to know just how much change to expect in a given period of time. If there has been no prior experience in quantitative goal setting, initial projections must, of necessity, represent kind of a stab in the dark. But as a backlog of experience grows, one will be able to be much more precise in the future because reference can always be made to what happened in similar situations in the past. Even though the goals as stated may be overly ambitious or, conversely, not sufficiently challenging, the specificity of statement provides the "tracks on which strategy must run" and also enables a clear measurement of effectiveness.[3]

Terminate the "Banking Concept" of Teaching

There is a commonplace philosophy of teaching found in all parts of the world that is labeled by Paulo Freire as the "banking concept."[4] The teacher's idea is to fill up what he or she considers to be an "empty pot" with more head knowledge within the frame of reference that the teacher wishes to maintain. In other words, the goal is to discourage critical thinking and to reinforce what are considered to be desired beliefs and behavior. When carried to the extreme, it is one-way communication designed only to bring about conformity.

The alternative is to view education as a means of helping the individual to pose problems, arrive at potential solutions, and take meaningful action to change unfavorable circumstances. As Freire puts it,

> The role of the educator is not to "fill" the educatee with "knowledge," technical or otherwise. It is rather to attempt to move towards a new way of thinking in both educator and educatee, through the dialogical relationships between both. The flow is in both directions.[5]

Mutual trust, of course, is a necessity if this approach is to work. Probably most essential is the requirement that those doing the teaching have confidence that people can and will behave in responsible ways if they are freed to chart their own destiny.

This approach, referred to by Freire as *conscientizacão,* is likely to run against the grain of practice of those churches that seem to be more concerned with conformity through legalism than anything else. This legalistic practice is nothing more than manipulation, regardless of the extent to which it is justified with seemingly spiritual terms.[6]

---

[3]A most helpful source is Robert F. Mager, *Preparing Instructional Objectives* (Belmont, Ca.: Fearon Publishers, 1972).

[4]Paulo Freire, *Pedagogy of the Oppressed* (New York: Seabury Press, 1968).

[5]Paulo Freire, *Extension for Communication* (New York: Seabury Press, 1973), p. 125.

[6]Everett L. Shostrom, *Man, the Manipulator* (New York: Bantam Books, 1967).

When the dialogical process is put into effect the teacher assumes a different role. It is his or her responsibility to help others to understand the dimensions of critical issues within a biblical context but not to hand down ready made solutions. Instead, skillful guidance is provided in the problem-solving process so that others are equipped creatively to "remake their own world."[7]

Jesus Himself was a master of this approach. He taught principles to His disciples in the process of day-to-day life, but they were expected to reason things out for themselves. Of course, He would apply rebuke and correction, but mostly He exemplified the teaching style of one whose greatest concern is to stimulate an ability for creative problem solving. The success of His disciples, when empowered and enlightened by the Holy Spirit, is proof that they were good learners.

Ongoing Measurement of Effectiveness

It is necessary to turn once again to research to document the extent to which the strategy followed actually succeeded in achieving the stated goals. Often the best method is readministration of a questionnaire given at the outset to reveal the extent of change that took place. This is a very simple form of educational testing that has been in use in the secular world for more than forty years. Yet the author has yet to see any extensive application of this standard methodology in Christian education. This allegation, by the way, is not mere conjecture. It is based on contact and interaction with most evangelical publishers and with the heads of a number of denominations.

Why are we so hesitant to engage in measurement and evaluation? In large part, it reflects lack of awareness and understanding. That can be easily remedied. More disturbing is the still not uncommon attitude that seems to say, "My mind is made up; don't confuse me with the facts." Now the problem becomes one of "hardening of the stewardship arteries," and it must be dealt with on that spiritual level. No amount of education will help in this latter case.

THE MEDIA OF CULTIVATION

The reader will recall this principle from Chapter 6: The mass media have only a contributory role in evangelism; their role is to

[7]Paulo Freire, *Education for Critical Consciousness* (New York: Seabury Press, 1973), p. 18.

build awareness and change belief and not to trigger a decision. The interpersonal media, especially face-to-face contacts, assume a more decisive role. The same generalization holds in the ministry of cultivation. At the very most, mass media are an important adjunct to the teaching ministry that takes place in the classroom, in small groups, and from the pulpit. Therefore, it is essential that the mass media be integrated into the work of the church if they are to be useful.

In this section we will examine, first of all, the teaching ministry within the church. Then the mass, platform, and group media will be discussed. Because many details on media were given in Chapters 6 and 7, exposition here will be more brief.

Media Within the Local Church

Nida has pointed out that "the sermon has become so focal a point of Protestant religious communication that we tend to equate the two."[8] Probably it still must rank as the most important teaching vehicle within the local church (apart from the Christian education program), but small groups also are coming to the fore as a useful channel for training.

The Sermon. According to Justin Martyr and other writers, worship in the early church contained both the liturgy of the Word and the liturgy of the Eucharist.[9] Through the former liturgy, God addresses His people; in turn, the people address God through the Eucharist and through other forms of adoration and praise. Something has happened, however, to shift the balance so that the worship service now has become little more than a lecture with hymns in many churches.

Perhaps the root cause of this shift in balance can be traced to about the time of the Reformation. As Gavin Reid has suggested, the pastor was probably the only educated person in the congregation.[10] Hunger for the Word of God had to be met somehow, and the spoken message delivered at the church, the most central meeting point of the community, was a logical means. But times changed. Bibles became available to the average man, and growing numbers acquired education. It has now reached the point where many in a congregation are as well-educated as the pastor, and perhaps even

---

[8]Eugene A. Nida, *Message in Mission* (New York: Harper & Brothers, 1960), p. 174.

[9]Quoted in Robert E. Webber, *Common Roots* (Grand Rapids, Mich.: Zondervan, 1978), pp. 79–81.

[10]Gavin Reid, *The Gagging of God* (London: Hodder and Stoughton, 1969), especially chs. 1–5.

better educated. Furthermore, the average church member has access to a wide variety of exegetical aids in the form of books, cassettes, and broadcast programs. Therefore, the sermon no longer plays such a central role.

Times have changed in yet another critical respect. In an earlier era a highly structured message given in linear form from the pulpit was quite appropriate. Today some would refer to this as a "hot message,"[11] meaning a highly structured presentation leading to an unmistakable and well-articulated conclusion. Those born in the post-World War II era, however, have been significantly influenced by television. This medium offers a montage of sight and sound that involves the viewer in a much less structured way. In other words, the "cool message," which lacks orderly presentation and the unmistakable conclusion, has become more commonplace. It is not surprising that a younger generation is not as responsive as its counterparts to the lecture format.

Regardless of these changes, the sermon retains its central role, and perhaps this is as it should be. Yet, the negative consequences cannot be ignored either. First, worship in its true sense tends to be minimized or eliminated altogether if the sermon is given undue prominence. The definition of worship used here is, ". . . a rehearsal of who God is and what He has done . . . the relationship which exists between God and His people."[12] Some might disagree with this definition, but there is no legitimate way to claim that the sermon captures the essence of this congregational expression.

Next, it is entirely possible that such reliance on the sermon is a reason why so many churches are composed mostly of Sunday-morning-only Christians. Come, listen, and leave. Nida comes right to the point here:

> In some instances the themes are so threadbare and the content so predictable that the "information" is almost nil. Too often the Sunday morning becomes the ideal time for the second Sunday morning nap or for uninterrupted planning of the afternoon's activities or the week's work.[13]

---

[11]McLuhan has claimed that media themselves are hot or cool. See Marshall McLuhan and Quentin Fiore, *The Medium Is the Message* (New York: Bantam Books, 1970). This is perhaps true, but one cannot separate the message from the medium. As a result, the author has come to the conclusion that message structure is the crucial factor. For elaboration see James F. Engel, Hugh G. Wales, and Martin R. Warshaw, *Promotional Strategy*, 3rd ed. (Homewood, Ill.: Richard D. Irwin, 1975), ch. 13.

[12]Webber, *Common Roots*, p. 78.

[13]Nida, *Message in Mission*, p. 174.

Yet another danger is that the sermon is viewed by some pastors as a way of attracting crowds. As was stressed earlier, there is a popular theory that people do not come back if they are upset or made angry. Therefore, the controversial is avoided. In fact, Stark and his colleagues found that only about six percent of all sermons given by Protestant ministers in nine major denominations dealt with such controversial issues as race and poverty.[14] Those in the theologically conservative ranks were most likely to have silent pulpits in this respect, whereas the overwhelmingly theologically and politically liberal clergy were much more likely to speak out.

Finally, the sermon generally is one-way communication, and this violates one of the most validated communication principles: Feedback is an essential aid to the accuracy of interpersonal communication.[15] This feedback must come in two ways. First, the preacher must have continued contact with congregational members so that there is awareness of their background and needs. Second, feedback must come afterwards as well so that there is some indication of what "got through." "I enjoyed your sermon" may make the pastor feel good, but that is about all.

So, does this mean that the sermon should be abandoned? Not at all. Rather the emphasis should be placed on remedying some of these weaknesses. Here are a few suggestions:

1. Those who are coming to church are seeking answers not abstract doctrine. Personal applications are imperative. In fact, the best messages are those that have been worked out by the speaker in his or her own life. Bill Gothard has made the astute observation that God works out His message through the day-to-day struggles in the life of each person. These lessons should then be shared.
2. Avoid theological jargon. Often this is just the "ingroup language" of the religious professional that means little to the average member of the congregation.[16]
3. Guarantee that there is feedback. This can be done in two ways.

[14]Rodney Stark, Bruce D. Foster, Charles Y. Glock, and Harold E. Quinley, "Ministers as Moral Guides: The Sounds of Silence," in Charles Y. Glock, ed., *Religion in Sociological Perspective: Essays in the Empirical Study of Religion* (Belmont, Ca.: Wadsworth, 1973), pp. 163–186.

[15]For one of the classic sources on this subject, see H.J. Leavitt and R.A.H. Mueller, "Some Effects of Feedback on Communication," *Human Relations,* vol. 4(1951), p. 410 ff.

[16]Most textbooks on homiletics stress this point. See, for example, Milton Crum, Jr., *Manual on Preaching* (Valley Forge, Pa.: Judson Press, 1977).

First the message may be pretested on a small group of perhaps six to ten people. Then these questions should be asked: (1) What was the main point? (2) What are you expected to do differently now that you have heard this sermon? (3) What do you think of what was said? The problem of sermon comprehension mentioned at the outset of Chapter 1 would rapidly diminish if this were done. Next, build in feedback after presentation in the form of some type of "talk it over group."[17] Both of these approaches have been used by David Mains with real benefit.[18]

4. Make sure the sermon is just one of many communication channels within the church.[19] In other words, do not expect it to carry the entire burden of cultivation.
5. Experiment with slides, tapes, overhead projectors, and other forms of visual aids both to provide variety and to substitute for the enervating effect of uninterrupted preaching.

In the final analysis, each church must assess whether or not the sermon is accomplishing the intended purpose of building the believer. While the ministry of *preaching* has always been a means for God to speak to His people, *preaching does not always require sermonizing.* There is a multitude of other ways it can be done, including drama, film, and so on.

Christian Education. The church has a clear biblical mandate to teach the believer, and one of the most visible means for the past hundred years or so is the Sunday School, at least in the United States. Usually it does not meet before 9:30 A.M. (this is to be sure everyone finishes milking his cows), and its program consists of opening exercises and thirty-five to forty-five minutes of teaching using materials prepared outside the church.

More often than not, the "banking concept" of education is the prevalent philosophy. The goal is to indoctrinate within some clearly stated theological and cultural guidelines, and dogmatic answers to honest, reasonable questions are given. Individuality either is quashed or not given opportunity for expression.

Secular education, on the other hand, is going in some different directions. Lecture is supplemented or replaced by audio-visual media. Content is less likely to be put forth in dogmatic fashion, and,

[17] A. Duane Litfin, "In Defense of the Sermon: A Communicational Approach," *Journal of Psychology and Theology,* vol. 2 (Winter, 1974), pp. 36–43.

[18] David Mains, *Full Circle* (Waco, Texas: Word Books, 1971).

[19] Litfin, "In Defense of the Sermon," p. 40.

of greatest importance, there is growing awareness that the student must be helped to cope with life in his or her adult ego state. Students are taught to think, and rarely is emphasis placed on the one "right answer" to controversial questions and issues. A learning environment of this type, in turn, requires dialogue between student and teacher.

Fortunately, the outmoded banking concept is beginning to break down in the church.[20] New materials are now being provided that capitalize upon modern trends in education. The learner is taught to reason and to cope with real issues within a framework of Christian doctrine and scriptural principle. Furthermore, Christian education is no longer confined to the Sunday morning time slot and is finding its way outside of church walls. Larry Richards has predicted that Christian education will increasingly become a nonformal process moving away from a schoolroom atmosphere, although he cautions that changes of this nature occur slowly.[21]

The Small Group. One of the best learning environments is the small group where free exchange of viewpoint is encouraged. Increasingly this channel is being viewed as a major method of building Christian maturity. If this is to happen, however, there must be more than unguided sharing. If trained leaders are provided along with structured materials, this has proven to be one of the best ways to uncover spiritual gifts, provide a ministry of healing, and to bring those to the surface who offer real leadership potential.[22]

Theological Education by Extension. Many churches on the mission field in particular suffer from an absence of trained leadership. As a result, discipleship materials have been put in an extension format for home or small group study without a leader being present. The method most often used is programmed instruction. As of 1977, approximately 35,000 people around the world were involved in theological education by extension (TEE), and the numbers are expected to grow dramatically.[23] Of those studying in this fashion, 52 percent are located in Latin America, 19.7 percent in Africa, 12.1 percent in Asia, and about 10 percent in the United States.[24]

---

[20]An especially useful source on this subject is Lawrence Richards, *A New Face for the Church* (Grand Rapids, Mich.: Zondervan, 1970).

[21]Remarks made by Larry Richards at a symposium of Christian leaders assembled by the Standard Publishing Company in 1975.

[22]This has been the experience of the Churches Alive organization. See Kay Oliver, "One Secret of Lasting Growth," *Moody Monthly* (June, 1977), pp. 27–29.

[23]*Missionary News Service*, vol. 25 (February 15, 1978).

[24]"World Survey of TEE—1977," *Emissary*, vol. 11 (published by the Evangelical Missions Information Service, January, 1978).

It has been the author's experience in offering a graduate-level extension course using audio cassettes and a workbook that learning often exceeds that possible in a classroom. Therefore, the use of this tool should expand by leaps and bounds.

Mass Media

Emphasis is placed here on Christian books, periodicals, and broadcasts.

Christian Books. As was pointed out in Chapter 6, more than 2,000 new Christian titles were introduced by publishers in North America during 1977, and this continued the average growth of 18.9 percent among evangelical publishers since 1971. An impressive record? Of course, but there are some clouds on the horizon of this otherwise rosy picture.

A great many Christian publishers are profit-making enterprises. This is not bad per se, but it is difficult to walk the tightrope between ministry to the believer and profit maximization. It is interesting that the best sellers focus around a few "hot" issues. One publisher succeeds with a title, and others are immediately in the ranks with virtual carbon copies. Probably most disturbing was the spate of books on prophecy mostly written from a dispensational point of view following the success of Hal Lindsey's *The Late Great Planet Earth.*

What happens, on the other hand, to the "little guy" who writes a book on the subject, say, of the contradiction between materialism and a truly Christian life-style? First of all, it will be difficult to get such a title published, because the market probably will be pretty small given the incidence of North American cultural syncretism. Next, the publisher probably will be reluctant to give it promotion even if it is published because of the drain on sales revenues, which will be meager at best. The net result: a tiny sale that does little to raise the consciousness of Christians on critical but nonpopular issues.

The discussion here could be taken from the pages of any secular marketing book. A basic principle is to market only those products that offer a substantial profit potential. Others are regarded as losers and are never brought to market or are given little or no marketing support. How does all this square up with a goal of ministry? Indeed, it is fair to ask whether it is possible for a prophet to make a profit.

Yet another problem is the probability that no more than ten percent of the Christians in the United States ever enter a Christian bookstore, according to a reliable source outside the publishing industry. Small wonder that only a handful of titles ever have sales beyond 100,000 copies, and the great majority have much less. If one conservatively estimates that there are twenty-five to thirty million evangelical Christians in America, this means that no more than one to five percent at the very most will read even the most popular titles, even taking account of the so-called "pass along" audience. No book is thus likely to make much of an impact unless it is an exceptionally big seller.

Perhaps the root of the problem is that publishers and bookstores have not generally focused much on the local church. Of course, product promotion will be aimed at this market, but reference is made here to a serious attempt to ask local leadership, "How can our ministry through books help in what you are trying to do in this congregation?" The reader will recall that a parachurch organization can justify its existence by providing a service that the church cannot provide for itself. If the attitude stated here is sincerely conveyed at all levels of the church, the ministry through the printed word can vault forward. Not surprisingly, profits will increase too!

The reader should not take this discussion as a condemnation of the Christian book industry, because that is not the intent. Rather, the objective is to provide a framework for an ever expanding ministry. Fortunately some publishers are taking these challenges quite seriously, and it is exciting to see the changes that are taking place.

Religious Periodicals. For purposes of convenience, newspapers and magazines are combined into one category, because they have some real similarities in ministry.

The periodical, and there are many throughout the world, has the opportunity for journalistic reporting and the ability to deal with topical issues in a way that would not usually be possible in the local church. Thus the opportunity exists for a dynamic and truly helpful ministry, but there are some factors which, unfortunately, inhibit this ministry potential.

There is an unresolved issue as to whether or not a magazine or newspaper should be reinforcing present values or be change oriented. To a degree it always must be reinforcing in the sense that historical Christian doctrine is maintained and affirmed. Furthermore, devotional articles, fictional pieces, poetry, and other features can augment and strengthen the ministry of the local church.

The issue concerns the degree to which there should be investigative reporting and prophetic commentary. James L. Johnson contends that the record is pretty bad in this respect:

> As far as the Christian press is concerned, it has never really arrived at a substantial opinion function role any more than it has arrived at investigative reporting. Too much of published "opinion" is confined to what everybody already knows so that it becomes "bland leading the bland."[25]

Johnson's point is that editors of many denominational or parachurch publications have little or no choice as to what they will cover and what they will speak out on editorially. They must live within a fixed policy. An example is a denominational leader who refuses to allow the editor to write a series of articles on abuse of installment buying by pastors. The reason given was that people will conclude that the denomination contains "undisciplined" ministers. The outcome was complete avoidance of the opportunity to help ministers cope with a problem in their lives.

There also is a muzzling effect when uncertainty surrounding audience reaction controls editorial content. One magazine avoided airing both sides of the biblical inerrancy question for fear that readers would think the staff was soft on the issue and withhold subscriptions. For this same reason another Christian magazine has yet to run an article on Christian feminism that gives anything but the traditional view. As Johnson says, this type of policy, ". . . casts the Christian press as a paper tiger as far as the world is concerned."[26] The great loser, of course, is the reader who is seeking objectivity.

Fortunately, the wheels of change are very much in evidence. In a published symposium with editors of four major periodicals, it is clear that these leaders are beginning to wrestle constructively with the need to speak out in a more forthright manner.[27] All agreed that there is a problem of alienation through change, but steps are being taken nonetheless.

Christian Broadcasting. Christian broadcasting on a large scale is primarily a North American phenomenon, and thousands of Americans will attest to the significance of the teaching ministry they have received first over the radio and more recently over television. Some

---

[25]James L. Johnson, "Role of Conflict and Journalistic Dysfunction," *Christian Communications Spectrum,* vol. 3 (Summer, 1977), p. 12 ff.

[26]*Ibid.*

[27]"The Changing Face of Magazines—How Much and Why?" *Christian Communications Spectrum,* vol. 3 (Summer, 1977), pp. 8–11.

long-standing programs have become household mainstays, and the effects of this ministry should never be underestimated. But, as was pointed out in Chapter 6, most syndicated programs and religious stations reach an older audience.[28] In fact, only one third of fifty-six religious stations in a recent survey reported making any attempts to reach those under thirty-five.[29] It is interesting in this context that a program designed strictly for teen-agers is listened to mostly by women between the ages of forty and sixty-four.[30] This means, of course, that a significant portion of the potential Christian audience is untouched by most programming. Fortunately there are such exceptions as the Southern Baptist program "Powerline," which features top 40 music and contemporary comment. It now is aired on 980 stations across the country (mostly secular), and ranks as the country's most-listened-to religious show.[31]

In recent years Christian broadcasting has received some careful scrutiny, and not all of the resulting comments are positive. Consider the words of veteran Christian broadcaster, Phill Butler:

> While most honest observers would acknowledge that our principal resources in Christian radio and television speak to the already-convinced, a large percentage of even this programming for Christians is not much more than a glossy pablum—spiritualized entertainment with little of the tough stuff of discipleship in it.[32]

Butler goes on to lament that the situation he describes definitely was not the case when Christian radio went on the air in the 1920s and calls for a return to its original concept.

Horst Albrecht, commenting from a non-North American perspective, uses an even sharper lance.[33] His claim is that we are middle-class people using middle-class symbols to present only a sterile middle-class religion that does not touch life at all. This may

---

[28]See, for example, David C. Solt, "Audience Profile for Religious Broadcasts, *International Christian Broadcasters Bulletin* (April, 1971), p. 3ff; Ronald Johnstone, "Who Listens to Religious Radio Broadcasts Anymore," *Journal of Broadcasting* (Winter, 1971–72); and *Family Radio News* (July/August/September, 1974), p. 3.

[29]James M. Birkett, "A Survey Study of Religious Stations," *Religious Broadcasting,* vol. 6 (June/July, 1974), p. 15.

[30]Tom Sommerville, Tom Hessy, and David T. Amster, "A Survey of the Family Radio Audience" (Family Radio Stations, Inc., 1974).

[31]*BEAM International,* vol. 29 (July, 1978), p. 3.

[32]Phill Butler, "The Christian Use of Radio and TV," *INTERLIT,* vol. 14 (December, 1977), p. 2.

[33]Horst Albrecht, "Who Says in What Channel to Whom With What Affect?" *WACC Journal,* vol. 22 (1975), pp. 22–28.

seem a bit harsh, but Charles Christensen, associated for many years with WMBI in Chicago (Moody Bible Institute), has said much the same thing.[34] He raises the question of whether anyone in radio will use a creative idea. He particularly singles out the local Christian station that presents back-to-back syndicated programming that makes the Christian life an "exercise in sermon tasting."[35]

Christian broadcasters also must walk the line between ministry and profit maximization, because there is money to be made in Christian radio. There are frequent announcements in *Advertising Age* or *Broadcasting* that another secular station is about to go "religious" in format because of profit. All that need be done is fully automate the station and run a steady diet of syndicated preaching and teaching programs, most of which pay to get on the air.

Probably the most critical question centers on the return for investment placed into this medium if the only intent is to minister to an over-fifty audience. There are growing numbers that are changing format to break out of this syndrome, and that is a favorable trend. Only a relative handful have any consistent measures of listening audience, however,[36] although that too is beginning to change. The issue that must be addressed is whether or not a placing of the same resources in other media will have greater effects in helping the believer to grow in the faith.

By the way, one of the answers often given to questions on audience impact is that there are over 125 million people exposed each week to some type of religious programming on television or over the radio in the United States. Let it be noted that there is no basis in fact *whatsoever* for such a claim. All anyone needs to do is examine the syndicated broadcasting ratings put out by ARB or Nielsen.

The reader should not infer that the author is down on religious broadcasting, because this is not the case. His life, after all, is now devoted to training professionals to take their place in the ranks of Christian and secular media. The fact is that he and his Wheaton colleagues stand with a large and growing group within this industry that are calling for some rethinking of basic assumptions and a restoration of a ministry cutting edge that seems to have been lost in some quarters. An enormous ministry potential remains untapped.

Critical Issues Facing the Christian Media. Publishers and broad-

---

[34]Charles Christensen, "Will Anyone in Radio Use a Creative Idea?" *Christian Communications Spectrum,* vol. 3 (Summer, 1977), p. 22 ff.

[35]*Ibid.*

[36]Birkett, "A Survey Study of Religious Stations."

casters are parachurch organizations, even if they operate from a denominational headquarters. This means that they exist primarily to serve the local church, and there is no automatic guarantee of continued existence if this is not taking place. Here are several issues that must be addressed by all who take the ministry of cultivation seriously within the ranks of Christian media.

(1) Are Activities Integrated With the Church? As has been said before, the essential question to ask is this: How can our publishing or broadcast ministry augment the discipleship ministry within the local church? The local church is placed in the driver's seat, so to speak, instead of the other way around. There is no better way to keep in touch with the grassroots and to guarantee that profit does not obscure ministry. For some to take this step would be a dramatic innovation indeed. Unless, it *is* taken, however, the parachurch organization will be hard pressed to justify a continued existence from any perspective other than profit making.

(2) Is Scripturally Valid Content Being Presented? This raises a thorny issue, but it cannot be avoided. Some of the things appearing both in print and over the air are not helping the Christian to build a scripturally based belief structure. In fact, more harm than good is done at times.

Let's take as an example the widely read books by Marabel Morgan, *The Total Woman*[37] and *Total Joy*.[38] In some ways Morgan has succeeded in helping wives to ". . . revive romance, reestablish communication, break down barriers, and put sizzle back into [their] marriage."[39] All this is well and good, but look at the basic premise on which all of this is built: *Please your husband—make him the center of your life—and you can have anything you want.* In other words, happiness in life comes by manipulating another person. How does that correspond to the writings of the apostle Paul on love in 1 Corinthians 13? This is far more a doctrine of manipulation than of love.

This is admittedly a somewhat extreme example, and the author does not wish to be unfair to Mrs. Morgan. But it is necessary to ask of all those who surface in the mass media to justify the extent to which they are contributing to a biblical life-style. Sub-Christian teachings should be labeled for what they are.

(3) What Effects Are Being Achieved in Lives. Here are some very pragmatic questions centering on the impact of mass media efforts:

---

[37]Marabel Morgan, *The Total Woman* (Old Tappan, N.J.: Spire Books, 1975).
[38]Marabel Morgan, *Total Joy* (Old Tappan, N.J.: Fleming H. Revell, 1976).
[39]Morgan, *The Total Woman*, p. 20.

a. Is anyone exposed? This is measured by copies sold, the number who tune in the program, and so on.
b. Has reader or viewer attention been attracted and held? Exposure does not guarantee attention. How many, for example, have read a given article in a magazine or have really listened to a particular radio program? Such information can only be collected by survey, and it is encouraging to see how many publishers are now beginning to conduct readership surveys with some regularity. *Campus Life* magazine stands at the forefront in this respect. Is it any surprise that it is the most-asked-for magazine among Christian youth?
c. Have the main points of the message been grasped? In other words, has there been comprehension as intended? Once again, surveys are mandatory to answer this kind of question.
d. What effects, if any, have taken place in the life of the viewer or reader? This is the least investigated yet most important issue of all. One research team in the Wheaton Graduate School asked readers of a very popular book whether or not they understood its message and have taken its suggestions seriously. This is one of a series of books, by the way, by an author labeled by Gary Collins of Trinity Seminary as a "pop psychologist." The results were mixed, at best, and one thing is sure: The author will not want to quote many of these readers as successful case histories in his next book.

Questions such as these cannot be answered without a continuing program of research. The problem is that research costs money, but so do mass media efforts that misfire. The issue is stewardship. Do we take our God-given mandates seriously or not?

The Platform Media

Reference is made here to seminars, drama, and film all of which can be used either in the local church or in cooperation with other churches. One authority has estimated that the number of films used in churches during 1974 increased by thirty-five percent over the preceding year.[40] Whether his figures are accurate or not, there has been a healthy upsurge. Moreover, there are a number of capable resource people who can augment church staff in such crucial areas

[40]Mal Couch, "Let it Be Done in Film," *Christian Communications Spectrum*, vol. 1 (Winter, 1975), p. 28 ff.

as Christian marriage, social action, and so on. There is little to be said except to encourage continued growth in this type of ministry.

Drama in the local church, however, raises some eyebrows. Remember that drama has the unique feature of highlighting the mysterious, the subtle, the artistic—things that cannot be captured any other way. Often its impact exceeds that of the spoken word as churches such as Willowcreek Community Church in Palatine, Illinois, have discovered.

The Group Media

The group media first mentioned in Chapter 6 are those specifically programmed to provide for two-way communication. The audio cassette has proved to be an especially effective teaching tool both to an individual and to a group. It assumes no literacy, and it can be tailored to speak to issues precisely in the language of those for whom it is intended. Complete programs of Bible teaching can be included, for example.[41] How else can good teaching be taken into areas where church leadership has not progressed beyond a primary education? The video cassette performs the same function when playback equipment is available. As yet, costs have kept this method from having much penetration, but that may change rapidly.

In the United States and certain other developed countries, cable television is an option. Senzig has advanced the useful suggestion that one or more churches go on the air with teaching programs to be viewed in the home, which can then be followed by group discussion.[42] In this way the ministry of the church can be dramatically extended beyond its walls. There are some programs now available for this purpose.[43]

A CONCLUDING WORD

The ministry of cultivation is entering a new era. Scholars are centering anew on the true meaning of "maturity in Christ," utilizing for the first time insights from the behavioral sciences to facilitate

---

[41]The basic resource here is Viggo B. Søgaard, *Everything You Need to Know for a Cassette Ministry* (Minneapolis: Bethany Fellowship, 1975).

[42]Richard J. Senzig, "Cable May Not Be Able," *Christian Communications Spectrum,* vol. 1 (Fall/Winter, 1975), pp. 28–30.

[43]Terry F. Phillips, "How to Get into CATV," *Religious Broadcasting,* vol. 10 (February/March, 1978), pp. 46–48.

understanding of biblical truth. In this sense, the field of Christian counseling, still in relative infancy, contains many of the keys to future understanding.

Also, we are now in the "era of accountability." This means that all who are in any phase of the ministry of cultivation must justify their stewardship on the basis of fact and not on spiritually pious claims. There will be an inevitable sifting out process as this practice becomes more widespread.

Finally, the "ball" is in the hands of the local church as it has not been for some years. Much of the burden of discipleship has shifted in the past, perhaps by default, to the parachurch organizations (publishers, broadcasters, etc.). The pendulum has now swung back, and it is hoped a more constructive partnership between both entities will be the result.

PART IV
THE CHURCH AND THE WORLD

Now that we have discussed and evaluated the subject of spiritual decision process from a variety of perspectives, it is necessary to broaden the focus to the issues facing the church and world evangelization.

The church always has had the mandate to "go unto all the world." From the very outset it has had to contend with the problems and opportunities of cross cultural communication. Chapter 12 reviews this subject from an anthropological perspective and attempts to lay a foundation for true partnership in a world church. Chapter 13 raises the issues of partnership between churches and parachurch organizations that are genuinely attempting individually and collectively to proclaim and exemplify the kingdom of God. It will become clear that unity is an imperative if world evangelization is to take place. Finally, Chapter 14 reviews the main points of preceding chapters and raises the issues and questions that make up the agenda for world evangelization in the coming decades.

CHAPTER 12
Cross-Cultural Communication

The year 1965 marked the beginning of a new era in the country of Indonesia.[1] The entire religious life of a nation had been altered following an abortive Communist coup and the savage deaths of approximately 400,000 Indonesians. A religious revival followed resulting in 2,000,000 baptisms between 1965 and 1971. Membership in the Baptist church alone more than doubled.

While this development is a real cause for rejoicing, it also triggered a series of critical problems for the Baptist church. The root cause was that the entire life of the church was based on a model imported from North America. The crisis was especially acute at the Baptist Seminary. Enrollment jumped sharply, but students were being trained to perpetuate a style of church life based on American theology and methodology. Students had been led to expect a missionary subsidy that would assure a salary plus a fully functioning and equipped church upon graduation. This arrangement did not materialize. Furthermore, the content of their education was pretty far removed from the issues of Indonesian life itself. In short, the seminary was no longer producing a graduate who could cope with the changes that had taken place. The most critical factor was a western style of training that insulated both pastors and church members from the indigenous forms and natural lines of communication in the culture. To use the words of Avery Willis:

[1]This discussion appears in Avery Willis, "Moving Toward the Contextualization of Theological Education: Extension Development at the Indonesian Baptist Theological Seminary," *Extension Seminary,* vol. 2 (1978), p. 1ff.

> The students had become victims, although willingly, of an instructional approach that made them dependent on foreign funds and expertise and which, at best, equipped them only to sustain an American model that was not viable in the culture.[2]

Fortunately a remedy was found in the form of extension education, which permitted church leaders to retain secular employment and study in their own locale. Furthermore, content was drastically altered to give it the "Indonesian flavor" it so desperately needed.

It is not necessary to elaborate further on the solution itself; the important point to note here is that the situation faced in the early 1970s by the Baptist church in Indonesia is quite common. The message itself, the church and its forms, and expected Christian life-style were not *contextualized* within the culture. As the late Sri Lankan church leader, D. T. Niles, put it, the gospel is like a seed that must be sowed. But our temptation is to bring along not only the seed of the gospel but our own plant of Christianity, flowerpot included. The need now is to break this flowerpot and let the seed grow as it should in its own soil.[3]

The term *contextualization* was coined in the early 1970s and originally had a somewhat technical and limited application only to the field of theological education. But the late Byang Kato and others have broadened it to mean, ". . . making concepts or ideas relevant in a given situation. In reference to Christian practices, it is an effort to express the never changing Word of God in ever changing modes for relevance."[4] It requires some rigorous analysis and thinking in these three dimensions:[5]

1. An understanding of the original context of biblical revelation so that the essence of biblical meaning may be abstracted apart from the cultural context in which it was communicated.
2. An understanding of the cultural filter through which each interpreter must evaluate biblical texts so that contamination may be minimized.

---

[2]*Ibid.,* p. 2.

[3]Quoted in Mortimer Arias, "Contextual Evangelization in Latin America: Between Accommodation and Confrontation," *Occasional Bulletin,* vol. 2 (January, 1978), pp. 19–28.

[4]Byang H. Kato, "The Gospel, Cultural Context and Religious Syncretism," in J.D. Douglas, ed., *Let the Earth Hear His Voice* (Minneapolis, Minn.: World Wide Publications, 1975), p. 1217.

[5]Harvie M. Conn, "Contextualization: A New Dimension for Cross-Cultural Hermeneutic," *Evangelical Missions Quarterly,* vol. 14 (January, 1978), pp. 39–48.

3. An understanding of the cultural context of the hearer so that truth is communicated with true biblical fidelity.

As we are applying the term here, then, contextualization goes far beyond theologizing. It pervades all of the life of the church—its message, its practices, its forms of Christian life-style. The goal is to achieve cultural relevance without sacrifice of biblical fidelity—quite a tight rope indeed! As the reader soon will discover, the tension focuses at a critical point: What exactly is the meaning of the gospel message?[6] Thus cross-cultural communication is a more difficult subject than it might appear to be at first glance.

In this chapter discussion centers, first of all, on the issue of what is culture. Once this basis has been established, we move on to the process of contextualization and end the chapter with some observations of how the church worldwide can achieve a higher degree of "partnership in mission."

THE CONCEPT OF CULTURE

Culture is a term that has been used in many varied ways, and there have been literally hundreds of definitions given. For purposes of this book culture is defined to encompass the *complex of values, ideas, attitudes, and other meaningful symbols created by people to shape human behavior and the artifacts of that behavior, transmitted from one generation to the next.*[7] We have now entered the domain of the cultural anthropologist, and it is interesting to note the extent to which this behavioral science has both pervaded and influenced the theory and practice of cross-cultural communication in the past two decades.[8] Probably more than anything else, this development has led to something approaching a science of missions practice, now referred to as *missiology.*

This brief definition of culture contains several implicit dimensions that were brought out in the *Willowbank Report,* a document

[6]F. Ross Kinsler, "Mission in Context: The Current Debate About Contextualization," *Evangelical Missions Quarterly,* vol. 14 (January, 1978), pp. 23–29.

[7]James F. Engel, Roger D. Blackwell, and David T. Kollat, *Consumer Behavior,* 3rd. ed. (Hinsdale, Ill.: Dryden Press, 1978), p. 65.

[8]For helpful introductions to missionary anthropology, see William A. Smalley, "Anthropological Study and Missionary Scholarship," *Practical Anthropology,* vol. 7 (1960), pp. 113–123; William A. Smalley, *Readings in Missionary Anthropology* (South Pasadena, Ca.: William Carey Library, 1974); and Paul G. Hiebert, "Missions and Anthropology: A Love/Hate Relationship," *Missiology,* vol. 6 (April, 1978), pp. 165–180.

prepared by theologians and missiologists who gathered to study the impact of gospel on culture:[9]

1. Culture includes an integrated system of beliefs (about God or ultimate reality).
2. It also comprehends values focusing on what is true, good, beautiful, and normative.
3. Customs are specified on how to behave, relate to others, talk, pray, dress, and so on.
4. Institutions are developed (government, law courts, places of worship, schools, and so on) to bind society together and give it a sense of dignity, identity, continuity, and security.

Methods of Cross-Cultural Research

There is increasing recognition for the need to conduct research that leads to an understanding of the norms and values of a culture. The methods described briefly here include mass observation, participant observation, content analysis, cross-sectional surveys, and longitudinal studies.[10]

Mass Observation. This technique refers to the process whereby researchers interact with members of a culture who appear to be especially knowledgeable, listen to conversations, and observe behavior and interaction patterns. Such an approach should be followed by everyone who has opportunity to enter another culture, but it has its limitations. As Duijker and Frijda put it, ". . . there is no systematic sampling; the situations are not standardized; much of the material gathered is irrelevant to the specific problem studied."[11]

Participant-Observer Studies. This is a step up from mass observation, because the ethnographic researcher lives among the people he or she is studying and attempts to become an accepted part of the culture itself. One authority has described the approach of the anthropologist in this manner:

---

[9]*The Willowbank Report—Gospel and Culture,* Lausanne Occasional Papers #2 (Wheaton, Ill.: Lausanne Committee for World Evangelization, 1978), p. 7.

[10]For an introduction to cross-cultural research, see Thomas Rhys Williams, *Field Methods in the Study of Culture* (New York: Holt, Rinehart and Winston, 1967); Louis J. Luzbetak, *The Church and Cultures* (Techeny, Ill.: Divine World Publications, 1970); and Marvin K. Mayers, *Christianity Confronts Culture* (Grand Rapids, Mich.: Zondervan, 1974).

[11]H.C.J. Duijker and N.H. Frijda, *National Character and National Stereotypes: Confluence,* vol. 1 (Amsterdam: North-Holland, 1960), p. 120.

> He studies his fellow men not solely as a dispassionate observer but also as a participant observer. He tries to feel with them, to see things as they see them, to experience some portion of their life with them. On the other hand, he tries to balance his identifications with detached objectivity.[12]

Participant-observer studies have two major weaknesses: (1) there usually is no systematic sampling plan,[13] and (2) the actual physical presence of an observer may introduce changes into the culture.[14] Thus this type of anthropological field study is sometimes criticized for lack of objectivity and comprehensiveness. Nevertheless, the compensating factor is the gain in richness of content and depth of understanding.

Content Analysis. Content analysis isolates values, themes, role prescriptions, behavioral norms, and other cultural elements from verbal or written materials.[15] The main advantages are first of all that it can be used where personal contact is difficult or impossible and secondly that it is unobtrusive—a culture can be studied without awareness by others. In actuality, it should be the starting point of all cultural research, especially given the growth of published materials in most countries today.

Cross-Sectional Surveys. The survey of a large group at a given point in time (ie., a cross-section) has some distinct advantages. First, it is possible to sample systematically and thus be relatively sure that the full scope of a population has been studied. Second, one can pry behind the mask, so to speak, to find underlying values and feelings on issues that might not be evidenced either in day-to-day behavior or in normal conversation. Finally, it is possible to probe deeply into the values of subcultures—those segments of the total that often escape analysis.[16]

---

[12]Clyde Kluckhohn, "Common Humanity and Diverse Cultures," in Daniel Lerner (ed.), *The Human Meaning of the Social Sciences* (Cleveland, Ohio: World Publishing, 1959), pp. 251–252.

[13]For a discussion of this problem see B.D. Paul, "Interview Techniques and Field Relationships," in A.L. Kroeber *et. al.*, eds., *Anthropology Today: an Encyclopedia* (Chicago: University of Chicago Press, 1953), pp. 430–451.

[14]See Eugene J. Webb *et. al., Unobtrusive Measures: Nonreactive Research in the Social Sciences* (Chicago: Rand McNally, 1966).

[15]The classic source on this method is Bernard Berelson, *Content Analysis in Communication Research* (New York: Free Press, 1952). Also see R.C. North *et. al., Content Analysis: A Handbook with Applications for the Study of International Crisis* (Evanston, Ill: Northwestern University Press, 1963).

[16]For an example, see Engel, Blackwell, and Kollat, *Consumer Behavior,* pp. 76–80.

The cross-sectional survey probably has been used more in North America than elsewhere, but it is by no means confined to that context. The fact is that surveys are now undertaken in most countries of the world with a high degree of success.[17]

Longitudinal Studies. Longitudinal research involves studies running over an extended period of time. While it is relatively new in cross-cultural research, it offers great promise.

The most practical longitudinal method is repeated study of representative samples within a culture. The objective is to assess shifts in values from one time period to the next. This type of polling has largely been confined to the United States (examples are the Gallup Poll, the Harris Poll, and the Yankelovich "Monitor"), but there is nothing in the methodology itself to prevent its use elsewhere. Unfortunately, it can be quite expensive, and that may prove to be the most potent barrier.

Culture in Biblical Revelation[18]

The Lausanne Covenant declared that Scripture is ". . . without error in all that it affirms."[19] Yet Scripture was given in a cultural setting. The New Testament, for example, is steeped in both Jewish and Hellenistic culture, and the apostle Paul drew heavily from the vocabulary of Greek philosophy. This gives rise to the heavy burden of discerning exactly what Scripture is trying to say.

There is agreement that some commands such as the veiling of women in public and foot washing refer to obsolete cultural customs. But how does one decide that which is strictly cultural and that which is normative? The writers of *The Willowbank Report* are helpful in this context:

> . . . we believe the right response is neither a slavishly literal obedience nor an irresponsible disregard, but rather first a critical discernment of the text's inner meaning and then a translation of it into our own culture. . . . We are clear that the purpose of such "cultural transposition" is not to avoid obedience but rather to make it contemporary and authentic.[20]

Fortunately, it is the ministry of the Holy Spirit to provide continuing illumination when making such judgments (Eph. 1:17ff).

---

[17]Surveys have been undertaken in tribal situations in Thailand. See Viggo Søgaard, *Everything You Need to Know for a Cassette Ministry* (Minneapolis, Minn.: Bethany Fellowship, 1974).

[18]This section is based on the discussion in *The Willowbank Report,* pp. 7–10.

[19]Douglas, *Let the Earth Hear His Voice,* p. 3.

[20]*The Willowbank Report,* p. 9.

Culture and Christian Witness

The Lausanne Covenant makes some pointed statements about culture. First of all:

> Because man is God's creature, some of his culture is rich in beauty and goodness. Because he has fallen, all of it is tainted with sin and some of it is demonic. The Gospel does not presuppose the superiority of any culture to another, but evaluates all cultures according to its own criteria of truth and righteousness, and insists on moral absolutes in every culture."[21]

Some aspects of culture, then, are rooted in goodness and reflect God's own handiwork in creation. But to say that one culture is better than another, a particularly common phenomenon in North America, is absurd. It must be recognized that cultures are inhabited by fallen mankind. Pure and simple, this means that everyone apart from God is destined to a life of self-seeking. Therefore, there is an element of self-centeredness at the heart of the world view of every culture. This seems to be particularly true at the moment in the United States, where individualism and achievement are enshrined and even made compatible with the Christian message in some quarters. As has been stressed repeatedly, this is one of the most insidious forms of syncretism in the world today.

It is apparent then that self-centeredness and Christianity are incompatible. You cannot have both, and that means that some aspects of culture must be renounced when one becomes a Christian.

On the other hand, there is much within most cultures that is not contradictory to Christianity and may be retained and even strengthened within the Christian life-style. There is no need to "deculturalize" a convert and require the forsaking of values and practices that are not forbidden by Scripture.

Finally, no one working in another culture has the right to bring his or her cultural world view and proclaim it as normative for others. The Lausanne Covenant is clear on this point:

> Missions have all too frequently exported with the Gospel an alien culture, and churches have sometimes been in bondage to culture rather than to the Scripture. Christ's evangelists must humbly seek to empty themselves of all but their personal authenticity in order to become the servants of others, and churches must seek to transform and enrich culture, all for the glory of God.[22]

---

[21]Douglas, *Let the Earth Hear His Voice,* pp. 6–7.

[22]*Ibid.,* p. 7.

THE PROCESS OF CONTEXTUALIZATION

Now it is time to get to the heart of the basic issue of cross-cultural communication stated by Nida: "Our real objective . . . is not a change of content . . . , but rather a fitting of the same content into such culturally meaningful forms as will be fit vehicles for the communication of the message."[23] This requires the hard work of contextualization, and the key is contained in the "dynamic equivalence model" to be discussed first in this section. Once it is grasped and operationalized, the remaining issues are largely those of strategy and procedure.

The Dynamic Equivalence Model

Every communication has both a form (how it is said) and a meaning (desired content and effect). When working with Scripture, a literal translation of the form (formal correspondence) may conceal or distort the true meaning. Here is an example given in *The Willowbank Report.*[24] A word-for-word rendering of the original Greek translates Romans 1:17 as "the righteousness of God is revealed through faith for faith." What in the world does this mean to modern man? Probably very little, but notice what happens when an attempt is made to preserve the original meaning in contemporary language form: "The gospel reveals how God puts people right with himself: it is through faith, from beginning to end" (TEV). What a difference! This is the essence of dynamic equivalence in which the *form* is changed to preserve the *meaning.*

By the way, Scripture translators who have had any degree of acceptance in the church have *always* followed the dynamic equivalence approach. Martin Luther is a classic example.[25] A word-for-word translation preserving original form becomes nonsense to a contemporary audience. Some degree of paraphrasing always will be necessary. One should evaluate a translation on these bases: (1) Does it accurately convey the meaning of the original text? (2) Is the meaning phrased in such a way that it is fully comprehended by those in the audience?[26]

---

[23]Eugene A. Nida, *Message in Mission* (New York: Harper & Brothers, 1960), p. 180.

[24]*The Willowbank Report,* p. 8.

[25]Some may raise their eyebrows at this statement, but a strong case can be made. See Hans Kasdorf, "Luther's Bible: A Dynamic Equivalence Translation and Germanizing Force," *Missiology,* vol. 6 (April, 1978), pp. 213–234.

[26]For standard sources on the theory of translation see Eugene A. Nida and Charles R. Taber, *Toward a Science of Translating* (Leiden: E.J. Brill, 1964) and William A. Smalley, *The Theory and Practice of Translation* (Leiden: E.J. Brill, 1969).

The Dynamic Equivalence Church. The theory of dynamic equivalence is by no means confined to scriptural translation. It also is applicable to both the form of the church and its traditions and practices.[27] A dynamic equivalence church would produce the same type of impact in its present context as the early church produced in its time. Therefore, a dynamically equivalent church,

> (1) conveys to its members truly Christian meanings, (2) functions within its own society in the name of Christ, meeting the felt needs of that society and producing within it the same Christian impact as the first-century Church in its day, and (3) is couched in cultural forms that are as nearly indigenous as possible.[28]

The most obvious starting point is avoidance of forms and practices exported from another culture, unless it can be explicitly demonstrated that they will function to bring about dynamic equivalence. The author has observed some flagrant violations of this seemingly commonsense point, but fortunately things are changing. Probably the worst examples lie in worship forms where such extremes as forbidding all types of local instruments and melodies in favor of the "great music of the church" (most of which did not mean a thing to the hearer) were practiced. There has been a breakthrough in this area through the growing study of ethnomusicology (a big word describing the analysis of indigenous music patterns).[29] Some of the resulting music sounds pretty strange to western ears, but maybe that will help some of us understand the bewilderment many non-North Americans experience when singing, "Let me raise mine Ebenezer" (from "Come Thou Fount of Every Blessing). (By the way, does the reader know what an "Ebenezer" is?)

It should be recognized that dynamic equivalence often is hard to achieve. The New Testament is not definitive when it comes to form and practice in the church. In fact, it only provides glimpses of first-century contextualization.

Dynamic Equivalence and Christian Life-style. It is not unusual to hear someone contend that we should live as the New Testament Christians did. That would lead to an interesting life-style. First, most of us would be in slavery and would be taught to accept that circumstance. Also we would have to worry about meat sacrificed to idols,

---

[27]For a very influential article on this subject see Charles H. Kraft, "Dynamic Equivalence Churches," *Missiology,* vol. 1 (January, 1973), pp. 39–58.

[28]*Ibid.,* p. 49.

[29]R. LaVerne Morse, "Ethnomusicology: A New Frontier," *Evangelical Missions Quarterly,* vol. 11 (January, 1975), pp. 32–37.

and coping with poverty would be a far more significant issue than coping with wealth. Obviously, times were drastically different, and no one would seriously contend that all of the appropriate behavioral forms from that period should be adopted today. Once again we must wrestle with dynamic equivalence.

One of the most common practices, not confined to the mission field by any means, is "de-culturalizing" a convert. Some evangelists insist that their life-style should now be imitated by the convert. That has meant in some situations that polygamy must be abandoned immediately, even though this practice left wives without any means of support and thus forced them into starvation or prostitution or both. This may seem an extreme example, but it has long been a critical problem in tribal settings. The basic question is this: Must the convert immediately forsake all elements of his old life in order to be a Christian?

The principle of dynamic equivalence in life-style was brilliantly enunciated in *The Willowbank Report:*

> True conversion to Christ is bound . . . to strike at the heart of our cultural inheritance. Jesus Christ insists on dislodging from the centre of our world whatever idol previously reigned there, and occupying the throne himself. This is the radical change of allegiance which constitutes conversion, at least its beginning. Then once Christ has taken his rightful place, everything else starts shifting. The shock waves flow from the centre to the circumference. The convert has to rethink his or her fundamental convictions. . . . Of course, the development of an integrated Christian world-view may take a lifetime, but it is there in essence from the start.[30]

The key point here is that dynamic equivalence begins once existing idols (money, success, or whatever) are dislodged and Jesus becomes Lord. That will lead to renunciation of some cultural practices that are explicitly prohibited in Scripture. Adultery is an example. Conduct begins to change as outlook changes, and this will require a long period of time. To insist on a strictly New Testament life-style as a precondition for becoming a Christian is to impose preconditions that Jesus did not set forth. He always started where people were and moved from there toward maturity.

In bringing about dynamic equivalence, several categories of customs should be distinguished. The first includes those practices that should be immediately renounced as mentioned above. A second category comprises behavior or ways of thinking that can be toler-

[30]*The Willowbank Report,* p. 20.

ated for a period but will be expected to disappear as the reality of Christ becomes demonstrated. Examples are caste, slavery, and polygamy. A third category relates to customs and not to morals and hence may be labeled as being indifferent. Here individual discretion is the guide. The mistake is to lump all three categories into one and to insist on renunciation and acceptance of an altogether foreign life-style, often that imported from another culture. The net result will be isolation of believers, both individually and collectively, from the mainstream of culture. In so doing, the church is rendered impotent as a force for change.

Making Contextualization Work

If dynamic equivalence is to be brought about in practice, here are the essential steps: (1) Begin with a proper hermeneutic; (2) find linkages between Christian ways and cultural patterns; (3) provide for a contextualized theology; (4) make every effort to avoid syncretism.

A Proper Hermeneutic. Hermeneutics has to do with the interpretation of scriptural texts. One of the most common ways to study the text is without any awareness of the original cultural context. The reader thus interprets what is read as if it had been written in his or her own language and cultural setting. Such an approach runs the risk of missing what God was trying to say in the context in which it was presented.

A second approach takes the original historical and cultural context more seriously and seeks to discover the meaning of the text in that setting. But it stops at that point and does not move to the critical issue of what the text may be saying in the contemporary situation.

The third approach takes the second approach one step further to address the cultural context of contemporary readers. It recognizes that a dialogue must develop between the original and the contemporary setting. Referred to as the "contextualized approach,"[31] the advantage is that our own culturally conditioned points of view are continually challenged while new truth is being revealed. In reality it is the only approach that makes contextualization possible. In essence, it asks (1) what really was being said back then? and (2) how can the basic principles put forth (i.e., the true meaning and not just the form) be applied today in diverse cultural settings? This is hard work to say the least, but it cannot be avoided.

Linking Christian Ways and Cultural Patterns. Luzbetak says that

[31]*The Willowbank Report,* pp. 10–11.

cross-cultural research must isolate the "soul" of a culture.[32] Others might use the term "world view" instead, but reference is made to underlying values and motivations. Once these have been uncovered, the challenge is to link the Christian message where possible to existing values and customs. This can be done in three ways: (1) adaptation of the message, (2) finding a redemptive analogy, and (3) replacing displaced customs.

(1) Adapting the Message to Existing World Views. At the very outset it should be stressed once again that the goal here is not to make the gospel relevant but to *communicate the relevance of the gospel.* This has been a central theme throughout this book, and the only new point to be discussed here is to illustrate how an understanding of world views can help. Two different examples will be used, one from Japan and the other from two subcultures within the United States.

During a seminar conducted by the author a group of Japanese Christian leaders isolated aspects of the world view and life-style they observed within some segments in that country. These were the points they made:

1. Social traditions require obedience to those who are perceived to be socially superior. Thus it would be somewhat unnatural for some to respond to a simple gospel presentation given by a peer. This may explain why the pastor is so important in conversion according to the Japanese decision process study cited in an earlier chapter.
2. Religions are expected, by older people at least, to be ritualistic and formalistic. The church will be suspect if it does not require some type of ceremony when it is joined. Also greater formality in worship would be expected.
3. The continued prevalence of ancestor worship makes it difficult to believe in Christ, and Christians often are accused of having no particular love and concern for their ancestors. This has been countered within the church by stress on a Christian funeral ceremony and the meaning of both death and life after death.
4. Those who are zealous for a religious cause are suspect in some quarters. Too much overt enthusiasm in the form of a

[32]Luzbetak, *The Church and Cultures,* ch. 7.

bubbly "life is wonderful" testimony, therefore, can be a barrier.

5. The true essence of a religion is felt by many to fall into the realm of the mysterious and incomprehensible. Short testimonies will usually be ineffective for that reason. Longer explanations are needed at the outset. Also decision processes tend to be lengthy, requiring at least one year and often many more.

Notice how both the message and church practices are adapted to these cultural idiosyncracies in a way that would be next to impossible if a strictly North American model were followed.

One does not have to go to the mission field, however, to find similar cultural differences. Within every society there are subcultures that vary sharply from one another, and one of the most pronounced contrasts also discussed earlier is the difference in world view between pre- and post-World War II generations in the United States.[33]

Over seventy percent of present-day Americans were not living during the Great Depression of the 1930s. Even World War II predates the personal history of the majority who are alive today. Yet, the severity of these two events had indelible impact on the lives of those who experienced them. For example, those living during the Depression were seriously deprived of material wealth, and the insecurity of wartime raised a further question of ultimate survival. Therefore, it is not surprising that those who experienced these events embrace values emphasizing job security, patriotism, and the acquisition of wealth and material goods. These were the things they lacked during childhood.

Instead of the ravages of world war and depression, the majority living at the present time have experienced the greatest period of prolonged economic expansion in the history of the United States. There has been a pronounced proliferation of affluence. The critical lifetime experiences of those in this age bracket vary greatly, but the following are among the prominent influences: the nuclear age, the civil rights movement, the existence of pockets of poverty amidst mass affluence, questions and doubts about continued space exploration, the Viet Nam War, concern about ecology, campus disorders

[33]Engel, Blackwell, and Kollat, *Consumer Behavior,* pp. 188–189.

and protests, inflation, Watergate, and a revolution in communication technology.[34]

In terms of life-style it is to be expected that a large proportion of the older, depression-oriented people will place greater emphasis upon material gain, financial security, patriotism, unquestioned belief in free enterprise, and maintenance of traditions with which they have become accustomed. No doubt the assurance of eternal life in the future is a positive aspect of Christianity from their point of view. They will tend to question changes in church liturgy and will favor the more traditional forms. The individualism inherent within much of traditional evangelicalism will be quite consistent with the value placed on economic wealth and achievement. Unfortunately, this can lead to serious excesses where wealth and Christianity are somehow seen as synonymous—a decidedly non-Christian viewpoint. Related to this same outlook is less felt need for what has now become known as "body life."

A younger generation, on the other hand, will not be satisfied, as a general rule, if the church does not take account of their world view. Often one of their greatest felt needs is for interpersonal relationships and love because of the fact that this is the very factor most often missing in their childhood. Therefore, the body-life phenomenon tends to be pretty largely confined to an under-forty generation. Material wealth, by and large, is assumed rather than sought after. Therefore, it ceases to be a motivating factor. This will call into question a noncritical acceptance of the free enterprise system and its various forms of excesses. Many will feel that the church should take a stronger political and social stand.

This discussion could be extended at great length, but it illustrates the importance of taking world views and life-styles seriously. Generally it is possible to adapt both message and church forms to capitalize on these differences, but there are distinct limits. When the existing values or customs fall into the nonacceptable category as discussed above, the church must clearly draw the line. It often has tended not to do so, and that has led to syncretism. What we are referring to here is adaptation to those values and customs that do

[34]These are adapted from several sources. Of particular importance is Margaret Mead, "The Generation Gap That Has No Parallels," *The Providence Sunday Journal* (October 4, 1970), p. N-43. Also see CBS News, *Generations Apart* (New York: Columbia Broadcasting System, 1969); and Elizabeth Herzog *et. al.*, "Teenagers Discuss the 'Generation Gap,'" *Youth Reports*, no. 1 (Washington: U.S. Department of Health, Education and Welfare, 1970).

not violate biblical norms and hence do not need to be displaced.

If the church does not make this adaptation, it will find to its dismay that converts will cling to their old ways of thinking without examining them in a Christian context.[35] Christianity thus becomes confined to the periphery of life. For instance, the church could err seriously with the post-World War II generation in America by confining religious practice to such things as avoidance of alcoholic consumption, nonattendance at questionable movies, and so on, while, at the same time, featuring only a Sunday-morning Christianity characterized by one-way pulpit communication. What happens, then, to the need for deep interpersonal relationships (*koinonia*) with others in the body? If it is not met in the church, then the church cannot be taken very seriously as the center for life itself. Make no mistake about it—existing needs and values will be met somehow. The essential question is whether or not the church will be viewed as a viable option.

(2) Finding a Redemptive Analogy. One of the greatest challenges in evangelism is to search among existing beliefs and customs to find a natural bridge for presentation of the ministry of Jesus Christ. This is what is meant by the term *redemptive analogy*.

Don Richardson has given an excellent illustration in his book *Peace Child.*[36] He struggled for a long period in a previously unevangelized tribal situation to find some way to present the gospel so that it could be comprehended. Finally, he discovered that one tribe made peace with another by offering an infant as a peace offering. Richardson quickly capitalized upon this custom and pointed out that God has done precisely the same thing through offering His Son. That proved to be the previously undiscovered key, and a true people movement toward Christ emerged leading to what is now a flourishing church. Richardson has elaborated this principle further in later writings.[37]

(3) Replacing Displaced Customs. Christianity often will lead to the necessity of abolishing existing customs that are in direct conflict with Scripture. Obvious examples, in addition to adultery mentioned earlier, are drunkenness, worship of idols, blood feuds, discriminations based on race or other factors, and so on. But customs

[35]See Luzbetak, *The Church and Cultures,* ch. 7, for an excellent discussion of this problem and some of the ways to find a solution.

[36]Don Richardson, *Peace Child* (Glendale, Ca.: Regal, 1974).

[37]For further discussion of this principle, see Don Richardson, *Lords of the Earth* (Glendale, Ca.: Regal, 1977).

or practices cannot be abolished outright without a clear and unambiguous Christian functional substitute. If severed functions are ignored, the corresponding needs probably will be filled in some other non-Christian way.

A good illustration comes from the dynamic example of the Quichua Indians in Ecuador previously discussed in Chapter 3. The reader will recall that the present-day Quichuas are direct descendents of the once proud Incas. When the Spanish conquered Ecuador, a form of Catholicism was introduced to this people with unfortunate consequences. For the most part it never penetrated the mainstream of culture and only remained on the periphery. The most serious error was the blending of Christian practices with existing pagan religious customs. This is referred to by Luzbetak, a Catholic anthropologist, as *Christopaganism.*[38]

One of the most outrageous forms of Christopaganism in this culture proved to be a continuation of periodic feasts originally undertaken to worship pagan gods. Drunkenness in extreme form was always the norm. The church merely continued this practice with a Christian veneer. It met a traditional need of the people, but the behavior tolerated can hardly be designated as Christian.

Once true Christianity took hold in 1967 the church immediately had to wrestle with such traditions as the feast days. If they were discontinued, the church would be placed in jeopardy in an important way. Therefore, a functional substitute was provided in the form of periodic large-scale gatherings of thousands of believers from isolated communities to worship, to celebrate their faith, and simply to have fun in the form of music and athletic competition. The major purpose (socializing) of the original feast days was maintained, but it now has been placed within a distinctly Christian context. The author has attended two of these celebrations and has been indelibly impressed by the genuineness and virility of the Christianity exhibited.

A Contextualized Theology. The next step in making contextualization work is to guarantee that theology is more than just a foreign import. This has become a critical issue in recent years, and it was here that the first thinking about contextualization emerged. As was mentioned at the outset, we have broadened the concept in this chapter to encompass far more than just theology.

Consider this situation. African scholars come to seminary with

[38]Luzbetak, *The Church and Cultures,* pp. 239–248.

high expectations that they will be equipped to minister to their people. For many months they study such topics as the proofs of the existence of God. Now this may be all well and good, but a problem emerges: Africans have no difficulty accepting the fact that there is a God. The proofs they learn are a part of standard systematic theology, dating, by the way, from the writings of Augustine initially. Augustine, of course, was writing in quite a different context.

The student then plows on through systematic theology, duly considering other important topics such as viewpoints on how the sin nature passed from Adam to the progeny. He or she finishes seminary and returns to the church with a justified sense of frustration. Never, for example, is anything said on witchcraft or demonism, just to choose one subject that is a critical problem for the African Christian to face. The net effect is that the leader is unequipped theologically to minister to his or her people.

Now, what is the reason for this? Seminaries traditionally are staffed by those who have studied in North America. They have learned systematic theology, to be sure, but it is a *North American or European theology.* When this is passed on, it is small wonder that the church then takes on an alien flavor.

What we learn from this example is that *theology must address the pressing issues of the day within a cultural context.* When Augustine, Calvin, Luther, and Hodge were writing, addressing pressing contemporary issues was precisely what they were doing. But to cite their writings as being normative for today seems absurd. This, by the way, is not to say that there is no gain from studying these resources under the heading of historical theology. Indeed there is much to be learned from the past. The need now, however, to quote Bayly, is for "fresh stones from the river-bed."[39] As he puts it in his discussion of the missing element in much of contemporary theology:

> The facts as God has revealed them in His Word (the Bible) are there, but they are not focused upon today. Instead, most evangelical theology is oriented toward yesterday. But yesterday is past. . . . And today's giants are different. . . . New stones are needed to slay new giants, although these new stones must come from the same river bed: the Word of God.[40]

[39]Joe Bayly, "Wanted: Fresh Stones From the River-bed," in Joe Bayly, *Out of My Mind* (Wheaton, Ill.: Tyndale, 1970), pp. 96–100.

[40]*Ibid.*, pp. 96–97.

The need, in short, is for a contextualized theology.[41]

This whole subject makes many Christian leaders uncomfortable. Often they will ask, "Why not a biblical theology?" The assumption is that there is one answer for all situations for all time. In reality, there should be many biblical theologies, all of which are focused within different cultural contexts providing biblical perspectives on different questions.

Probably the greatest hackles are raised by "liberation" theology, arising from Latin America.[42] It has Catholic roots, having been stimulated by the Latin American Episcopal Congress (CELAM) held in Colombia in 1968. Later it has been joined by such Protestant theologians as José Miguez Bonino, Luis Rivera Pagán, Julio de Santa Ana, and Emilio Castro. What the various writers have in common is that they are reflecting theologically on the issues of economic and political oppression and the need for liberation.

All writers, Catholic and Protestant alike, begin from the perspective of oppressed people living in abject poverty as victims of an exploitive society. The cultural context has the tragic theme of a few families growing progressively richer as economic development proceeds, while the mass remains largely untouched. It is hardly surprising that most are, to put it mildly, unenthusiastic about free enterprise and capitalism. Some have departed quite far from Christian roots in their speculation, and a few even are openly atheistic and outright Marxist.

Those who take the Bible seriously contend, with justification, that theology based on Greek thought forms leads to a conception of man as a duality of mind (or spirit) and body. This leads many Europeans and North Americans to spiritualize such biblical concepts as justice and peace. What the biblical liberation theologians have done is to separate the gospel from a narrow, personalized interpretation characteristic of much of the church and to highlight the imperatives of social and economic justice. They, probably more than others, have done much to bring the doctrine of the kingdom of God into sharp focus as the mandate for the church.

---

[41]For a very influential paper on this subject, see C. René Padilla, "The Contextualization of the Gospel," an address given at a conference sponsored by Partnership in Mission and later distributed by that organization.

[42]For a helpful review, see J. Andrew Kirk, "Theology in Latin America: What is it Today?" *Latin America Evangelist*, (May/June, 1978), p. 6ff. Also a useful background briefing paper was prepared on this subject by the Latin America Mission under the authorship of Clayton L. (Mike) Berg and distributed March 3, 1978.

Liberation theologians from Latin America and those grappling with similar issues outside the developed countries need to be taken seriously and not dismissed with a wave of the hand as being atheistic or Marxist (although there are some who fall into such camps and hence undermine their credibility). What the author is really saying here is that many of these writers are wrestling with real issues and have fortunately moved a long distance from the safe havens of the chairs of academic theology occupied by some of their North American counterparts. To an increasing degree they are the very ones who are grasping the "fresh stones from the river-bed" while the traditional bastions of theological thought focus their erudition in a narrower and narrower circle that fails to touch the mainstream of the church. Bayly rightly asks this question: "Where are the new stones, especially here in America? Who is finding them and fitting them to the sling?"[43]

Avoidance of Syncretism. When cultural elements that are intrinsically false or evil are assimilated into Christianity, syncretism is said to occur. The only corrective is to scrutinize all cultural elements in the light of God's revelation and the lordship of Christ. This is why we have emphasized so frequently the absolute imperative for a proper hermeneutic. When syncretism occurs, the church has blunted its cutting edge.

We tend to think of syncretism as taking place in so-called pagan cultures outside North America, but it must never be forgotten that *all* churches can fall into this sin. Consider the prophetic words about the western churches appearing in *The Willowbank Report:*

> . . . perhaps the most insidious form of syncretism in the world today is the attempt to mix a privatized gospel of personal forgiveness with a worldly (even demonic) attitude to wealth and power. We are not guiltless in this matter ourselves. Yet we desire to be integrated Christians for whom Jesus is truly Lord of all. So we who belong to, or come from, the West will examine ourselves and seek to purge ourselves of western-style syncretism.[44]

This statement, largely reflecting the views of those from developing countries, says something about how the so-called "evangelical renewal" in the United States is viewed elsewhere in the world. Those of us living in affluent situations who tend to fall prey to such syncretism would do well to heed these words from the Lausanne

---

[43]Bayly, "Wanted," p. 97.

[44]*The Willowbank Report,* p. 26.

Covenant: ". . . the salvation we claim should be transforming us in the totality of our personal and social responsibilities. Faith without works is dead."[45]

PARTNERSHIP IN MISSION

With more than 2.5 billion people yet to be reached with the gospel, it is all the more imperative for Christians to work together in the cause of world evangelization. As the Lausanne Covenant states, ". . . the responsibility to evangelize belongs to the whole body of Christ."[46] There is no question that the dominant role of western missions is fast disappearing and that God is raising up resources from younger churches elsewhere in the world. Hopefully, ". . . a growing partnership of churches will develop and the universal character of Christ's Church will be more clearly exhibited."[47]

In the spirit of developing partnership, the traditional practices of missions have been substantially rethought. The questions to be explored here have to do with relationships—power, control, and so on. While progress is being made, there still is quite a distance to go.

The Dead End of Indigenization

For more than three quarters of a century, some missionary statesmen have been rebelling against a strategy which, in effect, plants a North American church in an alien setting. We have seen earlier how futile this can be. Following the lead of Roland Allen[48] and others, the concept of *indigenization* gained popularity. The whole purpose, using the words of Henry Venn, writing many decades ago, is to undertake missionary strategy with the aim of, ". . . development of Native Churches, with a view to their ultimate settlement upon a self-supporting, self-governing and self-extending system."[49] The goal, then, is to establish a church that can function on its own without continuing reliance upon outside support.

---

[45]Douglas, *Let the Earth Hear His Voice,* p. 5.

[46]*Ibid.,* p. 6.

[47]*Ibid.*

[48]Roland Allen's writings have been reissued in recent years. See especially *The Spontaneous Expansion of the Church* (Grand Rapids, Mich.: Wm. B. Eerdmans, 1962) and *Missionary Methods: St. Paul's or Ours?* (Grand Rapids, Mich.: Wm. B. Eerdmans, 1962).

[49]Quoted in Kraft, "Dynamic Equivalence Churches," p. 39.

While no one can really quarrel with this goal, working it out in practice has been something else again. As Smalley warned in an influential paper written in 1959, "... self-government doesn't mean anything if we've indoctrinated a few people in western patterns and let them take over. All we've done is just replace ourselves by others with the same thought patterns."[50] What it comes down to is that *indigenization must be accompanied by dynamic equivalence* if it is to work, and this has only recently been recognized outside of a few innovative circles.[51] Dynamic equivalence, in turn, will never emerge if missionary practice is based upon a paternalistic model.

Paulo Freire has put his finger right on the problem.[52] As was mentioned in the previous chapter, he identifies a type of indoctrination (usually referred to as "education") where outsiders penetrate the cultural context of another group and impose their own view of the world upon those they are influencing. All this succeeds in doing is inhibiting the creativity of expression, and it will lead to an unwitting acceptance of the values, standards, and goals of the outsiders. Rather than liberating people to perform under the lordship of Christ, it only enslaves them. This can be the outcome in spite of the lofty altruistic goals of those from the outside.

Moving From Paternalism to Partnership

Ward and Graham have provided a useful model that describes the historical stages of relationship between missionaries and nationals (those who are the recipients of missionary efforts).[53] They have identified three distinct stages: (1) giving, (2) training, and (3) reciprocity.

In the first stage, one party has the resources and the other has the need. Hence *giving* seems to be the only logical strategy. But this very quickly leads to an unhealthy dependency relationship. As Taber has pointed out, the party with the resources will be the party with the power.[54] The net result is that the recipient is forever destined to assume a subsidiary role if this pattern is frozen.

---

[50]William A. Smalley, "Cultural Implications of an Indigenous Church," *Practical Anthropology*, vol. 5 (1958), pp. 51-65.

[51]Kraft's paper on dynamic equivalence cited earlier has been quite influential in stimulating rethinking on this important subject.

[52]Paulo Freire, *Pedagogy of the Oppressed* (New York: Seabury Press, 1974), p. 150ff.

[53]Ted Ward and Kathleen Graham, "Acts of Kindness: Motives and Relationships" (unpublished paper, Institute for International Studies, Michigan State University, April, 1977).

[54]Charles R. Taber, "Power and Mission," *Milligan Missiogram*, vol. 5 (Winter, 1977), pp. 2–6.

A second stage is *training,* and admittedly this can be a step forward. The intent is to build competencies so that giving may cease. In reality, this is the goal of the indigenization model discussed above, but, as we have seen, this also can encourage dependency if it is based on the wrong concept of education. Those on the receiving end are not just "empty pots" waiting to be filled with North American abilities and competencies. They must be equipped to cope with their own realities—to arrive at their own solutions following the lordship of Christ.

In this connection it should be stressed that it still is commonplace to have large numbers of foreign students attend Christian colleges and seminaries in the United States. It can be impressive to point to these alumni in various positions of leadership around the world, but how have they been helped through their education? Remember, they have been isolated from their context, and the material they are receiving usually is distinctly North American. They do gain the prestige of a western degree, and the training is not without value. Nevertheless, training is more effective if it can be undertaken on the local scene.

In spite of these limitations, we still hear grandiose schemes to bring "hundreds" from the third world to the United States for training in such diverse areas as broadcasting technology or theology. This makes little or no sense compared with the establishment of training centers throughout the world, staffed insofar as possible by leaders from within a given culture. Expatriots can also help in such training but only insofar as their goal is to develop problem-solving capabilities and *not* to export North American ideas and technology.

The third stage identified by Ward and Graham is *reciprocity.* Its essence is best captured by a comment made by Ted Hsueh, a leader in Christian communications in Hong Kong. When addressing North American colleagues he said, "I don't want a Paul-Timothy relationship with you, but rather a Paul-Barnabus relationship." In the Paul-Timothy dyad there is a sense in which the apostle was a superior dealing with someone who was inferior. Paul and Barnabus, on the other hand, were equal contemporaries offering themselves to one another (in those periods when they could get along) in a spirit of reciprocity. Reciprocity is based on awareness that everyone has something to offer in a relationship. When these resources are shared in relationship, the distinction between giver and receiver or even teacher and learner dissolves. If it is to work, it demands an attitude of mutual respect.

In the early 1970s the missions world was shocked by a call for a moratorium on further sending of missionary personnel to certain parts of the world, especially Eastern Africa. Those issuing this call were saying loud and clear that it is time to remove the dominance from the West and free the national church to stand on its own two feet. Pius Wakatama writing in this context agrees with the need for a selective moratorium, affirming the need for missionaries but only those who can impart needed skills in a spirit of partnership.[55] All who work cross-culturally would do well to heed what Wakatama has to say.

A CONCLUDING WORD

It is obvious that the author is indebted to *The Willowbank Report* as witnessed by the number of times it has been cited. It is helpful to conclude by noting what it has to say about the attitude of those who are involved in cross-culture communication.[56] The call is for humility and servanthood, and there are five important reasons:

1. Everyone is a prisoner of his or her own culture, and the ability to grasp both the culture of biblical times and the culture in which we serve is distinctly limited.
2. An attitude of genuine dialogue and empathy is required to understand and appreciate another culture.
3. We must follow the example of Jesus and begin our communication in terms of where people actually are and not where we would like them to be.
4. It must be recognized that even the most dedicated and trained communicator can seldom present the gospel to someone in another language or culture as well as a trained local Christian.
5. There must be humility to trust in the Holy Spirit, the Chief Communicator, who alone opens the eyes of the blind and brings people to new birth.

Clearly there is no role for an attitude of paternalism or cultural superiority.

[55]Pius Wakatama, *Independence for the Third World Church* (Downer's Grove: Inter-Varsity Press, 1976).

[56]*The Willowbank Report*, pp. 16–17.

CHAPTER 13

Proclaiming and Exemplifying the Kingdom of God

Just picture the scene. The Ramada Inn proclaims, "Welcome Kingdom Plan Associates!" Dozens of men (women are not allowed), mostly dressed in blue blazers and white shoes, scurry about with their thick notebooks emblazoned "Evangelio '79." You see, it is their responsibility to define a strategy to "finish the task" of world evangelization.

Now consider Al Krass's parody of what is going on inside:

> Organize, strategize, plan, *achieve* . . .
> Organize, rationalize, prioritize, *succeed* . . .
> The Holy Spirit's coming—he's gotta have an itinerary.
> The kingdom's coming—there's gotta be a plan.
> A Master Plan for World Evangelization.
> Ten Steps to More Effective Discipling.
> How to organize a Crusade.
> If only Jesus had planned it right—
> there mightn't have needed to be . . . a . . . crucifixion.
> Cybernetics
> Organizational Development
> Church Planning
> The Structure of a Mission
> Evangelio '79
> How to Reach More . . . Win More . . . Save More . . .[1]

---

[1]Al Krass, "In the Ramada Executives Come and Go, Talking of Evangelio," *The Other Side,* vol. 14 (April, 1978), p. 60. Reprinted by special permission of *The Other Side,* Box 12236, Philadelphia, Pa., 19144.

While these meetings drone on, the kingdom of God is coming silently, unexpectedly, and people are set free as the body of Christ functions. But,

> In the Ramada
> The Executives come and go,
> Talking of Evangelio.[2]

Apocryphal? Perhaps, but it does describe what often takes place when Christians gather to focus on issues of evangelistic strategy. We've already pointed out that the essential task of world evangelization still lies ahead of the church, and it *is* appropriate to address questions of strategy in meetings such as the (fictional?) Evangelio '79. But, the goal of such meetings should not be simply to design strategies unless there is a real focus on the problems existing in local areas and on equipping the local church to cope with those issues.

Unfortunately, there still is a tendency for Christian executives to manufacture outreaches that reduce evangelism to a finely honed set of Madison Avenue techniques. Slogans appear on billboards, bumper stickers, and T-shirts. Glowing testimonies find their way into television, magazines, and newspapers proclaiming in strangely identical terms how life changed from horror to heaven. The objective seems to be to *say it* as often and as loudly as we can through any means.

Mechanized sloganeering is bad enough, but the problem only intensifies when we bring the local church onto the scene. Yes, the executives at Evangelio '79 will talk about the church, but the emphasis will probably focus on how leaders and members can be persuaded to become trained and "involved." This merely perpetuates the common error of viewing the church as little more than an evangelistic medium.

There will be much talk about goals, usually in terms of "souls reached," whatever that means. Genuine conversion, of course, is always the goal of evangelism, but the usual tendency will be to overlook the decision process entirely and utilize decision-oriented techniques manufactured elsewhere and imported for the occasion. Later, glowing reports will appear, always stressing the numbers who "prayed" or showed some other overt response. Only recently has there been a parallel inquiry as to whether or not they ever

---

[2] *Ibid.*

appear on church rolls. But where in all this is the ultimate criterion raised: *Has the outreach helped equip the church and its new converts both to proclaim and exemplify the kingdom of God?* In other words, is the world any different once Evangelio has come and gone?

The author is of the conviction that unified, coordinated outreach undertaken for world evangelization is an *absolute necessity* but not unless the principles put forth on the following pages are taken seriously.

In this chapter, every effort will be made to draw together lessons learned from coordinated evangelistic outreaches undertaken during this century. Some firm principles are emerging, many of which have been discussed in depth or at least alluded to in previous chapters. It is the author's hope that a "road map" can be laid out to use as a general guide as the church collectively takes the imperatives of world evangelization seriously.

MOVING FROM GREAT COMMOTION TO GREAT COMMISSION

The intent in this section is to state the broad general principles that should be followed without giving much in the way of specific strategy guidelines. The detail will follow in the next section.

The Local Church Is the Starting Point

In 1975 a survey was undertaken among high-school-age youth in Quito, Ecuador, and they were found to be exceptionally open and receptive to the Christian message.[3] As the reader may recall from an earlier chapter, they seem to epitomize in every way the ideal "fertile field." Yet, those concerned with evangelistic strategy were forced to move slowly for the reason that the tiny evangelical church in Quito was utterly unprepared to engage in evangelism and to cultivate the new believers. In short, the church was in desperate need of renaissance, and any strategy for world evangelization must begin at that point. By the way, an evangelistic crusade undertaken in Quito in the early 1970s produced more than 3,000 supposed converts, but few showed up in these churches. This is just further

[3]This study is described in James F. Engel, *How Can I Get Them To Listen?* (Grand Rapids, Mich.: Zondervan, 1977), ch. 9.

evidence that one cannot proceed too rapidly with outreach when the church is not prepared.

Some might object at this point that a church listing in the spiritual waters should not be allowed to hold up the work of God. Why not just bring in others who can do the job? This option seems all the more attractive when it is accompanied by an appeal to urgency—the task must be finished now! The only problem is that it overlooks a fundamental principle stated again and again throughout this book: The local church is God's primary agency for world evangelization. It cannot be bypassed, and if it is presently unhealthy, that fact alone defines what must be done at the initial stages of any evangelization strategy.

In such situations it will be necessary to work simultaneously on both church revitalization and outreach. One cannot take place without the other.

Unity Is an Imperative

The church as the body of Christ was designed to function as a unified whole, but it seems as if this usually is an ideal rather than reality. The divisions that exist among those who accept both the authority of the Bible and the lordship of Christ defy all logic. But one point is quite clear: *Unless we have unity we do not have a message for the world.*

All too frequently those outside the church see our infighting and recoil from us. Here is just one example. During 1977 the NBC television network ran a special entitled, "Jesus of Nazareth." Without having viewed it in advance, a small group of Christian leaders condemned it as being heretical, and their opinion was widely reported in the secular press. The movie was aired and received appreciatively by a huge secular audience, and it also received high praise in most Christian quarters. Many secular commentators publicly asked why the Christians had to fight over this issue. The church, in turn, missed a golden opportunity to capitalize upon a media "happening."

By the way, the author joined many others in commending NBC for its programming decision and sent a copy to one of the dissidents. The answer received said this: "Anyone who is affiliated with such an apostate institution as you will have cause someday to repent for what you said." The author did not respond with fear over his salvation, but he was grieved to see the extent to which divisions have arisen over purely external factors. If this type of thing were not so widespread, it could be ignored. But it is time to label it for what it is—a totally unwarranted attempt to divide the body of Christ on peripheral issues. No one who takes Scripture seriously can justify such an action. We still have much work to do to get our house in order.

More frequently, unity is not especially evident on a local level simply because leaders who share the same Christian viewpoints have had little occasion to work together. All that it takes in many instances is a catalyst in the form of an individual or a parachurch organization that can provide new vision. Fortunately, barriers seem to be dissolving with encouraging rapidity. It is interesting to note that there often appears to be far greater unity once one moves outside Europe or North America. Our brothers in some of the developing countries have much to teach us in this respect.

World Evangelization Requires More Than Verbal Evangelism

All that needs to be done here is to restate what has been said so frequently before: Our lives may speak more loudly than our words. What, for example, does a church that condones excessive individual and collective wealth and other forms of materialism have to say to outsiders who are victims of the same strivings? The whole point, of course, is that the lordship of Christ over all phases of life must be lived as well as proclaimed.

It also does not do injustice to the cause of world evangelization to expand it to cover attacks on unrighteousness wherever it is observed in the structures of society. The author cannot help recalling in this context the statement of a few vocal evangelical leaders who have referred to one country in the world as being the most Christian society of all the leading countries. The reason given is that there are no restrictions whatsoever on open proclamation of the gospel. But they overlook that its government frequently makes the headlines in terms of outrageous corruption, and these spokesmen never raise voices of objection over the hundreds of Christian leaders who have been jailed or muzzled because they dared to speak out against injustice. Christ's good news cannot be proclaimed with fidelity if it is somehow abstracted from these political realities. We must get rid of a kind of tunnel vision that restricts the mandates of the kingdom of God only to evangelism.

Local Initiative Is Required

As the reader is aware, the author comes from a background in parachurch organizations. At one time he made a determined effort to export a strategy designed on one secular campus to reach and disciple faculty to every other major college and university in the United States. After a couple of years of futility he was forced to conclude that he, inadvertently, had fallen prey to the error of program orientation. No particular attempt was made to assess differences from one campus to another and, more critically, no real effort was made to derive principles of strategy to help local leadership cope with their own situation under the leadership of the Holy Spirit. Later this was changed with some very encouraging results.

A strategy that has worked elsewhere always is worthy of examination to discover if it might be utilized locally in whole or in part. But that decision is entirely to be made by those who are most affected, and it is not the task of the parachurch organization to override their evaluation. There have been instances in recent years, some of which were cited elsewhere in this book, where the so-called "arm of the church" (i.e., the parachurch organization) has attempted to control the body.

The author can say truthfully that the vast majority of parachurch organizations take their role as servant seriously. They can be of great help in building local unity, extending the church into unreached fields, imparting vision, mounting useful training programs, and so on. That type of work may be slow, but, in the long run, it accomplishes the essential purpose of equipping the church and encouraging local initiative. This, in turn, is God's agenda for world evangelization.

Careful Planning Is Required

It was stated in Chapter 4 that the planning process is a means to discover the mind of Christ. Prayerfully collecting facts, contemplating goals, and evaluating prospective outcomes provides a means whereby God can make His will known. Remember the words of John Stott in this context: "God cannot lead an empty head." Enough said?

Make Accountability a Way of Life

Stewardship and accountability have the same essential meaning. They require a determined effort to measure effectiveness in terms of carefully stated goals and to learn from what was done. This does not mean only counting the number of "souls reached" but goes far beyond that. How much church growth resulted? How many new converts are going on in the faith in succeeding years? What happened to those who did not respond to evangelism? Did they understand the message, or were they turned off and, in effect, inoculated against further evangelistic efforts? This latter possibility never is documented, but it is an ever present reality.

This inquiry also should center around the outcomes within the church itself. How has the life-style changed to more closely embody the mandates of the kingdom of God? Is moral and ethical behavior being exhibited? Are there signs that new converts are growing in maturity? Is the church being mobilized to meet the social needs of its area?

The purpose of this type of inquiry is *not* to provide material for press releases. If one were to believe all that is said in just one day's mail from Christian organizations, it would seem that the task of world evangelization is about over. What a bright and rosy picture! Is it possible that this represents a good bit of "evangelistic talk" designed to raise funds? Public relations is not the reason for measurement of effectiveness. Rather it provides data for those involved locally to ask God this question: *What would You have us learn from the past and do differently in the future as we follow You?*

Balance Urgency With Discipline

The task of world evangelization is an urgent one. After all, people are living in darkness in vast areas of the world, and God does not give us any justification for complacency. On the other hand, He has not mandated us to rush to all the world indiscriminately using whatever method might be at hand. He ordained the planning process, and His agenda calls for things to be done decently and in order. We can learn much from the simple fact that Christ Himself never ran; He always walked. Thus it is a matter of balance.

LETTING THE EARTH HEAR HIS VOICE

Given these principles, what should be done in a unified strategy of outreach on the local level to "let the earth hear His voice?" This question must be tackled by noting at the outset that strategies will differ depending upon the extent to which the area being evangelized can legitimately be considered a fertile field. Therefore, we will make considerable use of case examples drawn from Rochester, New York, a nonfertile field, and Luis Palau's experiences in South America where the situation is dramatically different. These are the steps to be followed, most of which are familiar to the reader by now: (1) analyze local Christian resources; (2) analyze the spiritual status of the target community; (3) establish measurable goals; (4) determine the strategy to be followed; (5) carry out the strategy; (6) measure effectiveness; (7) undertake a postmortem analysis. The entire approach is two-pronged, centering both on church revitalization and community outreach.

Analysis of Local Christian Resources

There are four essential questions to ask here: (1) How many churches presently exist? (2) How many could be expected to cooperate in a strategy focusing both on church revitalization and outreach centered on the kingdom of God? (3) What is the health of these churches? (4) What parachurch organizations are in existence?

The first question is easy to answer. In Rochester, New York, for instance, there are 330 places of worship in the city and surrounding suburbs, forty-three percent of which are Catholic, forty-two percent Protestant, and the remainder divided among the sects and non-Christian faiths. About thirty of these churches belong to the Greater Rochester Association of Evangelicals (GRAE) and have cooperated in such ventures as a Leighton Ford Crusade, Here's Life America, and a Bill Gothard seminar. It was felt during 1978 that perhaps ten would cooperate in a two-pronged strategy such as that being discussed here. This does not seem to be a large number, but many of these are strategic churches. Furthermore, a small number can have an impact far in excess of its size. Also, there is every reason to expect that other GRAE churches will join once they begin to see discernible results. The unfortunate problem here is that most are disillusioned about cooperative outreach after the outright failure of a recent joint effort.

The health of these churches is much more difficult to assess. The ideal means, of course, is some type of self-discovery program built around a congregational survey. This method was utilized with good results in the Greater Vancouver (Canada) Reachout undertaken by Leighton Ford. That particular Reachout obviously was designed to do much more than evangelism, and it was an early experiment in the type of strategy discussed here. Twenty or more churches were positively changed during this revitalization effort.

If surveys do not seem practical, the only recourse is to ask church leaders and others who are in a position to diagnose the cooperating churches. Both of these means were available in Rochester as local leaders worked in cooperation with staff and students at the

Wheaton Graduate School to design a unified strategy. These needs were uncovered within these churches:

1. Increase church attendance, especially from the large number of those living in the Greater Rochester area who are only occasional attenders.
2. Increase the involvement by church members in small groups designed to build greater discipleship and to meet an expressed need for interpersonal relationships within the church.
3. Increase the percentage of church members who evidence an active desire to relate Christianity to their personal needs.
4. Encourage greater stewardship among church members in terms of active Bible study and prayer.
5. Bring about a sharp increase in the number of members who can identify their spiritual gift(s) and exercise gifts both within the church and in the community.

A number of parachurch organizations are active in the community, and one of the most helpful is a group calling itself "Concerned Christians." This group consists of trained and experienced media people who have previously experimented with various forms of mass media outreach. In many ways, they have served as a key to unity among the GRAE churches.

Rochester is unusual in that both a degree of unity and vision already exist, but Luis Palau inherited something quite different in Rosario, Argentina. The existing church was very small, and most leaders felt that the community was totally nonreceptive to evangelism. Palau had good reason to believe differently and demonstrated through the mass media, especially radio, that spiritual hunger existed on a wider scale. That served to excite these pastors, and Palau was able to give them a vision both for church renewal and the starting of new churches prior to a concentrated evangelistic crusade. Thus he was able to act as a positive catalyst, and this is one of the most important roles to be played by those in the parachurch organizations. A church growth seminar was also extremely helpful in this process. In the final analysis, someone from the outside often can do more in a short time to build vision and stimulate action than those working from the inside.

The analyses discussed here serve to define the starting point of a unified strategy. If there is no present unity as was the case in

Rosario, then that must be the beginning step. If churches are caught up in a high degree of institutionalization as proved to be the case with some in Rochester, actions must be initiated to help move them toward becoming an organism. The goal, of course, is to leave the church community dramatically changed so that the effects of an outreach are not just temporary, as usually proves to be the case. The best measure of success is to discover continued action years later from the changes initiated at an earlier point.

Community Analysis

The steps in this analysis have been thoroughly discussed in Part II of this book. The reader will recall that the most important consideration is to isolate the most receptive segments of the audience (or fertile fields if you prefer). This is shown by the extent to which there are large numbers actively seeking or at least receptive to a changed life-style. It also is necessary to determine the felt needs of potential audience members to assure relevance in the appeals used. Furthermore, gospel awareness is an important consideration (i.e., fundamentals about God, man, Christ, and the Bible), because movement in decision processes occurs as this awareness is strengthened in the context of important motivations. Finally, it is necessary to know the manner in which most people make decisions, especially the sources of information to which they are exposed on a regular basis.

Whenever possible, a community survey should be undertaken.[4] This was omitted in the Here's Life America campaign described in Chapter 1, and the outcome was that the strategy designed for Atlanta, Georgia, proved to be pretty inappropriate for many other parts of North America. Without this information, it is difficult to avoid program orientation.

Luis Palau did not do formal surveying in either Argentina or Bolivia, but he was not without awareness of his audience. There was ample evidence that those with Catholic backgrounds already had a good grasp of the gospel, and their response to preliminary radio broadcasts showed that large numbers would be receptive to a decision-oriented strategy (as opposed to proclamation). In other words, he was assured in advance that there probably would be large numbers of decisions if proper methods were utilized. This is not to say, however, that greater response would not have been forthcoming had there been a formal inquiry into differences in various

[4]See Engel, *How Can I Get Them to Listen,* for methods to follow in this type of survey.

audience segments. Palau has readily admitted this point to the author and his students.

Leaders in Rochester, on the other hand, authorized a large-scale community survey, which was carried out by the staff of the Wheaton Graduate School. In general this survey showed a highly nonresponsive field. Bear in mind that previous evangelistic outreaches, especially Here's Life America, had not proved to be especially fruitful. As is typical in North America, over sixty percent said they were satisfied with life as it is and were not seeking change. Most had previous Christian backgrounds, and just under half were occasional churchgoers. The vast majority believed in God and His role in the life of an individual, but only twenty-four percent were interested in attending a church that preaches salvation.

About sixty-one percent of those surveyed said they try to live according to the Ten Commandments, but only thirty-eight percent claimed to try to carry religion into their life-style. Interestingly, the vast majority agreed that the Bible is God's Word, but less than one fourth open their Bible as often as once a month.

There is, in short, a high degree of biblical awareness among the people in Rochester (stage –6 in the decision process) but little apparent grasp of the implications for their life. Only thirty-five percent said Christianity has the answers for the problems in the world today, and under twenty percent would turn to the church if they had any kind of serious problem.

Although they evidenced satisfaction with life as it is, this never should be interpreted to mean that people are without problems. The thirty-five to forty-four-year-old segment, in particular, was designated a target audience because of their greater openness to change and the felt needs that they demonstrated. There were fairly large percentages who said they needed assistance in helping their children adjust emotionally, in knowing how to raise their children properly, in teaching spiritual values in the family, in expressing their feelings more freely, in building their self confidence, and in learning how to understand other people. This target audience, by the way, was highly educated, materially comfortable, and career-oriented. There was high interest in the printed page, and television was viewed during prime time hours of 9:00–11:00 P.M. Two radio stations, in turn, were listened to by more than two thirds in this segment.[5]

[5]Statistics in the above paragraphs are from Wheaton Communication Department Research Report #83.

From this information, then, it was possible to determine a target audience and derive a pretty accurate indication of where they stood spiritually. They were conventionally religious, but their beliefs were not reflected in life-style. They were career- and family-oriented, and there were some unmet needs. The strategy clearly could not center initially around a call for decision, but there were valuable clues for a strategy of proclamation.

Establishment of Measurable Goals

Because strategy is two-pronged, goals must be set both for church revitalization and evangelism.

Church Revitalization. The Latin American situation faced by Palau is usually characterized by a miniscule evangelical church. While it is in need of revitalization, the greater priority is establishment of new churches. Therefore, a major goal of the outreach is to specify the number of new congregations that will be planted. This, of course, forces existing churches to reevaluate priorities and engage in considerable evangelistic outreach themselves. It is in this area that the contributions of church growth concepts are especially notable. While there is also concern about the health within both existing and new churches, that has not been a primary focus of Palau's efforts other than to motivate greater outreach. Obviously, these broader issues must be faced soon, however, if the fruits of evangelism are to be conserved.

Rochester, on the other hand, is a city with many churches, the vast majority of which are not viewed by the public as viable options for their own life. The problem here, then, is to mount an effort that brings new light, so to speak, and stimulates problem recognition in a satisfied populace. In other words, church life-style must be so visible and attractive that it will give large numbers of non-Christians a standard against which to evaluate their life. Evangelistic outreach also is a concern, of course, but remember that many of these churches have been quite active on that front with only minimal impact on the community.

Several teams of graduate students wrestled with the problems of Rochester, and each prepared a strategy independently. One of these projects will be utilized here as an example of the thinking that took place. Here is a statement of possible goals for cooperating churches within the GRAE:[6]

[6]The members of this team were John Maust, Stan De La Cour, Marsha Quist, Christina Rees, Jeremiah Okorie, and Ruth Senter.

1. To stimulate a fifteen percent increase in church attendance during the first year that a church participates in the campaign.
2. To motivate at least twenty percent of the members in each cooperating church to become meaningfully involved in a small group discipleship program. In those churches where such an effort is already underway (there are healthy efforts in some churches), the goal is to increase the number of members involved by an additional twenty percent.
3. For the Rochester population as a whole, to encourage a ten percent increase in the number attending church each Sunday and a corresponding decrease in once-a-month and only occasional attenders.
4. For those churches that utilize a congregational analysis in the form of a survey and program reevaluation, the goal is for a ten percent shift after one year in these dimensions:

   a. The number of people who maintain daily Bible study and prayer habits.
   b. The number who are able to identify spiritual gifts and show evidence of their use in the community or in the church.
   c. The number who can show specifically that Christian solutions are found to their existing personal needs.

The latter goal, by the way, obviously is general and must be made specific within each church. Also, these are goals only for the first year in what must be a continuing effort. Therefore, they may seem to be modest, but this type of internal change always occurs quite slowly. Finally, notice that the goals are stated with sufficient numerical precision that measurement of effectiveness will be possible after one year.

Community Outreach. In Palau's strategy, it is possible to state goals in terms of attendance at an evangelistic crusade, the number of reported decisions, the number who become involved in churches as a result of their decision, and so on. It is unclear from published reports, however, how such goals were set, if indeed they were at all.

Once again Rochester presents a dramatically different situation. Those in the target thirty-five to forty-four-year-old audience and in the general population are anything but a fertile field. In fact, they might be considered a somewhat tired "worked over" field due to the lack of results of the most recent city-wide evangelistic effort. Therefore, it is not to be expected that many decisions will result during the first stages of a revamped cooperative effort of the type being discussed here. The most that can be expected is to "afflict the afflicted," so to speak, and to show Christianity in such a light both through Christian life-style and communication strategy that some will begin to reconsider their present indifference to spiritual concerns. If this can be accomplished and some can be helped to a greater understanding of what Christianity is all about, this will represent movement in their spiritual decision process. Therefore, goals must focus on proclamation outcomes rather than decisions. Eventually, when problem recognition occurs, decisions may be called for.

Here are possible goals suggested for consideration by the GRAE by the strategy team mentioned above for a one-year campaign directed primarily at the target audience but also to the Greater Rochester area as a whole:

1. There should be a minimum of sixty percent in the general audience who show an accurate awareness of the content of the themes of the media outreach. For example, at least sixty percent should be able to answer this type of question positively: "During the past several months, have you seen or heard over the radio or in the newspaper that there is a difference between talking about religion and living that religion?"
2. For those in the target audience, there should be a change in their present awareness and beliefs that Christianity relates to family and interpersonal needs. In particular, these changes should be evidenced in responses to questions asked on the initial community survey:
   a. "If you had a problem that concerned your personal development, to which of the following would you go?" Raise the percentage of those answering "church" from sixteen to twenty-five percent.
   b. "If you had a problem relating to your children or spouse of an emotional nature, to which of the following would you go?" Raise the percentage of those answering "church" from sixteen to thirty percent.
   c. "In my opinion, Christianity has the answers for the problems in the world today." Raise the percentage of those agreeing from thirty-five to forty-five percent.
   d. "I try hard to carry my religion into other areas of my life."

> Raise the percentage of those who agree from thirty-eight to forty-five percent.

As was mentioned in earlier chapters, the magnitude of change specified always will be a bit arbitrary. The important thing is not the numbers themselves but the specificity of the goal so that measurement of effectiveness is facilitated.

These goals also will probably appear to be quite modest, but such outcomes will not occur without a change in church life-style. Furthermore, the number of cooperating churches at the outset will be relatively small. As a result, less can be expected initially than one might hope for later.

What it all comes down to is to move people from stages –6 to –5 in their decision processes. At the moment they simply do not grasp the implications of Christianity for their life, and this must occur before many decisions can be expected.

Determination of Strategy

Palau's approach, of course, will be decision-oriented, and his strategy will be designed to utilize all means for that purpose while simultaneously starting new churches and strengthening existing churches. The suggested Rochester campaign has these phases: (1) church revitalization followed by (2) pre-evangelistic outreach.

Church Revitalization. Palau's efforts to build vision among present church leaders were described earlier. This also had to take place well in advance of actual outreach. A church growth seminar was helpful in both motivating and equipping pastors in the task of planting new churches. A resource frequently used for this purpose is a manual by Vergil Gerber.[7] A review of its contents will disclose much of the strategy that was followed both in Rosario and in Bolivia.

The strategy proposed for Rochester by the Wheaton team was fairly complex and cannot be described fully here. But its main elements can be given. The proposal called for a retreat to be sponsored by GRAE to build vision and to encourage participation. It would be followed by a period of intensive training in church revitalization using some of the resource people cited in Chapter 11. One of the primary purposes of this training is to establish the

---

[7]Vergil Gerber, *God's Way to Keep a Church Going and Growing* (Glendale, Ca., Regal, 1973).

importance of small group ministry and to begin implementation through trained leadership in each church.

Each church then would be responsible for selecting and training small group leaders who meet regularly with small group leaders from other churches. There is no one fixed curriculum but rather a set of options to meet the needs and problems existing in each situation. There are three suggested themes, however: (1) practical first steps in living and understanding the Christian faith, (2) identification and use of spiritual gifts, and (3) ways to be an effective witness at home and at work. One of the hoped for outcomes is to help those involved build bridges of friendship with neighbors and to make evangelism become natural and spontaneous. Also, groups can be structured so that non-Christians can be invited and involved from time to time. Many of the resources suggested come from the ministry of the Churches Alive team.[8]

It also was suggested that churches build means of encouraging interaction between family groups. Neighborhood block parties and family suppers are examples. The intent is to cement interpersonal lines within the church and to build a ministry of mutual encouragement from family to family.

It was recognized that not everyone in a church will want to become involved in small discipleship groups, especially since body life is known to be a largely under-forty phenomenon. Therefore, many suggestions were given for nongroup members encompassing books, tapes, seminars, and pulpit ministry.

One interesting suggestion is to call a gathering of all cooperating churches after about a year in the form of a "celebration." The intent is to give Rochester Christians a sense of group identity and awareness of strength in numbers.

Notice that the strategy discussed here really is not a strategy in the usual sense of the word, apart from the root concept of small group ministry. No fixed program was presented. Rather a variety of options was given in full recognition that the final strategy must be determined by each local church. This is a good example of the parachurch organization working as a servant to the local church, preserving their initiative at all costs. The churches themselves asked for this help, and suggestions were given in response.

Evangelistic Outreach. Because of the evidence of large numbers at

[8]For a description of the Churches Alive ministry, see Kay Oliver, "One Secret of Lasting Growth," *Moody Monthly* (June, 1977), pp. 27–29.

stage –3 in their decision process, Luis Palau and his team mounted a strong decision-oriented strategy in both Rosario and Bolivia. Use was made of large evangelistic meetings capitalizing on Palau's distinctive gift as a platform evangelist, but it did not stop there. A variety of mass media was used in addition, more for pre-evangelism, of course, than for direct decision. Yet call-in programs on radio and television gave unprecedented opportunity for both exposure to the gospel message and for direct response. This also was accompanied by person-to-person evangelism, which had begun earlier to aid church planting. All told, thousands of decisions resulted in both localities, and a high percentage of those who responded proved to be true converts as they joined the church and became involved in its life. This is an example of multi-media evangelism at its best.

The strategy in Rochester, of course, has to be dramatically different. Direct one-on-one evangelism had previously been tried and found wanting. Barriers of indifference have to be overcome first and interest stimulated in Christianity as people come to grasp its implications for their life.

Recall that the primary target audience in the thirty-five to forty-four-year-old age bracket is educated, wealthy, and career-oriented. They do not reject the Bible as being authoritative, and this means that many will take Scripture seriously if it is presented in a tasteful, nonpreachy fashion. This openness to the Bible is not always evident in such communities. They claim to have some kind of faith, but it is not applied to life. Therefore, a central element in the program in media outreach is designed to raise dissonance by highlighting this perceived discrepancy between faith and practice and showing how Christianity, properly related and applied, is an answer to their felt needs.

Once again strategy options were given only as suggestions for those in the GRAE and the Concerned Christians group to sift and evaluate. No attempt was made to give them a finished program. First of all, it was not wanted and, furthermore, too much in the way of specificity may discourage local initiative.

It was recommended that a thirteen-week media campaign be undertaken well after church revitalization begins. The first nine weeks will feature little opportunity for audience response, but the last four weeks will give direct opportunity for inquiry about the Christian life. That stage will require some type of counseling office with a telephone hookup to permit conversations on a "hot line."

The survey showed wide exposure to prime-time television and, especially during evening "drive time," to two radio stations. Thus about sixty percent of the budget logically can go in that direction. The rest can be invested in local newspapers or in national magazines that feature a regional edition for Rochester.

It is interesting to note here that the strategy team suggested that the all-city church celebration mentioned above be scheduled at the nine-week point, followed by the direct response media efforts. It is hoped the celebration will be highly visible in the community. Direct response, by the way, is to take the form of call-in or write-in. Counseling is to be given as needed, and the individual then is to be referred to the nearest local church. Ideally, direct contact can be made in the neighborhood, and this may take the form of attendance at a small group meeting. In any event, the contact is to be highly personalized and flexible. Where possible, of course, decision-oriented evangelism should be done, but further pre-evangelism in the form of friendship may be needed with many. The exact details here are entirely up to the church.

Some of the suggested media spots appear in an appendix to this chapter. The reader no doubt will be interested in how cleverly the "personal" is highlighted through skillful, nonjudgmental messages. Christianity really appears as a feasible option.

At the end of this fifteen-month campaign period, the hope is that churches will proceed together with more joining the outreach. If the effort has been successful, succeeding years should see an upsurge in the number of people who become Christians and join the local church. It might take at least several years, and those involved must be patient to allow the Holy Spirit to break down the skepticism with which the local church now is viewed.

The suggested budget for the entire effort is about $25,000. This would break down to about $2,500 for each cooperating church. Obviously it is assumed that most of the work will be done by local volunteers with only minimal outside involvement. The author feels that this budget is realistic and that the goals probably can be attained with only a modest expenditure. All too often we make the great mistake of assuming that evangelistic outreach demands budgets equivalent to those of national advertisers. This is because some have been carried away by the presence of expensive media hardware. This is yet another reason why every effort should be made to avoid the excesses of the "Madison Avenue" approach.

Execution of Strategy

When a cooperative effort of this type is undertaken, someone has to bear the responsibility for overall coordination and direction. Sometimes the parachurch organization such as the Luis Palau or Billy Graham teams are the ideal vehicle. Other times, a local group, such as the Concerned Christians in Rochester, is a more viable alternative. The only caution to be given once again is that the parachurch organization, if it is placed in charge, should be there mostly to encourage and facilitate local initiative. If their goal is to import their own program, there is not likely to be any lasting change. The important thing is that "ownership" must be established at the local level. All this means is that people become involved on a sustained basis if it is *their* program, not if it is someone else's. The author can remember all too many instances of the sighs of relief after an evangelistic outreach ceased where we said, in effect, "Wow, I'm glad that's over; now let's go back to normal."

Measurement of Effectiveness and Postmortem

The need for accountability has been well established throughout this book, and the starting point always lies in a statement of *measurable* goals. Furthermore, it is assumed that such misleading actions as praying a prayer or coming forward will not be misinterpreted as measures of success.

One of the criteria common both to Palau's crusades and the Rochester campaign is church growth. That can easily be assessed by head counts. Many of the other goals, however, require a before and after survey. This is true in both phases of the Rochester strategy. For example, there is no way to assess whether or not people have begun to see the church as a viable option unless they are asked. This type of research is not difficult, and it also does not need to be expensive.

Again it should be stated that effectiveness measurements are not undertaken primarily for purposes of public relations and fund raising. The whole intent is to assess what went well and what needs improvement. This is the meaning of the term *postmortem analysis.* How, for example, can the Rochester campaign be extended in future years unless an analytical postmortem is held? It demands an attitude of coming before the Lord and asking Him to teach His servants through the data that has been collected.

It should be noted parenthetically that the postmortem stage generally is completely missing in the business firm. The reason? No one wants to accept responsibility for what happens. The outcome, of course, is a continual reinvention of the wheel, so to speak, as succeeding generations of managers never are enabled to learn from the experience of their predecessors. Such an attitude has no place in Christian work. Luis Palau is a superb example of how a postmortem can be used effectively. He always has been frank to admit that Rosario was an experiment and that they fell far short of their goals. But he goes on to note that weaknesses were examined in Bolivia, and the lessons learned from there will be applied in the future. This is the very essence of a proper attitude of stewardship.

By the way, a lengthy period of so-called experience can be very misleading. It is not uncommon to see someone in Christian work who has had one year of experience repeated twenty or more times. What this says, of course, is that there never really has been an attitude of accountability, an attitude that should lead to continual modification and change.

ANOTHER LOOK AT EVANGELIO '79

The reader by now should grasp from the previous chapters that the author was profoundly affected by the International Congress on World Evangelization held at Lausanne. The extent to which the papers have been quoted throughout this volume attest to the fact that that gathering did not fall into the traps that the fictional "Evangelio '79" potentially could. Therefore, the intent of this chapter obviously was not to detract from such significant gatherings, but rather to place strategy meetings in a context in which they will be most fruitful in terms of impact on world evangelization.

The types of strategies discussed here are a far cry from Evangelio '79. The church is taken quite seriously, and every effort is made to equip it for purposes of evangelism. Programs and methodology are seen as tools and not as ends in themselves. In fact, a gathering such as Evangelio really becomes superfluous when the emphasis is placed on the local scene and on the encouragement of local initiative.

If Evangelio '79 or ('80, '81, . . .) were to be held, however, what could it do to help the cause of world evangelization? First, it should be stated unequivocally that no attempt will be made to determine strategy to be exported to the world. That can only be done locally under the guidance of the Holy Spirit. Grand strategies built by committees and then exported will do more harm than good.

Evangelio can be of major help if it focuses on what can be done to help the local church to cope with its situation collectively. Methods of analysis and planning then would take precedence over strategies. Leaders would be helped to analyze their situation and would be given training in approaches to strategic thinking. One of the greatest compliments the author ever received was in an Asian country where one of several hundred national leaders stood up with this word: "You have been one of the few who has ever come here with the goal of helping us think our problems through. Usually those who come have a program they want us to accept. They have hurt us, and you have helped us." The author hopes the reader will not misinterpret the motivation for including this statement. It was related only to say this: Such a response, if forthcoming from a gathering such as Evangelio '79, would make the whole meeting worthwhile.

APPENDIX

Examples of Radio and Television Evangelistic Advertisements Prepared as Options for Outreach in Rochester, N.Y.

Television Spot

VIDEO	AUDIO
(ZOOM SLOWLY IN ON MAN OR WOMAN SITTING AT TABLE IN LIVING ROOM OR WALKING IN A PARK. THE PERSON IS HOLDING A HANDFUL OF CHANGE. HE/SHE PICKS UP A COIN, STUDIES IT, AND READS . . .)	*MUSIC: SOFT AND LIGHT CLASSICAL*
	MUSIC: FADE UNDER
	MAN: (READING COIN) In God we trust. (LOOKS AT CAMERA) Do we?
(FREEZE)	

(WORDS ON SCREEN)

ANNCR: For more information call 765-4321 or write the Concerned Christians of Rochester, Box 222, Rochester, New York, 12345.

MUSIC UP AND OUT

Radio Spot

AUDIO

BRING UP SOUNDS OF YOUNG CHILDREN AT PLAY. INDIVIDUAL VOICES CAN BE HEARD.

FADE TO:

ADULT: Would you be happy if your children grew up to be just like you?

BACKGROUND SOUNDS OF CHILDREN'S VOICES.

ADULT: Concerned about it? So are we. Call the Concerned Christians of Rochester, 765-4321, or write the Concerned Christians, Box 222, Rochester, New York, 12345.

Radio Spot

AUDIO

ADULT? For the next five seconds we'd like you to think about God.

PAUSE FOR FIVE SECONDS

ADULT: Have any trouble? Were your thoughts confused

. . . or negative? God thinks about us and His thoughts toward us are positive. In the Bible it says: "For I know the thoughts I have toward you, thoughts for good and not for evil, to give you a future and a hope." Think about Him.
He's thinking about you.

ANNCR: This has been sponsored by the Concerned Christians of Rochester. For information call 765-4321, or write Box 222, Rochester, New York, 12345.

This last spot can have many variations, such as different voices for the "ADULT". Use children, old people, etc. Different verses can also be used, as long as they refer to God's thoughts about people.

CHAPTER 14

Restoring the Missing Cutting Blades

Two thousand years ago Jesus faced His followers and said, "Look at the fields—they are ripe and ready for the harvest. Come, follow me, and make disciples in all nations." Yet, two millenia have passed, and the granaries have yet to be filled. What is the problem? Certainly it is not a lack of harvesting equipment. Churches and parachurch organizations abound, especially in the western world, and the equipment chugs on making a lot of noise at times. But still not much harvest. Why? The equipment is there but the cutting blades are dull or missing altogether.

This was the analogy used by the author and Wil Norton in the book that is the predecessor to this volume, and the analogy still is apt.[1] The author's underlying purpose in these pages has been to tackle the cutting blade problem head on. Frequently it has been necessary to remove some serious cobwebs of misunderstanding and to dislodge what Ted Ward has called the "fuzzy fables of Christian Communication."[2] The goal always has been to bring needed clarity to our thinking processes.

There is an old adage for preachers that says first "tell them what you are going to say." That was done in Chapter 1. Then, "tell them." That was the purpose of Chapters 2–13. And, finally, "tell them

[1]James F. Engel and H. Wilbert Norton, *What's Gone Wrong With the Harvest?* (Grand Rapids, Mich.: Zondervan, 1975).

[2]Ted Ward, "Fuzzy Fables or Communications that Count," *Christian Communications Spectrum,* vol. 1 (1975), p. 10ff.

what you said." That is what this chapter is all about. The seven principles of Christian communications will be stated once again and the main points summarized. But also we need to take a look ahead and highlight the critical issues that the church worldwide must come to grips with in the next decade or so. Today's problems should always be looked upon as tomorrow's opportunities.

MAKING DISCIPLES IN ALL NATIONS

No single book could ever say all that needs to be said about the subject of making disciples in all nations. But the seven principles of Christian communications discussed and elaborated in this book, if followed seriously, provide some major pieces in the puzzle.

Goal-Oriented Communication Is Imperative

Christ's command to go unto all the world and make disciples is as contemporary today as it was when given to His first disciples. The church has no option but to continue this work until His return in glory. But it must be remembered that the Sermon on the Mount provided the key to the method—the church as "salt and light."

We have tended in this century to distort the entire meaning of what Christ was saying. First, we have imposed the term "Great Commission" as the great rallying cry of the church. Evangelism has been elevated as being the hallmark of a mature church. Christians have been mobilized, motivated, and maneuvered into almost a military-style verbal barrage on a lost world. But where is the salt and the light? Where is that behavior exemplifying the lordship of Christ that takes seriously the cause of the poor and oppressed, a love and concern for one another within the body of Christ, a life-style that stands in clear and distinct contrast to a world imprisoned to self-seeking? Christ was saying, of course, that the very life of the church is the essence of the message of Christianity.

There is a need now to tone down the "great commotion" that has replaced the Great Commission. But this does *not* mean to de-emphasize evangelism. Quite the opposite! The need is to take our eyes off the media hardware and Madison Avenue methods and regain once again a biblical perspective.

Furthermore, it is high time to come to grips once again with the fact that making disciples goes far beyond an initial conversion and reaches instead over a lifetime as the believer is conformed to the image of Christ. Christian maturity, then, is the goal of disciple-making efforts. We have become so enamored with evangelism in some quarters that maturity is almost taken for granted. Such an attitude, however, ignores the New Testament teachings, which have far more to say about Christian life-style than anything else.

The Bible Is the Only Infallible Rule of Faith and Practice

The Bible is the bedrock of Christian communications. It is the absolute and final authority for everything that is proclaimed. This has been the historic position of the church, and there is no reason to depart from this premise now. Human philosophies have come and gone over the past 2,000 years, while the Bible alone has retained an unchallenged position of eminence.

J. Robertson McQuilken no doubt is right that the infallibility and authority of the Bible may well be the most important issue facing the church in the next decade.[3] This is a crucial issue that cannot be avoided, but the "battle for the Bible" requires more than identification of those who presumably have departed from belief in inerrancy. This only serves to divide many who have precious little unity to begin with. It is disturbing that some who are most vocal seem to be the most reticent in raising their voices in protest over the degree to which cultural syncretism has invaded much of the North American church. One cannot fight for an infallible Bible on the one hand and ignore some of its most stringent teachings on the other.

The really critical issue in this whole controversy is one of hermeneutics. How can we achieve dynamic equivalence so that the historical meaning of biblical texts, church forms and practices, and Christian life-styles are understood in the original context, interpreted, and applied today so that the same meaning is achieved? Even more to the point, what will it take to motivate genuine obedience to these truths?

The author will never forget his first trip out of the free world into communist Europe. A pastor living close to the border of the Soviet Union made this prophetic statement: "For Christianity to be vital, there must be a balance between freedom and suffering. Our problem is lack of freedom—yours is lack of suffering. We pray for you because you have it too easy and have become impotent." Will it take

[3]J. Robertson McQuilken, address given to the Wheaton College Commencement, May 22, 1978.

externally imposed suffering to purify the church and cause it to take its message more seriously?

When it comes right down to it, the Bible has survived its critics for nearly 2,000 years, and it will continue to do so. What is needed now is proper interpretation and wholehearted obedience.

The Church Is Both Medium and Message

It must be said once again that the church as an organized body of believers is God's primary agent for world evangelization. It alone has divine permanence and a never-ending mandate, whereas the parachurch organization exists only insofar as it augments and serves the church.

We now come to the second great issue that must be faced in the next decade. What, exactly, is the church? As the reader will recall from Chapter 4, this is not an easy question to answer, and there is real diversity of opinion at the present moment. Is it primarily an institution, governed in a hierarchical manner, and operated by management principles? Or is it a spiritual organism, the mystical body of Christ, characterized by a sense of community and organized in terms of spiritual gifts? Or is it some mixture of these forms? Obviously it is both.

A related question is this: What is the purpose of the church? Is its great overriding mission to seek and save the lost? Or does it exist more for the purpose of Christian nurture and growth, with evangelism viewed as just one of its mandates?

The danger of the institutional model is that it will tend to substitute pragmatism for biblical fidelity. Bigness becomes viewed as a sign of greatness. Success in evangelism is more important than the motivation of a radically biblical life-style among the members. Activities center around a paid staff and a limited few from the membership while the remainder sit on the sidelines as little more than bystanders.

In the final analysis, those who are having the greatest success with the church seem to meet on an interesting common ground. On one side, for example, Robert H. Schuller contends that the church must gauge all that it does in terms of evangelistic outreach.[4] A strongly institutional form of organization is present, the pastor exercises a dominant role, and there is a flair for the dramatic in church buildings and public relations. It is all done to attract the non-Christians,

[4]Robert H. Schuller, *Your Church Has Possibilities* (Glendale, Ca.: Regal, 1974).

and this church is growing dramatically. Yet, there also is a strong ministry of cultivation within the church, and koinonia is achieved through a multitude of cells and small groups. Thus, there are elements of both the institutional and the organic. The church is more than just an evangelistic medium.

Gene Getz, on the other hand, stresses relationships within the body.[5] His church is definitely organic in organization, and they have no building. The expressed purpose of all that they do is to build the body to maturity. Yet, evangelism also is stressed and the church is growing, even though it is not particularly viewed as an evangelistic medium. Furthermore, there is a degree of institutionalization in the form of organization adopted.

What this says is that one cannot judge a church by externals. It must have a balanced ministry of outreach and cultivation and not unduly emphasize one over another. It cannot legitimately tilt toward an authoritative hierarchical organization, but neither can it be a body without gifted leaders. The essential question that all types of churches must wrestle with centers around the ways in which the balance can be achieved and maintained.

There is yet another important consideration that the North American church, in particular, must wrestle with, and that is its unbiblical tendency toward prophetic silence. Stuart Briscoe has put it well when he said that there seems to be a widespread misconception that God is nothing more than a "great felt need meeter in the sky." This is not to say that preaching and teaching should be of abstract principles devoid of the practical. On the other hand, it does not justify a pulpit and teaching ministry that is always positive and never controversial. Emphasis on the positive is the general principle of preaching put forward by Robert Schuller.[6] His contention is that modern man will not listen unless this stance is maintained. In fairness it should be pointed out that he views his preaching ministry as primarily being for the non-Christian, a position not taken by many pastors.

If this same preaching style is maintained for believers, however, the prophetic voice is silent. Materialism and cultural syncretism in any number of forms can reign supreme and never be challenged. It will not do to state that people do not want to hear a prophetic challenge. Is God still God or not? Is He content to allow for outright

[5]Gene A. Getz, *The Measure of a Church* (Glendale, Ca.: Regal, 1975).
[6]Schuller, *Your Church Has Possibilities.*

sin to exist in the church? Is it His will that poverty, nuclear war, unemployment, racial injustice, political and economic corruption, and any number of other ills permeate a society? If so, why does the Bible have so much to say on these subjects?

Maybe it is time that some comfortable Christians are confronted with the realities around them. Perhaps it is time that we emerge from our ecclesiastical ghetto with more than a Four Spiritual Laws booklet and take an active stance for social betterment. Tozer's words are powerful on this topic:

> The Church must have power; she must become formidable, a moral force to be reckoned with, if she would regain her lost position of spiritual ascendance and make her message the revolutionizing, conquering thing it once was.[7]

The Message Must Be Adapted to a Sovereign Audience

People are not obligated to listen just because they happen to be in proximity to a communicator. They have a God-given sovereignty to screen everything out at a point in time. This means, of course, that audience life-styles, needs, and spiritual background must be taken seriously. One of the most erroneous misconceptions, yet one that is so *very* common, is that mere exposure to the gospel will somehow bring about intended results. It is this type of thinking that has led to such strategies as house-to-house literature distribution without any attempt to assess potential audience reaction, strategies to blast the gospel in hundreds of languages simultaneously from satellites, and so on.

It must be made perfectly clear once again just what we mean by adaptation. It is such a subtle point that it can easily be overlooked. The goal is not to *make* the gospel relevant, but rather to communicate the relevance of the gospel. If one attempts to do the former, the tendency will be to overemphasize the abundant life theme, for instance, while playing down the costs of discipleship. In other words, it is very little different from an advertising strategy that sifts through the product appeals to find those that do the best in selling the product. In communicating gospel relevance, however, felt need *is* taken as the starting point so that biblical truths are seen as more than abstractions, but there is no attempt made to water down any aspect. It is worth noting again Briscoe's warning that God is more than a "great felt need meeter."

---

[7]A.W. Tozer, *Paths to Power* (Philadelphia: Christian Publications, Inc., n. d.), p. 5.

The author, of course, has a background in secular marketing, and much of his previous writing has been in the area of consumer research and advertising strategy. This perhaps explains why he has become increasingly uneasy about *manipulation* posing as audience adaptation. There are some who seem to feel that the end of conversion justifies the means. We would do well to keep Griffin's definition of manipulation before us: *"Any persuasive effort which restricts another's freedom to choose for or against Jesus Christ."*[8] Probably the most subtle form of manipulation is to give a half truth—"accept Christ and everything will be wonderful." If the costs of discipleship are ignored, self-seeking simply is transferred from secular life into the Christian life and still reigns supreme. This is one of the real dangers faced when Christian strategy turns to advertising sloganeering, featuring such themes as "I found it." What exactly did they find? An abundant life, of course, but what about the straight and narrow path that Jesus always seemed to stress? We might win huge numbers of supposed converts this way, but what kind of church is being built? It may be at this very point that cultural syncretism has its roots.

Becoming a Disciple Is an Unending Process With Many Influences

As we have stressed repeatedly, the so-called Great Commission always is in the process of fulfillment, because the making of disciples only begins once a person receives Christ as Savior. Evangelism simply cannot be stressed to the point that it obscures the cultivation of believers. The need is for a church that both proclaims and exemplifies the kingdom of God.

There are two important issues that must be faced in this context. First, what can be done to achieve better integration between mass media and interpersonal media? The mass media are primarily contributory at early stages of the decision process in the sense of stimulating attitude change, whereas interpersonal media usually play a greater role in the actual decision. Both must be united in a common strategy, for one without the other can prove to be ineffective. The first step is for the parachurch organization with a mass media ministry to take seriously its role as a servant of the local church. This will require a patient but determined attempt to utilize all forms of mass media as means of moving people in their spiritual

[8]Em Griffin, *The Mind Changers* (Wheaton, Ill.: Tyndale, 1976), p. 28.

decision process to the point at which they will be receptive to one-on-one sharing. But the local church also will have to move away from isolation and recognize that personal evangelism in a contemporary world will fall short of its potential if it is not coordinated with mass media outreach. This demands a true attitude of partnership.

The second issue centers strictly on the ministry of cultivation in the local church. Much is said and written about discipleship, but it still is a gray area. The basic question is this: What "product" will we see as an individual reaches a level of maturity where beliefs are changing both to reflect biblical truth and to enhance his or her uniqueness? What beliefs and behavior patterns, in other words, will exist at that point? We have seen the dangers of legalism, and it must be avoided at all costs. Once again we are forced back probably to the greatest question of our time: *What is the Bible really saying about life-style in a contemporary society?* Theologians must emerge from their ivory towers and join in dialogue with those at the grass roots so that real biblical scholarship emerges centering around the requirements of dynamic equivalence.

If the end product is not specified, the local church is merely spinning its wheels. There is no real purpose, then, in the pulpit ministry, Christian education, small groups, youth programs, and other activities in the church. Programs abound, of course, but this prior question remains largely unaddressed insofar as the author has been able to determine from extensive exposure both to denominational executives and local church leaders.

Christian Communication Is a Cooperative Effort Between God and Man

In its essence this principle affirms the essential point that the Holy Spirit is solely responsible for results in terms of movement in the decision process. The communicator, on the other hand, is obligated to proclaim a message that has both biblical fidelity and audience sensitivity.

Because of the ministry of the Holy Spirit, we are limited in our ability to draw upon and apply uncritically principles derived from the secular world. Schuller contends, for example, that retailing principles are a major key to building a large evangelistic church.[9] This type of thinking makes the author uneasy, even though Schuller is careful to make very clear that he also takes the sovereignty of

[9]Schuller, *Your Church Has Possibilities.*

God seriously. Such principles and strategies as large parking lots, attractive spacious buildings, and dramatic Sunday services are dangerously seductive. Success indeed can occur if they are applied, but is it success as defined in Scripture? There is a very real danger of building a church or an organization by human ingenuity with little or no role for God. As the searchlight of cultural syncretism is turned on segments of the North American church, one cannot help wondering how much of it really is built on cooperative ministry between God and man. This is a tightrope that each of us must walk, and the potential pitfalls are many.

Disciplined Planning Is the Obligation of the Church

God has ordained the planning process, and it is legitimately viewed as a primary means of achieving the very "mind of Christ." Collection of facts, prayerful consideration of goals, determination of strategy based on awareness of local situations, measurements of effectiveness, a postmortem analysis that asks God to teach His servants so they can be more effective in the future—all of this embodies the very essence of stewardship.

It is time to declare a moratorium on program orientation which, in the final analysis, immobilizes the planning process. Just as this chapter is being written, the author has heard yet another example of a certain parachurch organization taking its strategy for world evangelization built in North America and exporting it to the world with a very heavy hand. The whole approach, probably well meaning, says this: "Follow our strategy, and we will teach you what evangelism is all about." But the church in the great African city in question has successfully been doing evangelism for years. Now they are asking, "Just what do these people think they are doing by coming in with their ideas?" How much better it would have been had the parachurch group made a serious effort to encourage and equip local initiative so that the efforts that result will be appropriate for the locale.

Some Other Points to Keep in Focus

As we look to the coming decades, there are some additional points that also need to be restated and elaborated.

Power Is Shifting in the World Church. There was a period until recently when North America was in the position of giving to the world church. As Ward and Graham pointed out, it was more or less the old issue of the "have" and the "have nots."[10] As the North American and European churches joined hands, the gospel was taken literally to all parts of the globe through missions, and the very fact that there *is* a world church today reflects that fact.

But times are changing, and this fact was underscored most clearly at the Congress on World Evangelization held at Lausanne in 1974. Much to the shock of many from the traditional "sending" countries, the speakers who made the most impact, by and large, were from the developing countries. Who previously had heard much of such people as Kivengere, Osei Mensah, Escobar, or Padilla?

The fact is that the church in many countries of the world makes the United States, with its alleged evangelical "great awakening," appear mighty pallid by comparison. Dynamic leaders are coming forward, and the power no longer resides solely in the West. Today churches in the developing countries are sending missionaries, and some have even included the United States as a mission field.

What this says, of course, is that the forces of nationalism and the growing maturity of the world church demand an end to western paternalism. As the author has repeatedly stressed, missions have profoundly changed their strategies in this respect, and most are pursuing a healthy attitude of partnership. But there still are those organizations, such as the one mentioned above, swinging around the world exporting their made-in-the-USA methods. Why do they get away with it? Simply because they have money behind them and can find people who will cooperate because of that reason alone. But, in the long haul, the resentment building in the national churches toward this type of paternalism will inevitably surface and lead to a power struggle that would never need to happen.

What is it that makes some North Americans feel they have all the answers? Those who have traveled widely abroad, as the author has had much occasion to do, come home chastened and humbled. A short visit to Eastern Europe, for example, will disclose such a virility of Christianity under suffering that it is difficult for the visitor to return to his home church for a period. Many have made such an observation.

Servanthood! Partnership! Reciprocity! Here are the keys to cooperation in the world church. There is no role for western paternalism, but neither is there any role for isolation and avoidance

---

[10]Ted Ward and Kathleen Graham, "Acts of Kindness: Motives and Relationships" (Unpublished paper, Institute for International Studies, Michigan State University, April, 1977).

by nonwestern churches. The need is to join hands in God's work, and this *is* taking place in the post-Lausanne era.

Christian Leadership Must Be Trained. The need for pastoral education has been recognized for hundreds of years in the western church. Presbyterians have especially taken the lead in this respect. More recently, seminary training has been expanded to encompass Christian education, discipleship and evangelism ministries, counseling, and, to a limited degree, communications.

The seminary has played an important role in equipping the church today, but it stands at a crossroads. Is a pastor prepared for church ministry if he or she has become articulate in systematic theology, Hebrew, and Greek? That will train them for biblical teaching, but it does not necessarily make them better pastors. Are they really being equipped to be "shepherds of the flock" in the sense demanded as a church moves toward being an organism? Many have come to the conclusion that *much* more is required, and some seminaries are beginning to respond.

What about other activities in both the church and the parachurch organization? Does it make any sense, for example, to place a veteran pastor in charge of a denominational magazine? What does he know about contemporary journalism? The same could be said in broadcasting and all other phases of communication work. The day for amateurism is over! Professional training programs now exist for these more specialized ministries, and they cannot be ignored if the church is to be equipped to cope in a changing world.

Let it again be reiterated that North America, by and large, is *not* the place to train leadership from churches elsewhere in the world. There is a consistent and even demanding cry for training, and that need must be met. But to bring them out of their own context all too often results in indoctrination in western thinking. There are many cases where their leadership potential has even been impaired on their return because of an inability to contextualize.

Training programs, characterized by genuine contextualization, must be developed throughout the world. This is not easy to do, but it can be accomplished. The cooperative arrangement between the Wheaton Graduate School and Daystar Communications in Kenya is a case in point. It is possible for Africans to receive a fully accredited master's degree without ever coming to the United States. In addition, Daystar training is contextualized so that the danger of lack of contextual relevance is minimized.

It Is Time to End "Promotional Overkill." The author also teaches a course entitled "Marketing and Public Relations for the Christian Organization." The whole purpose is to help organizations relate meaningfully to their clientele. Here were just a few of the appeals for funds that were examined recently: (1) an American evangelist headed for mass meetings in Brazil advertising "one soul for every dollar contributed"; (2) an organization distributing tracts that promise "200 reached for every $5.00 contribution"; (3) a glowing report of unprecedented response in Hong Kong where "eighty-seven percent were exposed to the gospel." On and on and on we go. What are we to believe with such promotional barrages?

At the very outset, the individual Christian must recognize that he or she is not obligated to support *any* of these outreaches. The burden is on those making the appeal to justify such seemingly outrageous claims as "one soul for every dollar." What in the world does that mean? Can he really guarantee true converts who will take their rightful place in the church, or is this just promotional overkill? An attitude of healthy skepticism is warranted, because all too many so-called Christian causes have borrowed a bit too literally from secular promotional techniques.

Next, those who make such glowing reports of what they accomplished must be called upon to back up their claims. Frequently they dissolve when criteria such as church growth are utilized.

But, even more critically, why must we continually be subjected to these great victory stories? World evangelization that focuses on equipping the local church rarely will have as much to say in the respect of dramatic programs and large numbers, and support may suffer as a result. What is it about the American temperament that responds only to the dramatic? It is time for greater sophistication on the part of the average Christian, and the organizations could also help by "cooling it."

Trained Researchers Are Required. Finally, much has been said in this book about the need for research. This is not the province for amateurs. While sufficient methodological sophistication can be grasped by most people, there still is a need for training. Furthermore, churches and Christian organizations must make room for trained researchers on their staffs and use their expertise in the planning process.

Here and there trained researchers are being utilized in Christian strategy, but this still is the exception rather than the rule. In part this simply reflects the fact that research is a relative newcomer on the Christian scene, and any new idea takes a period of time before it diffuses very far. Much more serious is the not uncommon attitude that says, "I do my work only for God, and I don't need your research." That is nothing more than a spiritualized way to avoid accountability. No one is an island unto themselves, and all must be accountable for their work within the body of Christ. Those who persist in such an attitude will be nothing more than a serious impediment to any type of needed change.

SO, WHERE TO FROM HERE?

Much has been covered in this book. Not many success formulae have been given, and the author hopes the reader is not disappointed. Most of those formulae, by the way, do not work when taken out of their original context. Rather, the emphasis has been on ways of thinking about various aspects of Christian communication strategy. When analytical skill is utilized in full dependence upon the sovereignty of God, things will happen! Perhaps headlines will not be made, but the slow, grinding work of world evangelization will go forward.

We have centered at times on the erroneous concepts and strategies that have sometimes infiltrated Christian communications. This has been necessary in order to provide the needed clarity. What the reader probably has not realized is that most of the mistakes talked about here have been made by the author at one time or another in his life. Maybe that is why he feels so deeply about the need for some radical rethinking.

It is hoped that the reader will be encouraged to keep abreast of new developments. This book will be out-of-date in a few years, and so will the reader if he or she does not take precautions. Notice the periodicals footnoted throughout the book; these are the sources the author finds to be invaluable. Make every effort to spend time reading and contemplating implications of what is read. Change is always threatening, but it cannot be avoided.

Perhaps of greatest importance—build accountability into Christian work and learn from successes and failures. Nothing is more guaranteed to minimize "hardening of the spiritual arteries" than that step.

Finally, approach Christian work with humility. No one has all the answers. Some may have only a tiny piece of the puzzle at best. We need one another if progress is to be made. There is no place for the "Christian guru."

Is the author optimistic about the future? Of course! The church still is alive and functioning, frequently with renewed vitality, throughout the world. The signs of a healthy emphasis on stewardship are increasingly evident, thus giving rise to the likelihood that Christ's lordship over all phases of life *will* be proclaimed and exemplified to the ends of the earth.

Bibliography

The following are titles of books referred to in this work. Journals and unpublished papers are not listed. All authors of books, journals, articles, and other materials are listed in the index.

Abelson, R. F. et. al. (ed.). *Theories of Cognitive Consistency: A Sourcebook* (Chicago: Rand-McNally, 1968).

Allen, Roland. *Missionary Methods: St. Paul's or Ours* (Grand Rapids, Mich.: Wm. B. Eerdmans, 1962).

———*The Spontaneous Expansion of the Church* (Grand Rapids, Mich.: Wm. B. Eerdmans, 1962).

Allport, G. W., Vernon, P. E., and Lindzey, George. *Manual for the Study of Values,* 3rd ed. (Boston: Houghton-Mifflin, 1960).

Argyle, Michael, and Bert-Hallahmi, Benjamin. *The Social Psychology of Religion* (Boston: Routledge and Kegan Paul, 1975).

Atkinson, John W. (ed.). *Motives in Fantasy, Action, and Society* (Princeton, N.J.: D. Van Nostrand Company, 1958).

Barnlund, D. C. (ed.). *Interpersonal Communication: Survey and Studies* (Boston: Houghton-Mifflin, 1968).

Barton, Roger. *Media in Advertising* (New York: McGraw-Hill, 1964).

Bauer, J. B. *Sacramentum Verbi* (New York: Herder & Herder, 1970).

Benson, Dennis C. *Electric Evangelism* (Nashville: Abingdon Press, 1973).

Berelson, Bernard. *Content Analysis in Communication Research* (New York: Free Press, 1952).

Berelson, B. R., Lazarsfeld, P. F., and McPhee, W. N. *Voting* (Chicago: University of Chicago Press, 1954).

Berkhof, L. *Systematic Theology* (Grand Rapids, Mich.: Wm. B. Eerdmans, 1941).

Berlo, David K. *The Process of Communication* (New York: Holt, Rinehart, and Winston, 1960).

Biderman, A.D., and Zimmer, H. (eds.). *The Manipulation of Human Behavior* (New York: Wiley, 1961).

Birnbaum, Jack. *Cry Anger* (Don Mills, Ontario, Canada: General Publishing Co., Ltd., 1973).

Blackwell, Roger D., Engel, James F., and Kollat, David T. *Cases in Consumer Behavior* (New York: Holt, Rinehart, and Winston, 1969).

Bleum, A William. *Religious Television Programs* (New York: Hastings House, 1969).

Borden, George A., and Stone, John D. *Human Communication: The Process of Relating* (Menlow Park, Ca.: Cummings, 1976).

Brehm, Jack W. *A Theory of Psychological Reactance* (New York: Academic Press, 1966).

Brehm, Jack W., and Cohen, Arthur R. *Explorations in Cognitive Dissonance* (New York: Wiley, 1962).

Brim, Orville; Glass, David; Lavin, David E.; and Goodman, Norman. *Personality and Decision Processes* (Stanford, Ca.: Stanford University Press, 1962).

Cohen, Arthur. *Attitude Change and Social Influence* (New York: Basic Books, 1964).

Colquhoun, F. *Harringay Story* (London: Hodder and Stoughton, 1955).

Costas, Orlando E. *The Church and Its Mission: A Shattering Critique from the Third World* (Wheaton, Illinois: Tyndale, 1974).

Crabb, Jr., Lawrence J. *Effective Biblical Counseling* (Grand Rapids, Mich.: Zondervan, 1977).

Crowsers, Robert G. *Principles of Learning in Memory* (Hillsdale, N.J.: Lawrence Erlbaum Assoc., 1976).

Crum, Jr., Milton. *Manual on Preaching* (Valley Forge, Pa.: Judson Press, 1977).

Dayton, Edward R. *Planning Strategies for Evangelism: A Workbook*, 6th ed. (Monrovia, Ca.: MARC, 1978).

DeFleur, Melvin L. *Theories of Mass Communication,* 2nd ed. (New York: David McKay Co., 1975).

DeVito, Joseph A. (ed.). *Communication: Concept and Processes* (Englewood Cliffs, N.J.: Prentice-Hall, 1971).

Dewey, John. *How We Think* (New York: Heath, 1910).

Dixon, Norman F. *Subliminal Perception—The Nature of the Controversy* (Maidenhead-Berkshire, England: McGraw-Hill Publishing Co., Ltd., 1971).

Douglas, J. D. (ed.). *Let the Earth Hear His Voice* (Minneapolis: World Wide Publications, 1975).

Duijker, H. C. J., and Frijda, N.H. *National Character and National Stereotypes: Confluence,* vol. 1 (Amsterdam: North-Holland, 1960).

Dulles, Avery. *Models of the Church* (Garden City, N.Y.: Doubleday, 1974).

Ellul, Jacques. *The Technological Society* (New York: Alfred A. Knopf, 1964).

Engel, James F. *How Can I Get Them To Listen?* (Grand Rapids, Mich.: Zondervan, 1977).

Engel, James F., Blackwell, Roger D., and Kollat, David T. *Consumer Behavior,* 3rd ed. (Hinsdale, Ill.: Dryden Press, 1978).

Bibliography

Engel, James F., and Norton, H. Wilbert. *What's Gone Wrong With the Harvest?* (Grand Rapids, Mich.: Zondervan, 1975).

Engel, James F., Wales, Hugh G., and Warshaw, Martin R. *Promotional Strategy,* 3rd ed. (Homewood, Ill.: Richard D. Irwin, Inc. 1975).

Fenelon, F. *Dialogues on Eloquence* (Princeton, N.J.: Princeton University Press, 1951).

Festinger, Leon. *A Theory of Cognitive Dissonance* (Evanston, Ill.: Row Peterson, 1957).

Fishbein, Martin (ed.). *Attitude Theory and Measurement* (New York: Wiley, 1967).

Fishbein, Martin, and Ajzen, Icek. *Belief, Attitude, Intention, and Behavior* (Reading, Mass.: Addison-Wesley, 1975).

Ford, Leighton. *Good News Is for Sharing* (Elgin, Ill.: David C. Cook, 1977).

Freire, Paulo. *Education for Critical Consciousness* (New York: Seabury Press, 1973).

———*Extension for Communication* (New York: Seabury Press, 1973).

———*Pedagogy of the Oppressed* (New York: Seabury Press, 1968).

Gerber, Vergil. *God's Way to Keep a Church Going and Growing* (Glendale, Ca.: Regal, 1973).

Getz, Gene A. *The Measure of a Church* (Glendale, Ca.: Regal, 1975).

Gillquist, Peter E. *Fresh New Insight Into Love Is Now* (Grand Rapids, Mich.: Zondervan, 1978).

Glock, Charles Y. (ed.). *Religion on Sociological Perspective: Essays in the Empirical Study of Religion* (Belmont, Ca.: Wadsworth Publishing Co., 1973).

Glock, Charles Y., and Stark, Rodney. *Religion and Society in Tension* (Chicago: Rand-McNally, 1965).

Goodenough, Ward. *Cooperation in Change* (New York: Russell Sage Foundation, 1963).

Graham, Robin Lee. *Dove* (New York: Harper & Row, 1972).

Greenway, Roger S. *An Urban Strategy for Latin America* (Grand Rapids, Mich.: Baker Book House, 1973).

Griffin, Em. *The Mind Changers* (Wheaton, Ill.: Tyndale, 1976).

Hastings, James (ed.). *A Dictionary of the Bible* (Edinburgh: T & T Clark, 1905).

Hendricks, Howard. *Say It With Love* (Wheaton, Ill.: Victor Books, 1972).

Holt, R. *An Approach to the Psychology of Religion* (Boston: Christopher, 1956).

Hodges, Melvin. *A Guide to Church Planting* (Chicago: Moody Press, 1973).

Horne, Charles M. *Salvation* (Chicago: Moody Press, 1971).

Hovland, C. I., Lumsdaine, A. A., and Sheffield, F. D. *Experiments in Mass Communications,* vol. 3 (Princeton, N.J.: Princeton University Press, 1949).

Howard, David A. *The Great Commission for Today* (Downers Grove, Ill.: InterVarsity Press, 1976).

James, Muriel, and Jongeward, Dorothy. *Born to Win: Transactional Analysis with Gestalt Experiments* (Reading, Mass.: Addison-Wesley, 1973).

James, William. *The Varieties of Religious Experience* (London: Longmans, 1902).

———*The Principles of Psychology,* vol. 1 (New York: Henry Holt and Co., 1890).

Janis, I. *The Contours of Fear* (New York: John Wiley & Sons, 1968).

Jones, E. E., and Gerard, H. G. *Foundations of Social Psychology* (New York: Wiley, 1967).

Kennedy, James. *Evangelism Explosion* (Wheaton, Ill.: Tyndale, 1970).

Klapper, Joseph T. *The Effects of Mass Communication* (Glencoe, Ill.: Free Press, 1960).

Kroeber, A. L., et. al. *Anthropology Today: An Encyclopedia* (Chicago: University of Chicago Press, 1953).

Larson, Bruce. *The One and Only You* (Waco, Texas: Word Books, 1973).

Lazarsfeld, Paul F.; Berelson, Bernard; and Gaudet, Hazel. *The People's Choice* (New York: Columbia University Press, 1948).

Lerner, Daniel (ed.). *The Human Meaning of the Social Sciences* (Cleveland, Ohio: World Publishing, 1959).

Levine, Phillip (ed.). *Attitude Research Bridges the Atlantic* (Chicago: American Marketing Assoc., 1975).

Lewis, Gregg. *Telegarbage* (Nashville: Thomas Nelson, 1977).

Lindzey, Gardner, and Aronsen, Elliot (eds.). *Handbook of Social Psychology* (Reading, Mass.: Addison-Wesley, 1968).

Little, Paul. *How to Give Your Faith Away* (Downers Grove, Ill.: InterVarsity Press, 1966).

Lucas, Darrell B., and Britt, Stuart H. *Advertising Psychology and Research* (New York: McGraw-Hill, 1950).

Luzbetak, Louis J. *The Church and Cultures* (Techeny, Ill.: Divine World Publications, 1970).

Mager, Robert F. *Preparing Instructional Objectives* (Belmont, Ca.: Fearon Publishers, 1972).

Mains, David. *Full Circle* (Waco, Texas: Word Books, 1971).

Maslow, A. H. *Motivation and Human Behavior,* rev. ed. (New York: Harper & Row, 1970).

Mayers, Marvin K. *Christianity Confronts Culture* (Grand Rapids, Mich.: Zondervan, 1974).

Mazze, Edward M. (ed.). *1975 Combined Proceedings* (Chicago: American Marketing Assoc., 1975).

McClelland, David C. *Personality* (New York: William Sloane Assoc., 1951).

McDowell, Josh. *Evidence That Demands A Verdict* (Arrowhead Springs, Ca.: Campus Crusade for Christ, 1972).

McGavran, Donald A., and Winfield, C. Arn. *How to Grow a Church* (Glendale, Ca.: Regal, 1973).

———*Understanding Church Growth* (Grand Rapids, Mich.: Wm. B. Eerdmans, 1970).

McKeachie, W. J., and Doyle, Charlotte L. *Psychology* (Reading, Mass.: Addison-Wesley, 1966).

McLuhan, Marshall, and Fiore, Quentin. *The Medium Is the Message* (New York: Bantam Books, 1970).

Moberg, David O. *The Church as a Social Institution* (Englewood Cliffs, N.J.: Prentice Hall, 1972).

Morgan, Marabel. *The Total Woman* (Old Tappan, N.J.: Spire Books, 1975).

———*Total Joy* (Old Tappan, N.J.: Revell, 1976).

Mortensen, C. David. *Communication: The Study of Human Interaction* (New York: McGraw-Hill, 1972).

McQuilkin, J. Robertson. *Measuring the Church Growth Movement* (Chicago: Moody Press, 1974).

Miller, Keith. *The Becomers* (Waco, Texas: Word Books, 1973).

Muggeridge, Malcolm. *Christ and the Media* (Grand Rapids, Mich.: Wm. B. Eerdmans, 1978).

Neisser, Ulrich. *Cognitive Psychology* (New York: Appleton, 1966).

Nida, Eugene A. *Message in Mission* (New York: Harper & Brothers, 1960).

Nida, Eugene A., and Taber, Charles R. *Toward a Science of Translating* (Leiden: E. J. Brill, 1964).

Nichols, Alan. *The Communicators* (Sydney: Pilgrim Publications, 1972).

Nickel, Ben J. *Along the Quichua Trail* (Smithville, Mo.: Gospel Missionary Union, 1965).

Norman, Donald A. *Memory and Attention* (New York: Wiley, 1969).

North, R. C., et. al. *Content Analysis: A Handbook With Applications for the Study of International Crisis* (Evanston, Ill.: Northwestern University Press, 1963).

Oppenheim, A. N. *A Questionnaire Design and Attitude Measurement* (New York: Basic Books, 1966).

Packer, J. I. *Evangelism and the Sovereignty of God* (Downers Grove, Ill.: InterVarsity Press, 1961).

Posner, Michael I. *Cognition: An Introduction* (Glenview, Ill., Scott Foresman, 1973).

Pruyser, Paul W. *Between Belief and Unbelief* (New York: Harper & Row, 1974).

Quebedeaux, Richard. *The Worldly Evangelicals* (New York: Harper & Row, 1978).

Raimy, Victor. *Misunderstandings of the Self* (San Francisco: Jossey-Bass Publishers, 1975).

Reid, Gavin. *The Gagging of God* (London: Hodder and Stoughton, 1969).

Richards, Lawrence. *A New Face for the Church* (Grand Rapids, Mich.: Zondervan, 1970).

Richardson, Don. *Lords of the Earth* (Glendale, Ca.: Regal, 1977).

———*Peace Child* (Glendale, Ca.: Regal, 1974).

Rogers, Carl R. *Client-Centered Therapy* (Boston: Houghton-Mifflin, 1951).

Rogers, Everett M. *Diffusion of Innovations* (New York: Free Press, 1962).

Rogers, Everett M., and Shoemaker, F. Floyd. *Communication of Innovations: A Cross-Cultural Approach* (New York: Free Press, 1971).

Schaeffer, Francis A. *How Should We Then Live?* (Old Tappen, N.J.: Revell, 1976).

Schramm, Wilbur (ed.). *Mass Communications* (Urbana, Ill.: University of Illinois Press, 1949).

———*Mass Media and National Development* (Stanford, Ca.: Stanford University Press, 1964).

Schramm, Wilbur, and Roberts, Donald F. (eds.). *The Process and Effects of Mass Communication,* rev. ed. (Urbana, Ill.: University of Illinois, 1971).

Schuller, Robert H. *Your Church Has Real Possibilities* (Glendale, Ca.: Regal, 1975).

Scobie, Geoffrey E. W. *Psychology of Religion* (New York: Wiley, 1975).

Sereno, K. K., and Mortensen, C. D. (eds.). *Foundations of Communication Theory* (New York: Harper & Row, 1970).

Shannon, C., and Weaver, W. *The Mathematical Theory of Communication* (Urbana, Ill.: University of Illinois Press, 1949).

Shaw, M. E., and Wright, J. M. *Scales for the Measurement of Attitude* (New York: McGraw-Hill, 1967).

Sheehy, Gail. *Passages* (New York: Bantam Books, 1976).

Sherif, C. W., Sherif, M., and Nebergall, R. E. *Attitude and Attitude Change* (New Haven,Conn.: Yale University Press, 1961).

Shostron, Everett L. *Man, the Manipulator* (New York: Bantam Books, 1967).

Smalley, William A. *Readings in Missionary Anthropology* (South Pasadena, Ca.: William Carey Library, 1974).

———*The Theory and Practice of Translation* (Leiden: E. J. Brill, 1969).

Snygg, Donald, and Combs, Arthur W. *Individual Behavior* (New York: Harper & Row, 1949).

Snyder, Howard A. *The Community of the King* (Downers Grove, Ill.: InterVarsity Press, 1977).

———*The Problem of Wineskins* (Downers Grove, Ill.: InterVarsity Press, 1975).

Søgaard, Viggo B. *Everything You Need to Know for a Cassette Ministry* (Minneapolis: Bethany Fellowship, 1975).

Starbuck, E. D. *The Psychology of Religion* (New York: Charles Scribner & Sons, 1901).

Stark, Rodney and Glock, Charles Y. *American Piety: The Nature of Religious Commitment* (Berkeley, Ca.: University of California Press, 1968).

Stedman, Ray C. *Body Life* (Glendale, Ca.: Regal, 1972).

Steiner, Gary A. *The People Look at Television* (New York: Alfred A. Knopf, 1963).

Stott, John R. W. *Christian Mission in the Modern World* (Downers Grove, Ill.: InterVarsity Press, 1975).

Tippett, Alan R. *Church Growth and the Word of God* (Grand Rapids, Mich.: Wm. B. Eerdmans, 1970).

———*Verdict Theology and Missionary Theory* (Monrovia, Ca.: William Carey Library, 1973).

Toffler, Alvin. *Future Shock* (New York: Random House, 1970).

Tozer, A. W. *Paths to Power* (Philadelphia: Christian Publications, n.d.).

Trueblood, D. Elton. *A Place to Stand* (New York: Harper & Row, 1968).

Turner, Steve. *Tonight We Will Fake Love* (London: Charisma Books, 1974).

Waardenburg, Jacques. *Classical Approaches to the Study of Religion: Aims, Methods, and Theories of Research,* vols. 1 and 2 (The Hague: Moeton, 1973–4).

Wagner, C. Peter. *Frontiers in Missionary Strategy* (Chicago: Moody Press, 1971).

———*Your Church Can Grow* (Glendale, Ca.: Regal, 1976).

Wakatam, Pius. *Independence for the Third World Church* (Downers Grove, Ill.: InterVarsity Press, 1976).

Watzlawick, P., Beavin, J., and Jackson, D. *Pragmatics of Human Communication* (New York: Norton, 1967).

Bibliography

Webb, Eugene J. et. al. (eds.). *Unobtrusive Measures: Nonreactive Research in the Social Sciences* (Chicago: Rand McNally, 1966).

Webber, Robert E. *Common Roots* (Grand Rapids, Mich.: Zondervan, 1978).

Wells, Alan. *Mass Communications, A World View* (Palo Alto, Ca.: National Press Books, 1974).

Williams, Thomas Rhys. *Field Methods in the Study of Culture* (New York: Holt, Rinehart, and Winston, 1967).

Woodside, Arch G., Sheth, Jagdish N., and Bennett, Peter (eds.) *Consumer and Industrial Buying Behavior* (New York: Elsevier North-Holland, 1977).

Wuest, Kenneth S. *Studies in the Vocabulary* (Grand Rapids, Mich.: Wm. B. Eerdmans, 1945).

Yinger, Milton. *The Scientific Study of Religion* (New York: MacMillan, 1970).

Index

Index

Index

M

N

Index

XYZ

BOOKS FOLLOW IDEAS 12
COMMUNICATION 20
EXPOSURE/COMPREHENSION 22
SERMONS 22
CHURCH MEMBERS 23
MEDIUM/MESSAGE 25
GRIDS 26
27